Introduction to Buddhist Meditation

Sarah Shaw's lively introduction to Buddhist meditation offers students and practitioners alike a deeper understanding of what meditation is, and its purpose and place in the context of different Buddhist schools. She describes the historical background to the geographical spread of Buddhism, and examines the way in which some meditative practices developed as this process occurred. Other chapters cover basic meditative practice, types of meditation, meditation in different regions, meditation and doctrine, and the role of chanting within meditation.

Although not a practical guide, *Introduction to Buddhist Meditation* outlines the procedures associated with Buddhist practices and suggests appropriate activities, useful for both students and interested Buddhists. Vivid quotations from Buddhist texts and carefully selected photographs and diagrams help the reader engage fully with this fascinating subject.

Sarah Shaw teaches for the Oxford University Department for Continuing Education and practises with the Samatha Association of Britain. She is the author of *Buddhist Meditation: An Anthology of Texts from the Pali Canon* (Routledge 2006).

Georgios Halkias is Visiting Associate Researcher at the Faculty of Oriental Studies at the University of Oxford and Researcher at the Warburg Institute, University of London.

SARAH SHAW

With a chapter on Tibet by Georgios Halkias

Introduction to
Buddhist Meditation

Routledge
Taylor & Francis Group

LONDON AND NEW YORK

First published 2009
by Routledge
2 Park Square, Milton Park, Abingdon, Oxon. OX14 4RN

Simultaneously published in the USA and Canada
by Routledge
711 Third Avenue, New York, NY 10017, USA

Routledge is an imprint of the Taylor & Francis Group, an informa business

Typeset in Joanna by
HWA Text and Data Management, London

British Library Cataloguing in Publication Data
A catalogue record for this book is available from the British
Library

Library of Congress Cataloging in Publication Data
Introduction to Buddhist meditation / Sarah Shaw with a chapter
   on Tibet by Georgios Halkias.
      p. cm.
   Includes bibliographical references and index.
   1. Meditation – Buddhism. I. Halkias, Georgios, 1967– II. Title.
   BQ5612.S53 2008
   294.3'4435--dc22   2008003290

ISBN10: 0-415-40899-7 (hbk)
ISBN10: 0-415-40900-4 (pbk)

ISBN13: 978-0-415-40899-8 (hbk)
ISBN13: 978-0-415- 40900-1(pbk)

For Jeremy, Roland and Lucy

Contents

Figures

Preface

Recently I attended the annual Vesakha conference in Bangkok to celebrate the Buddha's birth, awakening and entry into nirvana. Delegates and visitors from hundreds of Buddhist localities and traditions had been invited. Alongside the great variety of lay practitioners, I found I kept on looking at all the myriad different robes, styles and dress amongst the monks and nuns. These were different shades of maroon, scarlet, russet, aubergine, lemon-yellow, ochre, gold, cinnamon, orange, cream, ivory, tangerine, brown, rust, dove-grey, silver, slate, charcoal, black, blue, coral-pink and white: the formal dress of many different orders. These colours were all outward manifestations of slightly different approaches, doctrines and attitudes to personal and public practice. This image came to mind when I started to write this book: it made the subject inspiring but intimidating. How can any book do justice to this richly coloured variation?

So I have to start by saying that I do not think it can. This book is a general introduction to the practice of meditation in a few of the leading Buddhist traditions. It gives some historical information, some account of the geographical spread of some schools and some indications of the basis of meditation practice in a few key areas. It gives a few samples from a few key texts, alongside one or two more personal accounts. It does not offer specific instruction. This, in most schools, is felt to be best given by an experienced meditation teacher. The book cannot pretend to be comprehensive, or to give enough information about the fast movements in the development of meditation centres or the accessibility of specific teachings. It does try to give some sort of context, in the ideas and cultural background that lie behind the practice of meditation. This is inextricably linked to other aspects of what many Buddhists call the eightfold path: theory, behaviour in the world and ways of seeing and interpreting events. As I hope this book indicates, these factors are shaped by and influence methods for meditation practice. Sometimes ritual gives a seed understanding of meditative procedure; sometimes theory is applied to the movement of the mind. These areas all work on one another and together. So this book includes some material on ritual and theory as supports and expressions of the practice of meditation.

Historically, meditation has usually been taught in cultures where there is great respect for privacy and confidentiality, and much grace in these matters. While some people might talk about the fact they practise meditation –

though many do not – it has often been regarded as a private, little discussed affair. The cultures in which it has flourished sometimes have centuries of custom concerning, for instance, privacy of consultation. So the information in this book is largely derived from what is in the public domain – what the texts, traditions, history and the published material of any group or school say. It must be filled with all kinds of assumptions and preconceptions. It seems to me that the best anyone can do is to be reasonably conscious of such things and hope one is not too wrong. If I have misrepresented any tradition, I am sorry and hope those concerned find some creative way of correcting this.

I have been a practising Buddhist for some years, with the Samatha Association in the UK, and have studied a few of the texts and customs of a few areas of Buddhist practice. I have tried to be disinterested, but I cannot pretend not to be interested. It is an awe-inspiring subject.

Acknowledgements

This long list of acknowledgements is a reflection of the amount of consultation needed and, luckily, given. Lesley Riddle suggested the book and encouraged me, as did Gemma Dunn and Amy Grant. Sarah Norman invited me to use the excellent library at the Oriental Institute, Taplow Court, and helped with many details. Others who have advised me are L.S. Cousins, Dr Paul Dennison, Professor Richard Gombrich and Dr Julia Hegewald. I would also like to thank the following: Brian Appleyard, Jo Backus, Geoff Bamford, at the Oxford Centre for Buddhist Studies, Dr Steven Collins, Jamie Cresswell, Ven. Dr Dhammasamai, Dr Gillian Evison, Dr Sanjukta Gombrich, Professor Peter Harvey, Ven. Wan Doo Kim, Dr Randolph and Dr Judith Ivy, Phra Dr Maha Lau, Dr Elizabeth de Michelis, Allen Miles, Peggy Morgan, Ven. Pannyavamsa, Jungnok Park, Diana Randall, Dr Peter Skilling, Dr Alan Sponberg, Sun Shuyun, Dr Gillian Warson and the staff at the Oriental Institute and Indian Institute libraries. Professor Chris Minkowski's continuance of the Sanskritists' lunch means that some Indologists in Oxford eat one meal a week sitting down. Jacqueline Callow, Amanda Lindop, Fiona Thomas and many friends in the Samatha Association have offered comment. Students in Oxford and Reading have asked useful questions. I am grateful to many practitioners who have given modern interpretations. Cherry Mosteshar was a great help in finding pictures. I am particularly grateful to Boonman Poonyathiro and his wife Deng, who have given constant encouragement, teaching and hospitality.

Two people generously stepped in right at the last minute. Special thanks are due to Dr Georgios Halkias, for writing his clear chapter on Tibet, and to Professor Peter Harvey, for making exhaustive corrections and comments.

As always, it is my husband Charles who has seen me through this book. All my thanks are to him and my family.

Aruna Publications, Aruna Ratanagiri, Harnham Buddhist Monastery, Belsay, Northumberland, UK

Chulalongkorn University Press, Bangkok: pictures from K.I.Matics, *Gestures of the Buddha*, 4th edition (2008)

Dr Paul Dennison, The Samatha Trust

Jeremy Edwards, photo from istockphoto.com

Dr Georgios Halkias

Aruna Publications

Texts

Buddhist Publication Society, Kandy: extract from Khema Ayya, *Within Our Own Hearts: Twelve Dhamma Talks on Meditation Practice* (1988)

Hightower, TV: 'The One Voice Chord' (2004) http://home3.inet.tele.dk/hitower/voice.html

Inward Path, Penang: extract from Ven Dhammasami, Ven, *Mindfulness Meditation Made Easy,* (1999)

Jain Publishing Company: extract from I.-J. Koh 'Introduction to Ch'an (K. Son) in the Later Silla' in L.R. Lancaster and C.S. Yu (eds) *Assimilation of Buddhims in Korea: Religious Maturity and Innovation in the Silla Dynasty,* (1991) Berkeley, CA: Asian Humanities Press. Reprinted by permission of Jain Publishing Company, www.jainpub.com

The Kwan Um School of Zen, Cumberland, and S. Sahn: 'Chanting with English Translations and Temple Rules, The Kwan Um School of Zen, Cumberland' (1996). www.kwanumzen.com/pdf/chantbk.pdf

Samatha Trust, Llangunllo, UK: extracts from U. McNab, *Samatha: Insight from a Meditation Tradition* (1997) and *The Suttanta on the Marks* (1996)

University of Hawaii Press, Honolulu, HI: extracts from R.E. Buswell, *Tracing Back the Radiance: Chinul's Korean Way of Zen* (1981)

Key

In Japan there are some Zen stone-gardens where it is never possible to see all of the stones from any given spot on the 'field': the garden can only be appreciated fully by walking around and taking in the few that one can see from a given angle. The use of terminology in various Buddhist contexts is a little like that. To someone familiar with Pāli texts, it seems strange to see Sanskrit terms used in the context of Pāli *suttas*; those more familiar with Sanskrit terms understandably find the Pāli inappropriate for *sūtras* they regard as equally authoritative. There are versions of many texts in both, as well as in Chinese and Tibetan. Variations of some terms are given as they occur and in the glossary, but it seems easier for students if the ones used in a particular region are adopted. In the early part of the book the terminology is mostly in Pāli, as the texts are; after that the Sanskrit is usually given.

The use of the term Chan in China, Seon in Korea, Thien in Vietnam and Zen in Japan needs mentioning. The term in these contexts derives from *jhāna*(P)/*dhyāna*(Sk), the deep meditative state that forms the basis of many Buddhist traditions, but does not always mean precisely that in these countries. It refers to a kind of school, common to those areas, where meditation practice forms a key component. This is sometimes of a different kind from the state denoted by the term in other Buddhist contexts.

For ease of reference, at the end of each chapter a list is given of works consulted or suggested for further reading. Within each chapter references are made by giving name, date and page reference to a work cited at the end of the chapter.

TRANSLITERATION SYSTEMS

Both Pāli and Sanskrit for some key terms are used where suitable. Transliteration systems for other languages are:

Chinese: Pinyin (for key terms and names, Wade-Giles romanization is given in brackets in the Glossary)

Hangeul: rule provided by the National Institute of the Korean Language on 19 July 2000, see (2008): http://www.korean.go.kr/eng/

Tibetan: 'Wylie', see Wylie, T. (1959) 'A Standard System of Tibetan Transcription', *Harvard Journal of Asiatic Studies*, 22, Dec., 261–7.

ABBREVIATIONS

BPS = Buddhist Publication Society
CUP = Cambridge University Press
OUP = Oxford University Press

For Pāli texts, editions used are those of the Pali Text Society (http://www.palitext.com/). They also have translations of all the texts quoted here. The reference to the text can be found by looking in the translation at the top inside corners.

A = *Aṅguttaranikāya*
Dhp = *Dhammapada*
D = *Dīghanikāya*
M = *Majjhimanikāya*
S = *Saṃyuttanikāya*
Sn = *Sutta-Nipāta*
Th = *Theragāthā*
Th = *Therīgāthā*
Ud = *Udāna*

Three kinds of Buddhism

For the purposes of this book Buddhist traditions have been arranged under three broad headings. The three groups could perhaps be seen as groupings of overlapping circles in a Venn diagram, with elements from one sometimes found in others and sometimes not. Some scholars prefer now not to employ these categories at all, but they are helpful and pertinent as long as they are not seen as too rigid.

SOUTHERN BUDDHISM

The first is that of the Southern forms, called, by the thirteenth century, the Theravāda, or the teaching of the elders. This is predominant in Thailand, Cambodia, Laos, Myanmar and Sri Lanka. The main source of text for this group is the Pāli canon. At one time it was thought this canon was the earliest and thus the most authoritative of the Buddhist textual traditions: Pāli is a development of the local Indo-Aryan language probably spoken at the time of the Buddha. There are many elements of truth in this but it has long been recognized that later texts in other languages such as Chinese and Tibetan sometimes retain elements that may be older than some Pāli texts. Writing was not introduced into India until after the Buddha's death; texts were still orally transmitted for many centuries after that and hence liable to all kinds of creative accretions, modifications or, as some would argue 'editing'. Southern Buddhism, as recorded in Pāli texts, does however contain many elements that must have come from the earliest strata of the tradition. Its meditation systems are primarily based on canonical and commentarial guidelines, but also include newer features, derived from a long process of acculturation and development.

NORTHERN BUDDHISM

This is the development from the form of Buddhism that evolved in India in the first two centuries CE, which is principally practised now amongst Tibetan Buddhists. In the early stages of its evolution it was not clearly differentiated from what became Southern Buddhism, and there seems to have been considerable interchange of ideas and practice. In the early centuries of the first millennium, many monks would follow the same *Vinaya*, or monastic rule, while following slightly different practices and adopting different doctrinal viewpoints. Sometimes called 'Mahāyāna', or 'greater vehicle', this school further develops the idea of the Bodhisattva, the being bound to or for enlightenment, to include many aspirant beings as well as one who became the historical Buddha. It uses visualization as a meditative tool and *Abhidharma*, the philosophical teachings, to direct the mind towards what was termed emptiness (*śūnyatā*). There is sometimes a vindication of both a politicized pacifism and physical violence in different Mahāyāna movements. The inspired, visionary nature of Indian Buddhism led to a stream of new Buddhist texts, up to the period 650 CE, which are used by many Mahāyāna schools to this day. Meditative texts of this tradition become quite different in form and content from texts of the Southern schools, and are sometimes characterized by great faith and the use of hyperbolic description.

EASTERN BUDDHISM

This refers to the forms of Buddhism adopted by the Chinese, Koreans, Japanese and many Vietnamese, which, for the most part, represents a development from texts that either are, or anticipate, the Mahāyāna. In China, however, Buddhism spread in separate waves through Central Asia on the Silk Road. Over centuries this encouraged the development of new schools of Buddhism, sometimes on the basis of textual and practice traditions imported from India and Central Asia and sometimes through the fusion of those elements with local customs, theory systems and practices. The emergence of Zen and Pure Land Buddhism are part of this Eastern form of the tradition.

It is customary to think of the various schools of Buddhism as in some way opposed to one another, or the byproduct of major schisms, though the features contributing to Buddhist pluralism are more complex than this, involving doctrinal, philosophical, social and even straightforwardly geographical developments. There are great varieties of Buddhism, not necessarily defined by the categories named above: some speak of Buddhisms, rather than Buddhism. For practical purposes in this book, material has been broadly arranged under country headings. As will become clear, there are many other factors, such as changing boundaries and varied ethnic, cultural and linguistic groups which qualify this sort of categorization. Many groups cover large areas that transcend geographical boundaries, though some sort of local identity is usually evident too. There is no central authority or institution which supervises all Buddhist traditions, an absence of centralism perceived by many Buddhists as a source of great strength.

The Eightfold Path and Meditation

One

In this fathom long body, I declare, is the world, the arising of the world, the ceasing of the world and the path leading to the ceasing of the world

INTRODUCTION TO BUDDHISM AND THE MIDDLE WAY

The historical Buddha, Gotama, claimed that one simple experience in meditation changed his life. According to his own account, he sat down one day as a child under a rose-apple tree and discovered it was possible to achieve a state he called jhāna. This was accompanied by initial thought, exploration of the object, joy, happiness and one-pointedness, or unification of mind, from which he saw his whole existence in a different way. In the commentaries that were composed after the Buddha's death, the practice he is said to have undertaken was one which he later described as the most 'sublime' of all meditations. This was the observation of the simple motion of the breath in and out of his body, which brought his body and mind to a state of completion and rest. When he remembered this joyfully peaceful state later in life he came to the conclusion that he did not have to fear the great happiness of being free from the pull of the senses. Rather, it was the wisdom derived from such peace that was actually helpful to understand things as they really are.

'I remember that when my father the Śakyan was busy, while I was sitting in the cool shade of the rose-apple tree, quite secluded from sensual pleasures, secluded from unskilful states, I entered upon and abided in the first jhāna, which is accompanied by applied and sustained thought, with the joy and happiness born of seclusion. Might that be the path to awakening?' Then, following on that memory came the consciousness: 'This is the path to awakening.' 'Why am I afraid of a happiness that has nothing to do with sensual pleasure and unskilful states?' And then, Aggivessana, this thought came to me: 'I am not afraid of this happiness, for this happiness has nothing to do with sensual pleasures and unskilful states'

(M I 246–7)

Figure 1.1 **Figure of the Buddha**

On the night of the full moon of Vesākha he defeated the armies of Māra – the various hindrances, fears and uncertainties that beset the mind. Sitting under a bodhi tree he explored meditative states further and recollected many of his past lives as well as seeing the arising and passing away of other beings. Just before dawn, he become enlightened, or, as he said 'awake', the word from which his title, Buddha, is derived.

The story of the Buddha's enlightenment – or awakening – is now familiar to most people. Less is known about the nature of the meditative exercises that brought about that experience, and the way that it is linked theoretically and practically to other aspects of his teaching. Much of the history of Buddhism has been written with an emphasis on the Buddha's ideas: how he formulated his theories and how he created what he called a path for others to follow. This book, however, attempts to give some information and historical context to meditation itself: the practices that were taught by the Buddha, and which were developed from his teaching, around the fifth century BCE

Around the time of the Buddha there were all sorts of meditation teachers, debaters, ascetics and holy men. If we can go by Buddhist texts, people seemed to go from one teacher another, learning what each had to offer and perhaps staying longer if they felt they needed to. Certainly this seems to have been the case with the historical Buddha. After leaving the palace in which he had lived a life of luxury with his wife, he joined those practising self-mortifications on an ascetic path, and practised with them for six years. At that time a number of harsh practices were common, which involved suffering, staying in one posture for a long time or starvation. These were all thought to lead to wisdom. The Buddha tried them and decided they did not. He also tried two meditations, known as the sphere of no-thingness and the sphere of neither perception nor non-perception. These, he found, did not lead to peace on their own, though he subsequently incorporated them into his own system as useful when practised with other aspects of his teaching. In the end he decided to eat food, build up strength, and remembered the meditation he had practised as a child. Recollecting this, he went to the Bodhi tree and attained enlightenment.

THE TURNING IN MOTION OF THE WHEEL OF DHAMMA

After attaining enlightenment, the Buddha taught what is sometimes known as his first sermon, 'the turning in motion of the wheel of *dhamma*' (the teaching). This first teaching attributed to the Buddha was delivered to a group of ascetics who were probably experienced meditators. In this he posited the idea of a middle way – an ongoing and creative equipoise that transcends the two extremes of self-punishment and over-indulgence of the senses. In order to achieve this, experience needs to be approached

Figure 1.2 **Eight-spoked wheel from Jokhang monastery in Tibet**

through four truths, each of which are to be apprehended in a different and complementary way. This requires extensive and, usually, sustained moral, emotional and intellectual maturation of factors that enable the mind to be free, while living in a world governed by the four principles that form the cornerstone of the Buddhist doctrine:

1. The first truth, dis-ease, is to be *understood*.
Dukkha literally means 'hard going': it is as if a cart were going over a road with a lot of bumps and stones on it. This first truth of existence is sometimes misinterpreted as being that everyone is going around being miserable all the time. This is not the case, though it may apply in some situations! It is rather that there is an inherent, moving tension or dynamic that inheres in all existence, of any kind.

2. The second noble truth, that of the craving that leads to dis-ease, is to be *abandoned*.
The cause of *dukkha* is the wish for things to be other than they are. This makes us overlay our experience with what is wanted and rejected, rather than acceptance. This leads to more desire, and the mind is said to create 'I's on the basis of this: these are the many egos through which our desires are temporarily gratified.

3. The third noble truth, the realization of the end of dis-ease, is to be *realized*.
The third noble truth is the end of suffering or dis-ease, nibbāna, meaning literally the putting out of a flame, taken as the extinction of desire. While the end of suffering is attractive, it is often said, quite reasonably, that nibbāna does not sound like something one would actually want. Indeed if it is seen solely in terms of desires that are supposed to disappear when it is attained, it is difficult to see it as something to be desired. It is worth mentioning, however, that the language used to describe it would seem very attractive in an Indian context. The 'cool' for instance, an epithet that is sometimes used, is clearly a pleasant prospect when living in the blistering heat of the kind that is found there. The word for happy or comfortable, *sukha*, is constantly used to describe *nibbāna*. Perhaps this is best demonstrated by a short verse from a Buddhist story which the scholar T. W. Rhys Davids once said distilled the essence of Buddhism:

Impermanent indeed are conditioned things!
For they partake in birth and old age.
What arises, ceases
Happiness is the calming of these things.

Jātaka no. 95

It is argued by the Buddha that the very fact that we feel that things are not quite as we would like them, impermanent and sometimes unsatisfactory, is because some part of us knows and intuitively recognizes what it would be like to be free from these conditions. Later Buddhist traditions formulate this in terms of a latent knowledge, which needs to be discovered or realized. Throughout Buddhist history, when poems are written about an experience of realization, the natural world is described with a vivid and delighted appreciation. Images like that used by the thirteenth-century Vietnamese monk, Tran Thai Tong, who compared the state to a return to a native land, from which one has been exiled, reinforce this:

On the long way, one does not walk but one arrives at home

From this point of view, the absence of the craving that characterizes the second truth is perceived not as the crushing of a natural impulse, but more the fulfilment of a deeper one: there is no craving, because what the human mind wishes for most is found.

4. The fourth noble truth, the path that leads to the end of dis-ease, is to be *brought into being*.
This last truth uses the word that is used for any thoroughfare or road. It is to be approached with the verb associated with bhāvanā, the term used by early Buddhists to describe what we would call meditation. Bhāvanā also includes many activities, such as appropriate generosity, attentiveness to others, as well as sitting meditation. These are all things to be 'brought into being'. Throughout all Buddhist traditions, the idea that meditation itself involves and needs other factors constantly recurs.

In the Buddhist path 'there are four truths and one knowledge'. The most important feature of these truths is that they are known altogether. They all exist because of each other and are 'true' because the others are. In practice many texts in the Buddhist tradition seem carefully designed to communicate a weaving in and out of them all. Where there is a description of an unhappy state, with a troubled mind, its cause is suggested. Where a state with an untroubled mind is described, the way to achieve this is described too.

Most of us are aware of one or other of the truths as some possibility – that things are not as we would like, or that there may be a state where there is freedom from that. The Buddha identified the human problem as in the way these are 'known': knowledge is partial, or corrupted by irritation, if there is annoyance with a friend or a job at work, or by desire, or disappointment. The Buddhist path gives recommendations to be 'brought into being' so that knowledge, when it does arise, is liberating and associated with peace. For this it needs to be associated with and transformed by loving-kindness, compassion, sympathetic joy and equanimity. It also needs to have expression in action in the world that does not cause harm or anxiety, to oneself or other beings. It gives some illustration of the way the Buddha taught that experience was to be apprehended and understood as much by work on the mind that comes to the truth as on the insight into the truth itself; or rather, it is only true if it is known rightly. So from the Buddhist point of view how we think is as important as what is thought, and the things we do are as important as the things we feel and think. This is quite a tall order, so a long path may be necessary for most beings to 'bring into being' the action, speech, and thought that will allow insight to arise that brings freedom, not fear or disappointment.

THE BUDDHIST EIGHTFOLD PATH

1. Right view
2. Right intention
3. Right speech
4. Right action
5. Right livelihood
6. Right effort
7. Right mindfulness
8. Right concentration

1. Right view

The first path factor, right view, is taken from the word to 'see'. The first part of the Buddhist path is not to 'see' the world through rigid lenses, opinions, and judgements, but to be able to look and watch without forming views.

If there is a fixed view that things are permanent, have a lasting identity and go on for ever, then the natural flux of the world is ignored and there is wrong view. The Buddha called this view eternalism. But if there is the fixed view that, in changing all the time, things have no coherence or continuity, and 'no self' at all, that is also wrong view. This was termed by the Buddha annihilationism. Most of us feel we do have a self: from the Buddhist point of view this is brought into being by many factors and causes, and many other ones will come into play in the future. It is not, however, permanent.

The 'middle way' does acknowledge the responsibility of an agent and that a bad or a good action will have a consequence upon that agent. It also respects individuals, institutions and many things, ranging from one's own football team, country, family or spouse which, while changing, certainly do adhere together as entities and are worthy of love and respect. The text (*sutta*) on the 'net of views' suggests that wrong view lies in the effect a view has on the mind. The *suttas* describe this with the statement 'This is true; all else is falsehood'. According to Buddhist philosophy, where there is strong view the mind, and the body, become rigid and fixed. Where there is right view, the mind becomes more pliant and soft, without losing strength. Right view frees the mind: it is said not to impose a rigid form, so that emergent and new identities can be respected and both flux and identity can be acknowledged. From a positive point of view, when the three signs of discernment of impermanence (*anicca*), unsatisfactoriness (*dukkha*) and the absence of an abiding self (*anattā*) are seen without hatred, coldness or fake 'detachment' – often the product of views of some kind – this is right view. When these are seen, the mind is said to become free from the clinging and suffering brought about by views.

2. Right intention

This is described in early Buddhism as a placing of the mind which does not involve cruelty, sense-desire or hatred; also, from an active point of view, an intention that does involve loving-kindness. Ven. Saddhatissa, a renowned twentieth-century meditation teacher and scholar, described it as:

> ...that quality of consciousness wherein there is no obstruction to the thought processes. State of consciousness that is limpid, cool, free from the limiting considerations of self-interest, without tension or veiled uneasiness.
>
> Saddhatissa (1971: 49)

A modern example would be the kind of intention that can operate at work. If one gets annoyed with something someone has organized in the office and sends an email with some hatred to someone else, then right intention will not be present. If one thinks of the person with some friendliness, there is less likely to be violent distaste or anger, and perhaps a more helpful and appropriate response: the action would have arisen from right intention. From the Buddhist point of view, volition (*cetanā*) is everything. The first and the second path factors are often taken together under the general heading of wisdom (*paññā*). This word is found throughout the history of all Buddhist traditions as the pre-eminent quality of spiritual development. The point is constantly reiterated by Buddhist teachers from all traditions that the wisdom described in Buddhism is not knowledge about things, or a kind of knowingness, which separates and makes the practitioner feels superior to others. Rather it is an apprehension that is both intuitive and realistic. The two path factors of right view and right intention are said to need to work together for wisdom to operate.

The next three path factors are concerned with behaviour in the world, and are grouped together under the category of *sīla*, variously translated as virtue, good conduct or good behaviour. The word concerns what one actually does and says in the world.

3. Right speech

This is speech that does not lie, speak falsely, divide people from each other, slander, or cause harm because it is savage or harsh. It also describes the kind of gossip that drains the mind or runs people and situations down. From an active point of view, it is described as speech that creates good will and is 'embracing'. The three path factors concerning behaviour (*sīla*) are sometimes thought of as less important than the others for salvation. Yet the Buddha does not say that one is more important than the others. Speech is considered particularly significant, not only for the effect wrong speech can have on the wellbeing of others, but also for its effect on the person who practises it. This does not mean that one never talks about other people: Buddhist texts are filled with people doing this. Rather, if the speech is of a damaging kind, the mind of the person who speaks will become damaged. This is considered particularly important for anyone practising meditation. On modern meditation courses there is sometimes a silence rule, except where speech is necessary or helpful. While this is obviously not a good idea for usual circumstances, it can be quite a relief and does mean that for that time the mind is free from some of its usual clutter. The Buddha sometimes spoke of a noble silence – and kept to it when asked about things he did not see fit to talk about. Clearly most of the time people need to have conversations and enjoy them. Right speech is perceived as not allowing that to become unkind or divisive and, in practice, enjoying silence sometimes.

4. Right action

This involves action in accordance with the five basic precepts of Buddhist practice, particularly the first three. The five precepts are the undertakings to avoid killing, stealing, causing harm to oneself or others through sexual misconduct, lying or becoming intoxicated. It can seem very odd to Westerners to see these as anything other than negatives: we tend to remember omissions rather than the things we have done that have not been harmful. Traditionally in Buddhist countries, however, simply refraining from harming another living being, or stealing, or refraining from breaking any of the precepts is considered actively good, and even likely to bring good luck. One Buddhist meditation, described in Chapter 4, involves the recollection that one has kept these basic precepts, even if only for a short period. Just bearing this in mind is said to help the practitioner from feeling disturbed or troubled in meditation, promotes a feeling of wellbeing and arouses happiness in daily life. It is not intended to arouse complacency or pride, but, from the meditator's point of view, is said to bring about peace of mind. On festivals and holidays, practitioners are asked just to remember that they have kept the precepts for a day and so find happiness in that. Sometimes extra precepts are taken, to bring them to eight or ten, and practitioners wear white, as a way of the making the day different.

5. Right livelihood

This is a way of life and deriving one's living that does not involve harming others. Not taking part in arms dealing, drugs dealing or dealing in human beings constitutes right livelihood. From a positive view, right livelihood is said to act in beneficial way on the mind, as it involves things that are done repeatedly, each day. The idea is that if these are undertaken with skill the mind will be less likely to have wrong intention or wrong view. One of the examples cited of right livelihood, perhaps surprisingly to the modern mind, is a mother looking after small children.

The last three path factors are closely linked to meditation. This is the triad sometimes known as the concentration (*samādhi*) part of the eightfold path. They are more involved with mental states.

6. Right effort

This is described in four ways. As (1) the effort that keeps unhelpful states at bay, (2) the effort that puts aside things which are unhelpful or harmful, (3) the effort that brings about helpful states and (4) the effort that ensures that helpful states are maintained. This is the effort that enacts the 'middle way', in meditation and in daily life, in part the balance between being too tense or too lax.

7. Right mindfulness

This is awareness of what is going on in the physical, emotional and mental experience, and events involving them. It includes awareness of the physical body, of feelings, of the tenor of the mind and of things going on around in all of these three areas. Mindfulness is sometimes said to be the quintessence of the path: it is an ongoing awareness that is compared in some Buddhist texts to a gatekeeper, who guards the mind from harm. Most commonly, mindfulness is advised in all traditions for the physical body first: touch, taste, smell, sound and sight.

8. Right concentration

This is the stilling of the mind in concentration. By concentration, the Buddhist path means the state of the mind when attention is fully engaged, aroused by an object of interest, such as a flower, a view of a wide area of sea or countryside, or a pattern of frost on a window pane. Where there is interest that is accompanied by mindfulness, so that there is neither excessive fascination or indifference, this can be deepened in a meditation practice, set apart from other activities in the day. The texts do warn that concentration can arise in a lot of negative situations, so that it is wrong concentration: it is possible to be very focused when having an argument. When it is right concentration, it is said to be characterized by mindfulness and an absence of any wish to harm or spoil. This happens when the mind comes to rest on an object with interest and mindfulness, and without hindrance. It becomes then an alert attention that can be deepened to take the mind into a refreshing and restorative meditation, known as jhāna.

RIGHT BEHAVIOUR, CONCENTRATION AND WISDOM:
SĪLA, SAMĀDHI AND *PAÑÑĀ*

The path factors are not considered to be sequential, but rather as elements which can be worked on together: they are often shown now around an eight-spoked wheel. They also demonstrate three areas of life, all of which can come under the heading of bhāvanā, 'bringing into being' the factors of the path. Simple action and behaviour in the world are often forgotten elements in this process. It is supposed to give the freedom from fear and anxiety that allows meditation to be practised, and ensures that there is no harm to oneself or others. Concentration, or the right attention of the mind, is cultivated in practices that lead to samatha, the calm found in meditation. Wisdom is associated with practices leading to vipassanā, or insight. In early Buddhist texts and in modern teaching the two are usually taught together, though some schools of meditation have a greater emphasis on one. The Buddha said that samatha and vipassanā should be 'yoked together'. They are sometimes compared to two wings of the same bird, or two sides of a plank of wood. The factors of the eightfold path are taught as working on one another and are all needed to follow the teaching and to bring the middle way into daily life and meditation. Mindfulness is nearly always enjoined. In Buddhist texts the three elements of behaviour, concentration and wisdom are rarely considered apart from one another, and it can be difficult to find a discourse delivered by the Buddha in the Pāli canon that teaches one in isolation from the others.

THE TEACHING (*DHAMMA*)

At this stage it would be useful to say something about the kinds of texts in which the Buddha's teaching has been passed down. In Indian languages the word dhamma, or, in Sanskrit, dharma, has all sorts of connotations, meaning in different contexts justice, what is right and even law. In Buddhism it can also mean these things, but one of its most usual meanings is the teaching of the Buddha, which sees things as they really are. The teaching of the Buddha is divided into three categories, assembled together as oral traditions in the councils that occurred in the years after the Buddha's death. Many of these exist now in Chinese translations, the Āgamas. Many are also recorded in the Pāli language, a form of middle Indo-Aryan that is probably much like the Prakrit spoken by the historical Buddha himself. At some point the 'canon', as it is called, became closed and subsequent texts and commentaries in Pāli are termed 'post-canonical'. Although greater weight is attached to the canonical texts, the writings that supplement it are also considered important and, for those interested in the practice of meditation, indispensable. Some of the commentaries include material, not in the Pāli canon, which records practices that must date from a very early period. This includes general guidance, physical procedures and basic tips for actually doing a specific practice. They explain how to go about conducting the practice of loving-kindness, for instance, or the best place and posture to choose for a meditation sitting. Such information is not always given explicitly in the canon. What is difficult is dating the material: many of the commentaries were not committed to writing until about the fifth century.

This means that the issue of whether a text is 'early' or not can be tricky. Certainly the Pāli canon seems to contain much of the earliest strata of the tradition. Many Sanskrit texts, however, were composed and recorded in the first centuries of the millennium, before some Pāli texts were written down. Some of these are lost, some recorded only in Chinese or Tibetan versions of a much later date, and some are still extant. Some emerge from a number of different schools of Buddhism about whom we know very little. The upshot of this is that a text found, say, in translation in China in the sixth century may well contain ancient material. A Pāli commentary may include an addition that is quite 'late'. As the subject is debated, scholarly consensus agrees, however, that the Pāli canon itself probably represents our earliest evidence for the nature of Buddhist practice and doctrine in its initial stages. It is divided into three categories or 'baskets': the *Vinaya*, the *Suttas* and the *Abhidhamma*.

THE THREE BASKETS

Vinaya

The *Vinaya* describes rules of conduct for monastics: 227 for monks and 311 for nuns. Said by the Buddha to be a heritage for his followers, this code has remained almost intact amongst Southern schools of Buddhism and is observed with some modifications by monks in many other traditions. There are a number of different *vinayas* in the many schools of Buddhism that exist now. As Buddhism travelled, certain features were changed in accordance with local custom or new doctrinal position. The issue of vegetarianism is an interesting example of this. In the Pāli canon the Buddha decides against an insistence on vegetarianism, on the grounds that as a guest a monk should be willing to accept any food offered. He did, however, insist that monks should not eat meat from animals especially killed to feed them. In practice, many monks from the Southern schools are vegetarian, as are some of the laity, but the principle of a willingness to accept what is being given is maintained. In Eastern Buddhist countries, vegetarianism did become popular and even enjoined as part of the Bodhisattva path. In practice some orders live by a vegetarian diet, but in other countries, like Tibet, it would have been impossible to maintain this and survive.

The *Vinaya*'s prime concern is with applied ethics and conduct: it does not for the most part involve discussion of meditation or mental states. Despite this, those in the monastic order often state that in order to fulfil its conditions, such as careful eating and behaving with proper respect to other monks and the laity and even, for a newcomer, wearing the robes correctly, requires a level of alertness and vigilance that aligns its maintenance to bhāvanā. There is one important regard, however, specifically relating to meditation. There are four offences, which, if committed, mean that the practitioner immediately ceases to become a monk. The first three are taking another person's life, sexual intercourse and stealing. The fourth is to boast wrongfully about one's own level of meditation practice. The reason for this was pragmatic: if a monk claimed to be of a high spiritual standing, he might receive more generous offerings from people anxious to get merit. The effect of this ruling has been important, however, in the teaching of meditation in the East. While many regions of South East Asia are full of stories of monks who have allayed tigers, or demonstrated psychic powers, monks should not make any false claim about such things themselves. In practice, this means that monks are reticent about making any overt claims to meditation states. This contributes to a striking feature of dhamma teaching given by the monastic orders, and in practice, lay teachers: while their guidance may indicate obliquely to those of meditative experience the teacher's level of attainment, no public claims are made.

Sutta

This is the main body of texts that describe the Buddha's teachings, discourses, conversations and meetings with others and where most of his meditation teaching is found. It also describes his followers' teaching and the settings, debates and situations that prompted them. A richly complex group of texts, it includes genres we would call dramatic dialogue, lyric poetry, bardic narrative, epithets, adventure stories, exempla, fabliaux and biographical account.

Abhidhamma

The *Abhidhamma* is known as the 'higher' teaching, and varies in content from school to school and in some of its underlying assumptions. It involves a close examination of what is going on in meditation in the mind and body of the practitioner, as well as consciousness in daily life. It works on a moment-by-moment basis, so that each slight shift in the state of mind and in the thought process is delineated. While some have argued that the study of *Abhidhamma* is solely an intellectual and scholastic exercise, which it certainly can be, those that use it in Asia regard it as a meditative tool. Its purpose is to lessen a sense of 'self' and to loosen rigidity of mind – and hence the meditation – through awareness of fluidity and impermanence in the movement from one mental state to another. The content of much of the *Abhidhamma* material, in its close description of the mental and bodily state in *jhāna* and the process whereby the mind enters meditation and leaves it, supports such a hypothesis. There even seems to be some actual meditation advice in the *Vibhaṅga* and the *Paṭisambhidāmagga*, an *Abhidhamma*-type text, that includes detail of the practices of loving-kindness and breathing mindfulness. Certainly in Thailand and Myanmar, a country with an unusually strong *Abhidhamma* interest, the material is employed in some meditation schools as a means of such investigation, in what could be called a phenomenological rather than an ontological approach. To put it more simply, in such schools the material is used to investigate the mind and its mental states with particular regard to meditative experience, in an attempt to loosen attachments to any state. The exercise also awakens investigation and ensures that good debate about such matters, a key element in some meditational schools, is allowed to enliven the meditation for those who need and benefit from this kind of analysis.

THE IMPORTANCE OF MEDITATION ON THE BUDDHIST PATH

Sister Ayyā Khemā was born in Berlin in 1923. A Jewess, she escaped in 1938 to Scotland while her parents went to China. Her father died in a Japanese camp. After the war she went to America, married and had two children. In 1979 she became a nun in Sri Lanka, where she founded centres for women. She died in Germany in 1997. Through her teaching and writing she became one of the most highly respected nuns of the twentieth century. In this passage she describes the reasons for practising meditation, voicing in simple vernacular the Buddha's conclusion that the happiness of being free from attachment to the senses was not to be regarded with fear:

It is, therefore, immaterial which method of meditation we practise, as long as it will be a useful key. However, the breath has been the traditional and much favoured subject from the days of old until now. Breath and mind are intrinsically connected. When the mind becomes quiet and tranquil, the breath follows suit. When the breath becomes calm, it also becomes so fine and subtle that it is difficult to find. Meditators are sometimes afraid at this point that they are losing their breath and with it their life force and begin to breathe forcefully. There is no need to fear: as long as there is life, there is breath. As the breath becomes shallow and quiet, a pleasant physical feeling arises...

Why should it be important to experience a blissful physical feeling in meditation and what can be learnt from it?

First of all, the Buddha said that in order to meditate successfully, we need to be comfortable in body and mind. Secondly, the impermanence of this most pleasant feeling will show us how fleeting all our pleasures are and will eventually make us dispassionate towards the gratification of the senses, which are keeping us bound in the realm of birth and death. Furthermore, our meditative absorptions act as a purifying method for our defilements. While we are pleasantly absorbed in blissful feelings we have no negativities in our mind, so the mind carries less darkness around with it, as we practise steadily. Also during our daily lives, we realize that the difficulties which all of us encounter can be considered minor irritations and not major tragedies, since we have a trained mind now which is able to reach a blissful feeling on demand.

Possibly most important of all, the reason for the necessity to achieve meditative absorption is the fact that only a mind which is well trained to concentrate steadily is strong and powerful enough to penetrate the illusion in which we live and see the absolute reality, which underlies it.

Khemā (1988: 108–9)

THE STAGES OF AWAKENING

There are said to be four stages in the process of attaining enlightenment.

1 Stream-entry. This is a stage when there is the eradication from the mind of doubt and wrong views and means that nibbāna will be attained within seven lifetimes.
2 Once-return. This weakens the hold of sense desires, hatred and ignorance and means that nibbāna will be attained within this or the next lifetime, or have rebirth as a non-returner in the heaven of the Pure Abodes.
3 Non-return. This eradicates sense desires and hatred, and means that there will be no more rebirth in the sense sphere, but rebirth in one or more of the heavens of the Pure Abodes.
4 Arahatship, the state of 'being worthy'. This eradicates all vestiges of the defilements. The mind is free from rebirth and 'I'-making.

Seclusion is happiness, for the one who has heard the teaching and sees.
Non-harm is happiness, restraint towards living beings.
Being free from passion is happiness, the transcending of desires.
But getting rid of the conceit that makes 'I's — that really is happiness!

(Ud 10)

CONCLUSION

This chapter discusses the four noble truths and the eightfold path. It notes that all elements of the eightfold path are enjoined and are rarely taught in isolation from one another. The categories of behaviour in the world (sīla), concentration (samādhi) and wisdom (paññā) are described.

FURTHER READING

Conze, E. (1956) Buddhist Meditation, London: George, Allen and Unwin.
Gethin, R. (1998) The Foundations of Buddhism, Oxford: OUP.
Gombrich, R.F. (1988) Theravāda Buddhism; A Social History from Ancient Benares to Modern Colombo, London/New York: Routledge and Kegan Paul.

Harvey, P. (1990) *Introduction to Buddhism: Teachings, History and Practices*, Cambridge: CUP.

Keown, D. (1996) *Buddhism, A Very Short Introduction*, Oxford: OUP.

Khemā, Ayyā (1988) *Within our Own Hearts: Twelve Dhamma Talks on Meditation Practice*, Kandy: BPS

Rahula, W. (1967) *What the Buddha Taught*, P. Demieville foreword, 2nd edn., Bedford: Gordon Fraser.

Saddhatissa, Ven. H. (1971) *The Buddha's Way*, London: George, Allen and Unwin.

Shaw, S. (2006) *The Jātakas: Birth Stories of the Bodhisatta*, New Delhi: Penguin.

Early Buddhist Guidance on Meditation
Two

This chapter discusses basic features of Buddhist meditative practice, such as finding a teacher and a school, various objects for practice and posture. It also explores some qualities aroused by meditation. An ancient pairing, mindfulness and concentration, is discussed. The relationship between calm (*samatha*) and insight (*vipassanā*) is introduced. Breathing mindfulness, a practice particularly recommended by the Buddha, which can be used for either calm or insight, or both, is briefly described. As an indication of the diversity of methods of meditation taught today, a supplementary meditation, walking practice, is discussed.

THE GOOD FRIEND

As in ancient India, where people used to look around for a method and teacher, the most important single requisite for meditation is finding a school and someone from whom to learn. From the time of the Buddha, and before that, meditation seems to have been taught personally. Considerable emphasis is placed on the teacher, or 'good friend', who assigns an object and gives instruction in it. This is based on the temperament (*carita*) of the person involved. Some meditations are suitable for certain temperaments, some for others. Some are suitable for all temperaments, but it is usually best to ask advice as to how to practise them. Breathing mindfulness, for instance, is often recommended now. As both texts and modern teachers advise, there are certain stages when the meditator needs guidance. This can happen at any time, and the meditation can become boring or hard if advice is not sought: sometimes people make too much effort, sometimes the attention is too slack. It is often compared to someone learning a musical instrument, or how to sing, who needs to be given advice on posture, breathing and effort. At the time of the Buddha one monk, Soṇa, wore his feet out pacing up and down and making too much effort. The Buddha compared the meditation practice to a lute: if the strings are too taut, the note will be harsh and painful to hear; if too slack, it will be off-key. Soṇa was subsequently successful in his meditation. When the right balance is found, with the help of a teacher, the practice will develop.

THE TEACHER OR GOOD FRIEND

In an Asian context teachers generally are accorded immense respect. Early Buddhist texts differ, however, from those of some other traditions in that there is not a 'guru', but rather an adviser, who helps the practitioner with meditation practice and can assess the basic needs of his or her temperament. While no specific instructions are given about this relationship, friendship of all kinds is highly regarded in early Buddhist texts. The 'good friend' should be someone who 'gives what is hard to give, does what is hard to do, endures what is hard to endure, reveals his own secrets, guards the secrets of others; he does not forsake one at times of need and does not despise one for any loss' (A IV 30). The need for consistency and a willingness to take advice is implied. One famous text describes an enthusiast, Meghiya, who did not want instruction, but to 'get there on his own'. Although obliquely warned by the Buddha not to try this, Meghiya wilfully goes off to practise without guidance (Ud 34–7). According to later commentaries, he happened to pick a spot where he had once had a pleasure garden as a rather fast-living king. His mind is described as 'encircled' by highly coloured distractions, like a tree surrounded by creepers or a hive by bees: similes that certainly ring true for any meditator, whether or not the 'past lives' are taken as literal or metaphoric intrusions. Hardly surprisingly, his meditation does not work. So, defeated and perplexed, Meghiya returns to the Buddha and is given by him a series of practices to pursue. Some of these are based on behaviour (*sīla*), some on arousing calm (*samādhi*) and one, given at the end, is for arousing wisdom (*paññā*). This sort of method, which approaches a meditator's needs in a personalized and comprehensive way, is frequently employed by the Buddha, who seems to tailor his teaching according to the needs of the questioner and audience. Meghiya is in effect told to practise each element of the eightfold path, in a way suitable to his temperament and attainment.

As if to ensure the perpetuation of this low-key and practical attitude towards teaching meditation, the Buddha often recommended the teachings given by his followers, approving their creative touches when they used similes 'never heard before'. Some eloquent testaments to friendship occur in verses composed by or delivered to early Buddhist disciples: many of these become awakened or enlightened and in turn teach others. At the beginning of the famous *sutta* on breathing mindfulness, groups of monks teach other groups of monks in the presence of the Buddha, an image presumably in part included to ensure the continuance of the teaching transmission in the eventual absence of the founder.

WHO CAN PRACTISE MEDITATION?

At this point it is also worth noting that on the issue of meditation, the Buddha did not see any deficiency in the attainments of laymen – or women, who were considered equally capable of attaining all the stages of enlightenment and of teaching others. In this regard the Buddha was a revolutionary innovator, at a time when most spiritual traditions, with the exception of the Śvetambara Jains, felt that the attainment of liberation was not possible as a woman. He was hesitant to found an order of nuns – indeed it was considered socially unacceptable and potentially dangerous for women to live outside the home – but did so when requested by his disciple Ānanda three times. Many of these early women meditators attained all stages of awakening, just as the men did. His list of those with pre-eminences amongst his followers includes many nuns, highly skilled in various aspects of meditation and insight, and some lay women, whose merits occasionally included meditation. The *suttas* include meditative teachings given by such women.

Within the Pāli canon all kinds of people become teachers of meditation, once they have reached attainments themselves. One nun gives instruction to her ex-husband, and the lay man Citta, famous for his attainments, also gives advice on meditation practice.

OBJECTS FOR MEDITATION

There are many and varied objects of meditation. Some of these are listed by Buddhaghosa and discussed in Chapter 4. They include colours, the four elements, the body, and collections of attributes, such as the excellences of the Buddha. Some involve the development and purification of emotions, such as loving-kindness or compassion. According to Buddhist texts and practices, different objects are suited for different temperaments. According to the tradition, they are suggested by the teacher to answer needs that may also vary at different times: the Buddha sometimes gives a different object to a questioner on different occasions, when it is appropriate for that person. The list of meditation objects could be extended if one looks at the way Buddhism develops in various countries and contexts. Aurally based objects, such as mantras, and complex visual ones, such as visualizations of the Buddha or Bodhisattvas, for instance, become particularly important in Northern Buddhism. The same object may be looked at from a different angle elsewhere: chanting is often used to calm the mind, for example, but in some traditions, like Zen, is frequently employed as the object of insight practice.

Saddhatissa, a distinguished twentieth-century Sri Lankan monk, described the variety of possible objects in the following way. He aligns objects for concentration with those in other contemplative traditions:

With all forms of *samatha* meditation, the chosen subject, whether it be breathing, a coloured disc, or the repetition of a special phrase, is only a stepping stone, or an aid to concentration. The meditator focuses his attention on the chosen subject until the mind becomes quiet and one-pointed. At this stage a conceptual image (*nimitta*) will arise. Buddhist literature abounds in descriptions of various types of *nimitta*: essentially it is a 'sign' that appears in front of the closed eyes. If the meditator was using a *kasiṇa* subject, then the *nimitta* that eventually arises will probably take the form of a disc. If the *ānāpānasati* practice [mindfulness of breathing] was used, then the *nimitta* may take the form of a wisp of smoke or a flurry of clouds. If the 'formulated utterance' practice – *araham sammāsambuddho* (free from all impurity, by his own efforts completely enlightened) was being repeated then the resultant *nimitta* may be a vision of a Buddha statue or a painting. Or – to apply Buddhist terminology to the practices of the Christian contemplatives – if a *maṇḍala* consisting of an image of Christ is used as a *samatha* meditation subject, then the *nimitta* that will arise may well be a 'vision' of that same Christ. …The *nimitta* – however holy or awe-inspiring its appearance – is a perfectly natural occurrence, the *vipāka* [result] of a certain kammic development.

Saddhatissa (1971: 77)

kasiṇa = device for meditation: see Chapter 4

nimitta = mental image derived from meditation

Figure 2.1 **Sitting in meditation** (by kind permission of Aruna Publications)

POSTURE

The Buddha described four postures, standing, walking, sitting and lying down, all of which may be used to observe the mind and practise meditation. The most common, for meditation conducted in seclusion, is sitting. The recommendations given in the canon for this are sparse: that the back should be straight and the legs crossed. This probably meant a lotus position, or a half-lotus. This is where one foot rests on the opposite thigh; the knees should touch the ground, though this is not always possible at first. The 'Burmese posture' is sometimes simpler, in which one foot is placed alongside the opposite leg rather than on the thigh. Most schools say that the important thing is to be stable and comfortable, and not to strain too much when first starting. Thai women often sit with both legs to one side. Modern meditators sometimes use chairs, though this is mildly discouraged in some systems as the posture cannot be sustained as long and not enough strength is developed in the lower part of the body. If it is the only way to be comfortable, though, it should be taken. In *Jātaka* stories and in the idealized existence of the Universal Monarch, the Bodhisatta, the Buddha in a past life, sits on a palanquin to meditate – presumably then, as now, a large cushion-like couch. This would probably now be considered far too luxurious in most Asian meditative contexts! But it is an encouraging precedent. While many Asians are comfortable with sitting on the floor, most Westerners usually need a cushion when they start, and many as they continue. An alternative posture is for the meditator to kneel, sitting on the heels with, sometimes, a cushion as support. This posture, used in martial arts as a resting position in Eastern Buddhist countries, is often employed for Zen practice.

The main thing, as so often in early Buddhist texts, is not the particular injunction, but flexibility in its application. Just as a diversity of meditation practices are included in the Buddha's system to cover all temperaments, so the feature of posture seems to be important because it is, the texts imply, to be changed when it gets clearly uncomfortable. Most modern traditions strongly recommend sticking to one posture for a single meditation sitting, for half an hour or an hour. Postures vary slightly according to practice. Zen practitioners face the wall for 'just sitting' practice; they place the left hand over the right and keep the eyes half-open. The classic *samādhi* posture, with right hand over left, eyes closed and in an empty space, perhaps at the root of a tree, or, more likely in front of a shrine, is used for most South Asian practice. The eyes are kept shut. The Thais have a series of graceful movements whereby posture can be changed during a sitting practice without attention being taken away from the meditation object and without causing disturbance to others. The feet are pulled out, the practitioner moves position and the feet are returned to a new posture.

While the detail of such recommendations may have changed since the time of the Buddha, the spirit of the teaching of early Buddhism is maintained through a sense of balance in diet, exercise and sitting practice. The mind and body should not become strained, tense, or over slack. Frequency is more important than forcing things. Saddhatissa says, 'five minutes each day is of more value than one hour every couple of weeks'. In this way, the legs gradually become more adapted to the posture. Unlike some ancient Indian schools, which insisted on harsh postures, or used posture in an extreme way by long periods in one position, early Buddhist texts, on the rare occasions the subject is discussed, emphasize the middle way. One of the Buddha's followers who suffers from sleepiness is advised in the text to go for a walk; the Buddha himself lies down when he has back-ache. From the meditative point of view there are times when a slight realignment of posture can change the whole perspective of the practice. Practitioners sometimes find looking at an image of the Buddha helpful to provide a natural corrective to the mental state present when, say, the back becomes slumped or the shoulders tense.

MINDFULNESS

Once basics such as object, posture and a teacher have been chosen, the practitioner can move on to the practice of meditation. The word that has been most associated with Buddhist meditation in the West has been that of *sati*, now almost universally translated into English as 'mindfulness'. Derived from the word 'to remember', it is sometimes described as awareness, and has been termed 'the pivotal factor of the path'. It is the quality that teachers from all Buddhist traditions enjoin most in new practitioners – yet say is the most difficult to teach. The Buddha said it was impossible for mindfulness to be in excess and that it balances all other factors of the awake mind, which it is said to define by its very presence. As an aspect of meditation, one modern teacher has compared it to the taste of an orange: you know it once you have tasted it, but cannot really describe it to anyone else. In fact from a doctrinal point of view humans are said to experience this quality, naturally, fairly frequently, as it is a feature of consciousness whenever there is alertness and confidence. It may not be established as a foundation of mindfulness, however, unless cultivated: many Buddhist texts are devoted to explaining how it can be aroused.

THE FOUR FOUNDATIONS OF MINDFULNESS

Mindfulness is most commonly described in four categories: of body, of feelings, of mind, and of *dhammas*, events that include and encompass all of these. These arise inside oneself, internally, outside, externally, and in the movement between the outer and the inner world. Mindfulness, according to texts, knows each area of experience as it arises. So, when taking a walk, the feeling of enjoyment of sunshine, wind in the face, the foot's sensory contact with the ground and the movement when one's balance shifts in the body, are all known as they arise. They are part of the general, moving awareness between the inner and the outer world and the relationship between the two. The mind gradually becomes freed by not becoming lost or engulfed in the thoughts arising from any of these, but by the simple awareness of each sensory event and how it is experienced, and in being aware of the flow and process as one experience follows another. While mindfulness techniques, some of which are discussed in this chapter, may involve some labelling of events as they occur, according to neither traditional doctrine nor modern teaching is that function a property of mindfulness itself. The practitioner is not attempting to classify all experience under four foundations of mindfulness, nor, unless the meditative practice specifically enjoins it, to state to him or herself whether an event is occurring internally, externally or both internally and externally. Rather the aim is to be aware of all experience, for which this classification – often indeed employed as part of many meditation teachings – is considered the most comprehensive and all-encompassing. In early Buddhism, the 'labelling' part of the mind is called *saññā*, identification or perception. Said to be present in all states of consciousness, it is described as the way we interpret our experience, but is distinguished from mindfulness, which is a particular kind of awareness. Mindfulness of body is particularly emphasized by the Buddha and all schools of meditation.

One text, the *Satipaṭṭhāna-Sutta*, has ensured that Buddhist meditative practices associated with mindfulness have been communicated around Asia and the West. This describes the four foundations of mindfulness, and is considered a central teaching by many, if not most of the Buddhist traditions. Its contents were sometimes shifted around, added to or changed as it was translated repeatedly in China and other Buddhist regions, with different exercises and recommendations included as it was transported from area to area. Its intention, however, remained the same: to ensure that this quality was taught, in a comprehensive and inclusive way.

The practice of mindfulness in a general sense is encouraged at all times and in daily life, even when there is not a special attention just to the motion of walking, or the sitting meditation practice:

> And again, monks, a monk, when walking, knows, 'I am walking';
> when standing he knows, 'I am standing'; when sitting he knows, 'I
> am sitting'; when lying down he knows, 'I am lying down'; or, however
> his body is disposed, he knows it.
>
> In this way he practises, contemplating the body in the body
> internally, externally and both internally and externally... In this way
> too, monks, a monk practises contemplating the body in the body.

> And again, monks, a monk acts with clear comprehension when
> going backwards and forwards. He acts with clear comprehension
> when looking ahead or behind, when bending and stretching, in
> wearing his robes and carrying his bowl, when eating and drinking,
> chewing and swallowing, when defecating and urinating, when
> walking, standing, sitting, falling asleep, waking up, talking and
> keeping silent.
>
> In this way he practises contemplating the body in the body
> internally, externally and both internally and externally... In this way
> too, monks, a monk practises contemplating the body in the body.
>
> *Satipaṭṭhāna-Sutta*, M I 57

CLEAR COMPREHENSION AND WISDOM

A companion quality to mindfulness, clear comprehension, is also enjoined
repeatedly in Buddhist texts. This is clarity of intention: to take a modern
example, it is not much good to be extremely mindful of lifting one's foot,
if one is trying to find where sugar is stacked in the supermarket and have
lost clarity of intention about that. The aspect of 'clear comprehension' is
soon associated in the canon with the wisdom (*paññā*), the quality linked to
the first two path factors, in particular the first, right view. Work on wisdom
does involve more use of the labelling part of the mind. The three marks said
to characterize existence, impermanence (*anicca*), dis-ease (*dukkha*) and *anattā*
(not-self), are seen in events as they arise, so that the mind can be free from
attachments to things as being permanent, pleasant or 'mine'. As we see
later in this chapter, many meditation practices and, indeed, whole schools
of Buddhism have an emphasis on developing awareness and wisdom, the
ability to discern and discriminate, and the intuitive 'knowing' (*jñāna*) that
can be trained through meditation practice.

Teachings on mindfulness in the Pāli canon seem carefully structured to
arouse as well as describe the quality enjoined. This extract is part of a *sutta*
addressed to the parricide Ajātasattu, who visits the Buddha to ask about the
benefits of the holy life:

> And how, great king, is a monk a gatekeeper for the faculties of sense?
>
> Here, a monk, seeing a visible object with the eye, does not grasp at
> the appearance nor does he grasp at its various details. Because harmful,

unskilful states such as longing and discontent would assail him if he were to abide without restraint with regard to the eye faculty, he practises restraint, guards the eye faculty and achieves restraint over the eye faculty. Here, hearing a sound with the ear... smelling an odour with the nose... tasting a flavour with the tongue... touching a physical object with the body... apprehending an object with the mind, the monk does not grasp at the appearance nor does he grasp at the various details. Because harmful, unskilful states such as longing and discontent would assail him if he were to abide without restraint with regard to the faculty of mind, he practises restraint, guards the faculty of the mind and achieves restraint over the faculty of the mind. Endowed with this noble restraint over the faculties of sense he experiences within himself an untainted happiness.

In this way, great king, a monk is a gatekeeper for the faculties of sense.

And how, great king, is a monk endowed with mindfulness and clear comprehension? Here, a monk acts with clear comprehension when walking backwards and forwards, in looking ahead or behind, when bending and stretching, in wearing his outer and inner robe and carrying his bowl, when eating and drinking, chewing and swallowing, when defecating and urinating, when walking, standing, sitting, falling asleep, waking up, talking and keeping silent. In this way, a monk is endowed with mindfulness and clear comprehension.

From *Sāmaññaphala-Sutta*, D I 70

CONCENTRATION (*SAMĀDHI*) AND *JHĀNA*

A companion quality to mindfulness is concentration. This, according to Buddhism, is present in all our consciousness to a greater or lesser degree anyway. It brings together the factors in the mind at any moment. In daily life it may be intensified when doing something which arouse interest and sustained attention. Where it is cultivated in meditation, this interest is strengthened, and concentration involves the mind resting with attention on an object, often to the exclusion of others. In a meditative sense it is not the same as 'concentrating', say, on a piece of work. Rather it is perhaps more like the original meaning of the English word concentration: a bringing together and a unification. It can be seen, for instance, when the mind naturally finds happiness and peace in a single object, such as the sight of a vast expanse of blue sea or sky, or the lustre of a jewel or a crystal catching the sun. For this purpose, meditations involving concentration usually involve taking time out and practising meditation in seclusion. No one wants to become too one-pointed in a meditative sense when driving a car or trying to do the shopping! Concentration is sometimes compared to an unflickering candle flame, whereas mindfulness is like the light it emits.

The *jhānas*

All of these factors are described as coming together for the first jhāna. The mental image becomes settled and the mind becomes unified, happy and refreshed. At this point the faculties of faith, energy, mindfulness, concentration and wisdom are said to come into balance.

The first jhāna: accompanied by initial thought, sustained thought or examination, joy, happiness and one-pointedness. This is compared to a bathman taking water to moisten and knead soap powder into a malleable ball.

The second jhāna: accompanied by joy, happiness and one-pointedness. This is compared to a pool fed by underground springs.

The third jhāna: accompanied by happiness and one-pointedness. This is compared to lotuses seen blossoming under the water, pervaded by it.

The fourth jhāna: accompanied by one-pointedness and great equanimity. This is compared to a man sitting with a pure white cloth over his head, covering his entire body.

In the *Sāmaññaphala-Sutta*, the Buddha illustrates the *jhānas* with the images described above. Considerable emphasis is also placed on the bodily experience of meditation: jhāna does not just involve the mind. As is said of the fourth jhāna:

> And he sits suffusing this very body with a purified and translucent mind
> so that there is no place in his body that is not suffused with a purified and
> translucent mind.

FURTHER SIMILES FOR THE FOUR JHĀNAS

In one *sutta* the Buddha compared the mind to a city, with mindfulness as the gatekeeper, checking who is coming in and leaving the city. The meditations are compared to the fuel and provision of its storehouse, which ensure that the citizens are never hungry or malnourished. The similes are suggestive: the Buddha implies that the practice of concentration (*samādhi*) and mindfulness leading to jhāna gives long-term fuel and nourishment for the mind, so that it does not become 'hungry', drained or unhappy. The basics are provided by the first jhāna, which ensures the survival of the city. The second jhāna gives some staples to the diet, the third jhāna proteins and nourishing food. The fourth gives flavour, taste and the means whereby the other ingredients can be made into a palatable meal.

First *jhāna:* compared to stores of grass, wood and water
Second *jhāna*: compared to stores of rice and corn
Third *jhāna*: compared to stores of sesame, beans, and cereals
Fourth *jhāna*: compared to stores of ghee, butter, oil, sugar and salt.

A IV 111

In addition four other meditations are associated with jhāna. The formless spheres eventually came to be referred to as four further jhānas. The last two of these were practised by the Buddha before his enlightenment or awakening. In the *Mahāsaccaka-Sutta* he said that they did not then lead to peace, perhaps needing the presence of the others or a more balanced foundation.

The four formless spheres are:

1   The sphere of infinite space
2   The sphere of infinite consciousness
3   The sphere of no-thing
4   The sphere of neither perception nor non-perception.

JHĀNA

In Pāli texts, jhāna is described as being supported and developed by faith, mindfulness, energy, concentration and wisdom. In the *Sāmaññaphala-Sutta*, for instance, the meditator is described 'setting up' mindfulness before the practice of jhāna. The *Abhidhamma* text, the *Dhammasaṅgani*, lists mindfulness and wisdom as factors of all meditations. Clarity and 'mastery', the abilities to advert to, enter, sustain and to control at will meditation states are constantly enjoined. Such advice stresses, through implication, that meditation requires alertness and wisdom and is not a passive, quiescent state, as is sometimes suggested by translations that use words like 'trance' and 'hypnotic state' for *jhāna*. Within the canon, and within the teachings of the most reputed meditation teachers, wakeful flexibility and clear comprehension are constantly enjoined as essential for *samatha* meditation.

SAMATHA AND VIPASSANĀ

Mindfulness and concentration are essential for all forms of meditation. In meditation the mind needs to able to rest in a unified state upon an object and also to be aware of what is going on in internally and externally. With a basis in both these qualities, two strands of meditative practice emerged at the time of the Buddha, found in most Buddhist meditative systems to this day. They are that of calm (*samatha*) and insight (*vipassanā*). These two ways are in part a matter of emphasis. We can see this if we take an object like the breath, perhaps the most commonly pursued object in Buddhist meditative systems. It can be explored with an emphasis on feeling, and on its peaceful, enlivening aspects. Calm and joy in the breath can be aroused and the mind can enter into a peaceful state. A *samatha* school will use this feeling to develop the *nimitta*, an image that arises in the meditation, to enter *jhāna*, developing a balance of the five faculties of faith, energy, mindfulness, concentration and wisdom. The emphasis is on finding calm and contentment first, with insight as a supplement or associated factor: the practice of *jhāna* needs some wisdom. A *vipassanā* school may look at the breath from another point of view: it is impermanent, not always satisfactory and it is not owned: it is not 'self'. The meditator will not be encouraged to pay much attention to images, and may not arouse the faculties to the development of *jhāna*, but focus more on insight into what is going on in the breath and the body. The breathing mindfulness *sutta*, of which there is an extract below, teaches the interplay of both these approaches for the full development of the four foundations of mindfulness. Most meditation teachers recommend some *samatha* at the outset: Westerners in particular have lively minds that need some calm and restfulness. In practice, one school should develop the strengths of the other school in time, either in an ongoing balance, or by paying more attention to the other at a later stage. If one looks closely, one usually finds that other aspects of the eightfold path are taught in most schools, particularly in Asian contexts, where the balance has emerged from centuries of teaching. *Samatha* practices such as the meditation on loving-kindness and recollections of the qualities of the Triple Gem, the Buddha, the *dhamma* and the *saṅgha*, are taught in most traditions. Some schools of *vipassanā* insist on practitioners attaining jhāna, before moving onto insight. One meditation teacher has described calm as 'the increase of happiness' and insight as 'the diminishment of suffering'. A balanced path needs both.

> There are many meditators here in Thailand who ... claim *samatha* is not necessary. One must practise only *vipassanā*. To them there is even no need to observe the precepts. They point out that one reaches the Path and achieves the goal in *nibbāna* through wisdom ... here they forget another principle ... 'one who progresses well in the precepts has one-pointedness as one's merit ... one who progresses well in one-pointedness has wisdom as one's merit.' When one progresses well in wisdom, one will reach liberation, free from defilements. This is it. Those who explain or those that think that *samādhi* is not necessary are the ones who have not yet reached *samādhi*. That's why they cannot see the merit of *samādhi*. Those who have attained *samādhi* will never speak against it.
>
> Thate (1978: 93)

INSIGHT

At the end of a meditation practice the meditator is sometimes encouraged to 'let go' of any experiences, and to see them in the light of the three marks. All experiences, however joyful and peaceful, partake of impermanence (*anicca*). This, and other factors, makes them partake of unsatisfactoriness (*dukkha*). They do not contribute to a lasting or an enduring 'self'. They arise according to conditions and cannot be controlled. They are not 'mine', and are hence 'non-self' (*anattā*). The *Rathavinīta-Sutta* is one of the main texts in the Pāli canon on the practice of insight and wisdom (*paññā*). It compares each stage to a stage in a chariot-race and gives the seven stages of the purification of insight knowledge. The meditator starts with behaviour (*sīla*), goes on in the second stage to calm (*samatha*) and then works through levels of insight:

1   The purification of virtue (*sīlavisuddhi*)
2   The purification of mind (*cittavisuddhi*)
3   The purification of view (*diṭṭhivisuddhi*)
4   The purification by overcoming doubt (*kankhāvitaraṇavisuddhi*)

5   The purification by knowledge and vision of what is path and not-path (*maggāmaggañāṇadassanavisuddhi*)
6   The purification by knowledge and vision of the way (*paṭipadāñāṇadassanavisuddhi*)
7   The purification by knowledge and vision (*ñāṇadassanavisuddhi*)

The purification of virtue comes under the practice of *sīla* and the second purification, of mind, under the practice of calm (*samatha*). The next five form the basis of many modern insight meditation systems. In these, 'views' about meditation need to be seen. Doubt is then overcome and there is an increase in confidence. Ten 'defilements' of insight, such as joy or attachment to any one intuition, can arise and are purified. Knowledge arises as to what is path and what is not: some states, for instance, lead to further awakening, calm and insight. Others, however, lead to excitement or over-agitation and so do not contribute to the peace of the middle way. Through knowing and seeing, the path ahead becomes clear: direct knowledge of phenomena occurs and there is a 'turning away' from attachment to the continued flux in the mind and physical events. This includes 'equanimity about formations', in which the meditator transcends fear, terror or delight. Finally the necessary purification that will lead to awakening can be discerned: the meditator finally loosens all attachment or rejection with regard to events and conditions, and *nibbāna*, the unconditioned, is glimpsed.

BREATHING MINDFULNESS

Perhaps the most widespread object used amongst Buddhists as meditation is taught in the West, is that of the breath. Contemplating this is described by the Buddha as the acme of his teaching, 'the most serene abiding'. For this practice the movement in and out of the body of the breath is observed. This awareness is taught as something that can be going on gently in the background during the day, as a way of producing mindfulness and alertness. Or it can be developed as a sitting practice, where the breath becomes increasingly the single object of the mind. As suggested above, it can be pursued as a *samatha* practice, to produce a joyful alertness that leads to calm, or as a *vipassanā* practice, in which the emphasis is on insight, through the experience of the breath, into the arising and falling of all events in the body and mind.

Suttas on the subject explore the interplay of both calm and insight. Throughout Southeast Asia there are all kinds of practices associated with the simple watching of the breath. Inevitably practitioners of one method are likely to favour their own, but each school has its own techniques and customs, most of which are rooted in the recommendations of the *sutta*.

Extract from *ĀNĀPĀNASATI-SUTTA*

The *Breathing Mindfulness Sutta* has been one of the most popular texts in the history of Buddhist practice, and was one of the first to reach China in the second century CE.

And how, monks, is breathing mindfulness, cultivated? How is it frequently practised? How is it of great fruit and great reward? Here, monks, a monk goes to a forest, or the roots of a tree or an empty place and sits, folding his legs in a cross-legged position, making his body straight and sets up mindfulness in front of him.

Mindful, he breathes in; mindful, he breathes out.

1 As he breathes in a long breath, he knows, 'I am breathing in a long breath', or, as he breathes out a long breath, he knows, 'I am breathing out a long breath'.

2 As he breathes in a short breath, he knows, 'I am breathing in a short breath', or, as he breathes out a short breath, he knows, 'I am breathing out a short breath'.

3 He trains thus: 'Experiencing the whole body I shall breathe in', he trains thus: 'Experiencing the whole body I shall breathe out'.

4 He trains thus: 'Tranquillizing the bodily formations I shall breathe in', he trains thus: 'Tranquillizing the bodily formations I shall breathe out'.

5 He trains thus: 'Experiencing joy I shall breathe in'; he trains thus: 'Experiencing joy I shall breathe out'.

6 He trains thus: 'Experiencing happiness I shall breathe in'; he trains thus: 'Experiencing happiness I shall breathe out'.

7 He trains thus: 'Experiencing the formations in the mind I shall breathe in'; he trains thus: 'Experiencing the formations in the mind I shall breathe out'.

8   He trains thus: 'Tranquillizing the formations in the mind I shall breathe in'; he trains thus: 'Tranquillizing the formations in the mind I shall breathe out'.

9   He trains thus: 'Experiencing the mind I shall breathe in'; he trains thus: 'Experiencing the mind I shall breathe out'.

10   He trains thus: 'Gladdening the mind I shall breathe in'; he trains thus: 'Gladdening the mind I shall breathe out'.

11   He trains thus: 'Concentrating the mind I shall breathe in'; he trains thus: 'Concentrating the mind I shall breathe out'.

12   He trains thus: 'Liberating the mind I shall breathe in'; he trains thus: 'Liberating the mind I shall breathe out'.

13   He trains thus, 'Contemplating impermananence I shall breathe in'; he trains thus: 'Contemplating impermanence I shall breathe out'.

14   He trains thus: 'Contemplating dispassion I shall breathe in'; he trains thus: 'Contemplating dispassion I shall breathe out'.

15   He trains thus: 'Contemplating cessation I shall breathe in'; he trains thus: 'Contemplating cessation I shall breathe out'.

16   He trains thus: 'Contemplating letting go I shall breathe in'; he trains thus: 'Contemplating letting go I shall breathe out'.

This is how, monks, mindfulness of breathing is cultivated and practised frequently, so that it is of great fruit and great reward.

(M III 78–88)

In this *sutta*, we can see many elements that, in varying degrees, become prominent in subsequent forms of Buddhism. The first four stages are linked to mindfulness of body, the next four to mindfulness of feeling, the next to mindfulness of mind and the last to mindfulness of *dhammas*. There is also a slight emphasis towards calm (*samatha*) in the first three 'fours', with such features as gladdening and tranquillizing the mind, and a slight emphasis towards insight (*vipassanā*) in the last four, as the breath is seen as impermanent and as arousing dispassion, cessation and 'letting go'. It is considered to be the most comprehensive as well as the most balanced of all the Buddha's objects for meditation. A *samatha* bias is more likely to differentiate and develop a distinction between the long and the short breath described in the *sutta*. The recommended 'long' breath is employed by expanding the chest slightly on the inbreath, thus opening the diaphragm more and allowing a very long and peaceful breath to arise. This method is particularly favoured where the practice needs a light, peaceful attentiveness on the pleasant aspects of the breath to introduce a feeling of wellbeing.

Other schools do not exercise any control on the breath. The *vipassanā* way is more likely to follow this procedure. For such practices attention follows the rise and fall of the breath in the body as it occurs. Methods vary: some, for instance, investigate the distinction between 'name' (*nāma*, mind and its mental states) and form (*rūpa*), the fourth link of dependent origination, discussed in Chapter 3. In a breathing practice 'name' is the mind and its associated states, which perceives the breath; 'form' is the breath itself and the experience of the body. The relationship between these two, knower and known, is examined for the impermanence of both features. Some distinction may be made between fine materiality and the four elements, from which matter derives. Other objects which arise at the 'sense-doors' will also be investigated – a touch, perhaps – and the mind that knows the object that makes 'constructings' on the basis of that will be investigated too. From here the moving nature of the perceiving mind – also regarded as a sense in Buddhism – may be seen through its processes, sorting and responding with each breath to the changing nature of objects received at the 'sense-doors', in the body and the mind, as they arise.

It is worth noting that each school of meditation has its own methods and that if one is doing a particular kind with a specific teacher it is considered very important to follow the instructions as given. Most of the methods have evolved over a long period of time and provide their own correctives and balances.

Following the breath

Buddhadāsa was one of the most renowned teachers of meditation in the twentieth century. We can see, in his differentiation between the qualities of the long and the short breath, that he has been deeply influenced by the Pāli canon and subsequent commentaries. He intersperses rhetorical questions with comments, exhortation and straightforward advice, a method that also seems to have been characteristic of the way the Buddha is described teaching in the early texts.

Many kinds of Breath

For example, when the breathing is long, how does it influence our awareness? What reactions does the short breathing cause? What are the influences of coarse and fine breathing, comfortable and uncomfortable breathing? We observe the different types of breath and their different influences until we can distinguish clearly how the long and short breaths, coarse and fine breaths, and comfortable and uncomfortable breaths differ. We must know the variations in the reactions to and influences of these various properties of the breath, of these qualities that influence our awareness, our sensitivities, our mind.

Along with the above observations, we need to watch the effect or the flavor of the different kinds of breath. The flavors that arise are kinds of feelings, such as happiness, non-happiness, dukkha, annoyance, and contentment. Observe and experience the flavors or effects caused, especially, by the long breath and short breath, by the coarse breath and fine breath, and by the easy breath and uneasy breath. Find out how they have different flavors. For instance, we will see that the longer breath gives a greater sense of peace and well being, it has a happier taste than the short breath. Different kinds of breath bring different kinds of happiness. We learn to analyze and distinguish the different flavors that come with the different kinds of breath we have scrutinized.

Buddhadāsa (1989: 27)

BREATHING MINDFULNESS AS A PRACTICE FOR DAILY LIFE

To put in a few conscious, deep and calm respirations before starting any continuous work, will likewise be found most beneficial to oneself and to the work as well. To cultivate the habit of doing so before important decisions, making responsible utterances, talking to an excited person etc., will prevent many rash acts and words, and will preserve the balance and efficiency of mind... These are only some examples of how even a casual Mindfulness of Breathing as applicable in the midst of ordinary life, may have beneficial results.

Nyanaponika (1972: 62)

WALKING PRACTICE

Earlier on, in the discussion about posture, it was noted that some meditation practices are undertaken in postures other than sitting. At meditation centres, walking practices are recommended to arouse both concentration and mindfulness. Instructions are also given for meditators to take a longer, freer walk for exercise and, if in natural surroundings, to appreciate the countryside as well. But the act of walking itself may be taken as a meditation object. For this it is used as a supplement to sitting practice, usually in a monastic setting, or on meditation retreats. It needs some seclusion and, like a sitting practice, is not conducted during the usual events of the day. There is a simple reason for this: it needs concentration as well as mindfulness and would not be advisable on the pavement at rush-hour, or while doing the shopping!

The practice needs most of one's attention to be placed on the process of walking, and the sensation within the foot as it gently and evenly touches the ground, just as the attention is given to the breath or the development of loving-kindness as a sitting practice. In monasteries there is usually a space specially designated for this walking, known as a *caṅkamāna*. Modern meditation teachers give many variations of the walking practice. Some ask the practitioner to watch each stage of the process of walking, so that the movement as one lifts the foot, moves it and then touches the ground with the whole of the foot is observed. This can be done purely by being aware of the bodily feeling, while keeping awareness of the area around in the external world. The *Satipaṭṭhāna-sutta* speaks of awareness of each foundation internally, externally, and both internally and externally. So when people conduct this practice they are usually encouraged to be aware of sounds, wind, warmth or coolness and any movements in the world around. On meditation retreats the process of walking is examined in fine detail, so that the meditator becomes aware of the subtle shifts in balance as the body gradually moves from one step to another. Awareness is also maintained of the surroundings, the breath passing in and out of the body and the way the body rearranges itself as each step is taken.

This extract is taken from a modern Burmese teacher, Ven. Khammai Dhammasāmi. It is one of many kinds of practice of this kind. Although it is sometimes called 'mindful walking', its aim is to arouse a balance with concentration too.

Vipassanā meditation practice can be accomplished adopting various postures, standing, sitting, walking, eating, lying etc. It can be practised at any time. The most common postures are sitting and walking. People usually start with sitting and alternate it with walking.

Unlike sitting, in walking meditation you keep your eyes open. This is closer to how we would be doing in our working life. If you master walking meditation, you will be able to apply it to your working day and improve your awareness in daily life.

Similar to choosing breathing in and out as our primary object, the primary object in walking is the movement of our feet, lifting and placing. Contemplating lifting as we lift our foot off the ground and placing as we place it on the ground. However, we must not look at our feet. We look straight ahead and downward at an angle of 40 degrees or three meters ahead. This is to help us avoid the obligation of making any eye contact with other people. If we look straight down we may become dizzy and be unable to develop concentration (*samādhi*). It we look too far ahead, we will not be able to develop contemplation, as there will be many distractions...

You then walk slowly, much slower than usual speed, noting *lifting, placing, lifting, placing*, until you reach the end. Now stop, noting *stopping, stopping.* Turn back, observing *turning, turning, turning.* Stand for a while to make a mental note of *standing, standing, standing.* Then start walking again noting, *lifting* and *placing.* At the beginning, the distance must not be less than ten paces or more than thirty. It is preferred that one chooses to make between 20–30 paces if possible. If it is too short, your mind will tend to wander and you may feel frustrated. If it is too long, you will have difficulty in developing concentration.

...

Some find walking meditation easier [than sitting]. People should be encouraged to do it more as it is the first step towards achieving general mindfulness in daily life. Walking meditation helps to balance many things.

Dhammasāmi (1999: 33–4)

Dhammasāmi notes, 'Just have one awareness when you are crossing the road. Develop the awareness that you are crossing the road'.

BEGINNING AND ENDING A PRACTICE

One feature of early Buddhist teaching, and other Buddhist traditions, is the importance of making a clear start to a meditation practice and finishing it. The meditation object is adverted to, the meditation practice entered and then lasts for a certain period of time. After that, the meditator is encouraged to leave it behind, open the eyes and become aware of surroundings. Sometimes after that a recollection practice is done, quietly remembering each stage of the meditation. This is supposed to help settle the meditation in the mind before leaving the practice. The ability to do all of these things is known as five masteries: to advert, to enter, to sustain, to emerge and to remember. Almost all schools of practice have ways of ensuring that from the outset the meditation practice is put aside when finished, such as paying active attention to the senses and the world around.

CONCLUSION

In this chapter the role of the teacher, posture and some basic guidelines, suggested by most schools, are discussed. Certain features of meditation practice are described, including mindfulness (*sati*) and concentration (*samādhi*), an ancient pairing. The two approaches of calm (*samatha*) and insight (*vipassanā*), are considered. There are many objects of meditation. One of the most popular is that of breathing mindfulness, which may be developed with an emphasis towards calm, or insight, or both. The chapter also notes the importance of making a clear distinction between sitting or walking in meditation and going out into daily life.

FURTHER READING

Buddhadāsa, Bhikkhu and Santikaro, Bhikkhu trans. (1989) *Mindfulness with Breathing: Unveiling the secrets of life, A Manual for Serious beginners*, Bangkok: Evolution/Liberation.

Cousins, L.S. (1973) 'Buddhist Jhāna: Its Nature and Attainment according to the Pāli sources', *Religion*, 3: 115–31.

Cousins, L.S. (1984) '*Samatha-yāna* and *Vipassanā-yāna*', in Dhammapala, G., Gombrich, R.F. and Norman, K.R. (eds) *Buddhist Studies in Honour of Hammalava Saddhatissa*, Nugegoda, Sri Lanka: Hammalava Saddhatissa Felicitation Volume Committee.

Cousins, L.S. (1985) 'Buddhism', in Hinnells, J.R. (ed.) *A Handbook of Living Religions*, Harmondsworth, Middx: Penguin, 278–343.

Dhammasāmi, Ven. (1999) *Mindfulness Meditation Made Easy*, Penang: Inward Path.

Gunaratana, Mahathera H. (1985) *The Path of Serenity and Insight: An Explanation of the Buddhist Jhānas*, Delhi, Varanasi, Patna, Madras: Motilal Banarsidass.

Mahasi Sayadaw (1990) *Satipaṭṭhāna Vipassanā: Insight Through Mindfulness*, Kandy: BPS.

Nāṇarama, M. Mahāthera, Kariyawasam, A.G.S. trans. (1997) *The Seven Contemplations of Insight: A Treatise on Insight Meditation*, Kandy: BPS.

Nyanaponika Thera (1972) *The Heart of Buddhist Meditation: A Handbook of Mental Training Based on the Buddha's Way of Mindfulness*, London: Rider.

Rahula, W. (1967) *What the Buddha Taught*, P. Demieville foreword, 2nd edn., Bedford: Gordon Fraser.

Saddhatissa, Ven. H. (1971) *The Buddha's Way*, London: George, Allen and Unwin.

Shaw, S. (2006) *Buddhist Meditation: An Anthology of Texts*, London: Routledge.

Sumedho, Ven. (1985) *Mindfulness: the Path to the Deathless: the Meditation Teachings of Venerable Ajahn Sumedho*, Great Gaddesden: Amaravati.

Thate Desaransī, Phra Ācharn, Attagar K. trans. (1978) *Meditation in Words*, Nongkhai, Thailand.

Vajiriñāṇa, P. Mahāthera (1962; 2nd edn. 1975) *Buddhist Meditation in Theory and Practice*, Kuala Lumpur: Buddhist Missionary Society.

Tracing Back Radiance

Some features of the early Buddhist understanding of the mind

Three

This mind, monks, is radiant, but is defiled by impurities which come as visitors from outside. (A I 10)

THE KILESAS (*KLEŚA*) OR DEFILEMENTS

One famous early Buddhist text describes the mind as naturally radiant but defiled by adventitious defilements, or 'visitors', described as literally coming from outside to disturb it. While this statement needs some modification, in this chapter we will look at some of the doctrinal and practical implications associated with 'the radiant mind' in early Buddhism. It reflects an underlying attitude towards the practice of meditation that permeates all early Buddhist texts and modern practice in Southern Buddhist – now called Theravāda – countries. The chapter will also consider briefly the way that this idea is developed and takes a life of its own in many other schools, shaping the attitude towards what constitutes a meditation and how it is practised.

KUSALA AND AKUSALA

As a starting point it will be useful to give some analysis of the theory associated with the Buddhist psychological and philosophical understanding of the mind, in particular the one that takes rebirth in a human body. A familiar notion from Western schools of psychological theory is the idea that because humans block states such as anger or desire, they do not experience their full psychological potential. This doctrine to some degree rests upon an assumption that the human species has suppressed powerful instinctive drives which may need to find outlet and expression within daily life. The Buddhist philosophical tradition of *Abhidhamma* does not deny the great pull of such states, which are associated with existence in the lower, animal and ghost realms. It suggests also, however, that the powerful 'roots' of greed, hatred and ignorance are mixed up in nearly all humans with three positive roots, which define and bring about a human rebirth: non-greed or generosity, non-hatred or loving-kindness and wisdom. Basic patterns of response and volitional formations rooted in ignorance overlay these tendencies and produce some of the negative habit patterns, difficulties and mannerisms that accompany a human identity for the period of a single rebirth. So, from the point of view of early Buddhist philosophy, it is positive roots which humans often stifle and crush as often, if not more so, than other roots. The natural tendency of the mind to be free from greed and hence generous may not be given expression if there is meanness, avarice or worry. An innate predisposition towards non-hatred and hence loving-kindness is not allowed to be expressed where there is resentment or anger. Ignorance, although an innate part of a human rebirth, is said to be the active turning away from wisdom and from that which knows. Within any situation there is the possibility of knowing, or of finding wisdom from which to act, but much of the time, through the power of the hindrances, often conditioned by habitual responses and patterns of thinking, humans actively reject this option. So they perpetuate cycles and habits which produce suffering rather than freedom. 'Views' form and crystallize, which according to the *Abhidhamma*, stiffen and make rigid the body and mind; while pride or the idea that one is worse than others, in early Buddhism considered a form of pride, puffs people up or diminishes confidence and strength. Hence the cycles and innate predispositions, conditioned by earlier rebirths, become more deeply ingrained.

In Indian languages the word *kusala*, used so often in early Buddhist texts to describe the positive possibilities that inhere in a human rebirth, has connotations of skilfulness, flexibility, goodness, intelligence and even humour: it is the word employed for inquiring about someone's health. The mind that is disturbed by hindrances all the time becomes, however, *akusala*, unhealthy, unwieldy, unskilful and 'bad': it is like a kind of ineptitude or illness in one's dealings. These disturbances, which are seen to deaden the mind, arise much of the time, for most people, but mindfulness does not allow them to engulf consciousness so that it is no longer 'awake'.

The Pāli canon describes these hindrances as obstructions or obstacles: like weeds they crush and suffocate inherent skilful tendencies so that they cannot grow and flourish. The practice of meditation, and the alertness derived from applying mindfulness in daily life, is likely to weaken the hold of these habit patterns. It does this by allowing the health of the human rebirth, based on what is known as the skilful mind (*kusala citta*), to reassert itself and create a predisposition towards mindfulness, happiness and wisdom. This does not mean that the mind can become immediately free

[handwritten margin note: akusala: bad / negative   kusala: positive connotations]

from all defilements – while living in the world, and not enlightened, this is not considered possible. It teaches that where there is mindfulness and careful guarding of the senses, experiences are noted and appreciated, but do not pull the mind in different directions, so that a proper balance is found for the further development of calm and insight.

THE FIVE HINDRANCES

The defilements that obstruct the mind are summarized in early Buddhist texts by five hindrances that are successively removed in the stages of path, and whose vestiges only go from the mind when enlightenment or awakening takes place. These are finally eradicated when, with some sort of union of good behaviour (*sīla*), concentration (*samādhi*) and wisdom, their origin and arising is known with the mind that has been made mature with calm and insight. The practice of calm meditation also helps the mind to settle so that they can, for a while, lessen their hold. In one early text the Buddha speaks to a brahmin, Sangarāva, who tells him that he is unable to remember his most basic texts because his mind is so distracted. The Buddha compares the mind to a clear pool. The pool can be troubled, muddied or darkened by a number of different things. It may become stained or coloured, a comparison with desire. It may become turbulent and heated, compared to ill-will. It may become brackish and mossy, compared to sloth and torpor, or agitated, compared to restlessness and worry or, if it is shaded, simply very dark, compared to vacillating doubt (A III 229–36).

1 Longing (*abhijjhā*) or desire for objects of the five senses (*kāmacchanda*)
2 Ill-will (*vyāpāda-padosa*)
3 Sloth and torpor (*thīna-m-iddha*)
4 Restlessness and worry (*uddhacca-kukkucca*)
5 Vacillating doubt (*vicikicchā*)

According to early Buddhism, most human beings experience most of these states several times in one day, largely according to the habitual patterns established throughout a lifetime. In a meditation practice, however, the establishment of mindfulness and concentration are intended to set up different habits, which will start to lessen the pull of the hindrances. In time the practice aims to establish the positive qualities that characterize the active, skilful mind.

A PĀLI TEXT ON THE HINDRANCES

The following passage is taken from one of the most famous *suttas* in the Pāli canon, the *Sāmaññaphala-Sutta*, which travelled with Buddhism throughout Central Asia and China as one of the core texts of the tradition. It gives the classic formula for each of the five hindrances, and an antidote for each one, though other texts and modern practice offer many other ways of addressing the difficulties they pose in meditation.

Then he, endowed with this noble heap of virtues, this noble restraint of the sense faculties, this noble mindfulness and clear comprehension and this noble contentment, finds for himself a place of seclusion, the roots of a forest tree, a mountain cave or a mountain cleft, a charnel ground, a jungle thicket, or a heap of straw in the open air. After he has returned from the almsround and eaten his food he sits, folding his legs in a cross-legged position, makes his body straight and sets up mindfulness before him.

Abandoning longing for the senses he abides, with a heart free from longing, and purifies his mind of longing.

Abandoning ill-will and hatred, he abides with his mind purified of ill-will and hatred, and, compassionate, wishing for the welfare of all sentient beings, he purifies his mind of ill-will and hatred.

Abandoning sloth and torpor, he abides free from sloth and torpor, and, perceiving light, mindful and clearly comprehending, he purifies his mind of sloth and torpor.

Abandoning restlessness and worry, he abides in calm, and, with a mind made inwardly peaceful, purifies his mind of restlessness and worry.

Abandoning doubt, he abides having crossed over doubt, and, without being troubled about what is or is not wholesome, he purifies his mind of doubt.

...In this way, great king, a monk sees that when these five hindrances have not been abandoned in him, it is like a debt, a sickness, an imprisonment, and an enslavement and a road in a wilderness. But when he sees that these five hindrances have been abandoned in him, it is like freedom from debt, good health, release from prison, freedom from slavery and a place of safety. When he sees these five hindrances have been abandoned in him, gladness arises. In the one who is glad, joy arises. The body of the one who is joyful becomes tranquil. The one who is happy concentrates the mind.

(D I 71–2)

The similes are usually taken to describe each of the five hindrances in turn. Longing is compared to being in debt, ill-will to a debilitating illness, sloth and torpor to a kind of imprisonment, restlessness and worry to enslavement and vacillating doubt to being lost in a wilderness. The 'perception of light' as an antidote for sloth and torpor is commonly advised, and refers to the awareness of a source of light in the external world, such as sunshine or a lamp. From the earliest days of the tradition, meditations were assigned according to temperaments, for which some meditations are particularly suited. Those struggling with a particular hindrance were given special practices by the Buddha to deal with that one, and to cultivate its opposite quality. The underlying assumptions are that the human mind is capable of peace, happiness and alertness, indeed is innately predisposed towards these qualities, if work on the hindrances is undertaken.

HOW THE BUDDHA TEACHES OVERCOMING ONE HINDRANCE: HATRED
In Pāli texts the Buddha demonstrates a number of different methods for achieving this, so it is worth taking a short detour to notice some of the highly specific and diverse ways the Buddha actually taught people to overcome hindrances in particular situations. The second hindrance, for instance, is ill-will, a manifestation of hatred (*dosa*). Rather in the manner of a doctor or a therapist, the Buddha carefully tailors his recommendations according to his audience and purpose. Some variations on this can be seen by looking at a brief selection of texts on this one problem, which is treated as a difficulty that can arise both in daily life and in sitting meditation.

1 The first is highly specific to *a person* and *individual*. In many *suttas* the Buddha answers the challenge of a particular person, such as a proud brahmin, through debate that uses and thereby turns around his adversary's arguments. At other times he simply gets the questioner to see his situation from a different perspective. These verses were given by the Buddha to Tissa, who became a monk late in life and who seems to have had all kinds of problems in meditation, ranging from pride to sleepiness. The verses, from the *Dhammapada*, were recited to him, according to the commentary, after he had complained bitterly about the unkindness of his fellow monks. It is pointed out to him by the Buddha that as he has not behaved well or kindly towards them, he should not be surprised at this. The Buddha then tells him a story of a past life, in which Tissa had

picked a fight by clumsily lying down across a doorway so that a monk had unwittingly trodden on his hair. The tale, it is said, culminates in these verses being delivered. Tissa eventually attains enlightenment.

> He abused me, he struck me! In those who harbour such thoughts, hatred will not cease.
> He abused me, he struck me! In those who do not harbour such thoughts, hatred will cease.
>
> (Dhp 3–4)

2   *A statement of a cause*

Sometimes the Buddha simply gives a short aphorism or statement of the cause of a particular hindrance:

> These two things are causes of the arising of hatred. What two? The repulsive feature of an object and unwise attention [to it]. (A I 87)

3   *A list of recommendations*

Some *suttas* give a list of guidelines, and are delivered, presumably, to a group of monks rather than an individual. These employ one of the Buddha's favourite methods, a short grouping of antidotes to a particular problem. This one, explaining how to free the mind of resentment (*āghāta*), is typical of many lists to counteract hindrances in daily life and meditation, in this case a form of malevolence related to ill-will. The third divine abiding, sympathetic joy is left out, perhaps considered too 'near the bone' for this particular difficulty.

> Monks, there are these five ways of overcoming resentment, whereby all resentment should be overcome.
> What five?
> In the person in whom resentment has been born, loving kindness (*mettā*) should be cultivated. In this way resentment should be overcome.
> In the person in whom resentment has been born, compassion (*karuṇā*) should be cultivated. In this way resentment should be overcome.
> In the person in whom resentment has been born, equanimity (*upekkhā*) should be cultivated. In this way resentment should be overcome.
> In the person in whom resentment has been born, lack of thought and attention should be accorded to it. In this way resentment should be overcome.

In the person in whom resentment has been born, the fact that he has made his own *kamma* should be fixed in his mind, 'This *kamma*, good sir, is of one's own making: one is an heir to *kamma*, *kamma* is the womb, *kamma* is a close relative, *kamma* is a refuge: whatever one does, whether beautiful or unpleasant, one becomes an inheritor of that.'

In this way resentment should be overcome.

So, monks, these are the five ways of overcoming resentment, whereby all resentment should be overcome.

(A III 185–6)

4   A summary of principle

From time to time the Buddha describes a principle on which to base a cure for a particular hindrance. In the Mahāniddesa, for instance, he associates a kind of temperament with the hindrance of ill-will and recommends meditation on the 'beautiful' as an antidote. This is usually the meditation on loving-kindness, one of the most popular and widely taught meditations to this day in many Buddhist traditions. It sometimes refers to the kasiṇa (discussed more fully in the next chapter under 1–10 of Buddhaghosa's headings). In fact the practice of loving-kindness is particularly associated with the natural luminosity of the mind. This text stresses its importance as pre-eminent amongst various forms of bhāvanā:

Monks, if just for the moment of one finger snap a monk produces the thought of loving-kindness, such a one is to be called a monk. Not empty of result is his meditation. He acts in accordance with the teaching of the Blessed One, he follows his advice and is deserving when he eats the alms food. How much more so if he cultivates it!

(A I 10)

5   A story

In common with other Indian religious teachers, the Buddha frequently uses a story to make a point. The Jātakas, the stories of his past lives while he prepared for Buddhahood, are an example of this. In Jātaka 385 for instance, he remembers a rebirth as a deer in a park belonging to a violent king. When taken to be shot by him, he simply drops fear, does not permit ill-will to arise and lets his mind rest in loving-kindness: the king is so moved he cannot shoot his arrow.

In each of these approaches we can see a slightly different angle on one particular hindrance, which is finally overcome by an opposing quality, in this case loving-kindness. Indeed the story demonstrates that this can overcome ill-will in others too. Mettā can be developed in daily life, or, in meditation, to take the mind to jhāna. This can then lead to the application of insight, which will eventually eradicate hatred completely. Incidentally, it is worth noting that the Buddha also often recommends a number of meditations for different problems that can arise. As noted in Chapter 1, the eightfold path is rarely taught with its elements isolated from one another.

AJAHN CHAH

Ajahn Chah was one of the great forest tradition teachers of northeast Thailand. He was born in 1918 in a rural village and ordained as a novice at the age of nine and as a monk at the age of 20. He died in 1992. His pupils included an American, Ajahn Sumedho, founder of the English Forest Saṅgha, and a Canadian, Ajahn Viradhamma. He was renowned for his discipline, directness and humour and for teaching the importance of both samatha and vipassanā practice. As so often in the forest tradition, close textual understanding is transformed into a direct and forceful colloquial speech:

I'm telling you, it's great fun to closely observe how the mind works. I could happily talk to you about this one subject all day. When you get to know the ways of the mind, you'll see how this process functions and how it's kept going through being brainwashed by the mind's impurities. I see the mind as merely a single point. [Negative] Psychological states are guests who come to visit this spot. Sometimes this person comes to call; sometimes that person pays a visit. They come to the visitor centre. Train the mind to watch and know them all with the eyes of alert awareness. This is how you care for your heart and mind. Whenever a visitor approaches you wave them away. If you forbid them to enter, where are they going to sit down? There's only one seat, and you're sitting on it. Spend the whole day in this one spot.

This is the Buddha's firm and unshakeable awareness; that watches over and protects the mind.

Chah (2006: 53)

ABHIDHAMMA

According to the *Abhidhamma* traditions, known sometimes as the 'Higher Teaching', consciousness is changing and moving all the time, as momentary states of mind react and respond to thoughts and sense-impressions constantly received throughout the day. These sense-impressions in turn arise from momentary units of matter or energy, each of which has a lifespan many times longer than a moment of consciousness. These are also, however, rapidly moving clusters of energy patterns whose nature is often described in terms that anticipate the language of modern physics. The elements of earth, water, fire and air, sometimes also described as extension, cohesion, energy and movement, group together to form the impressions we receive constantly at the physical base. Our minds, reacting and responding to this abundance of information, constantly sort these stimuli, tending to group experiences in terms of familiar classifications, and act upon that. Contacts, feelings that arise on the basis of these and ideas that form on the basis of these feelings, contribute to the way each new event is identified and explained. Although the timescale of such activity is supposedly momentary, it follows principles that can be detected on a slower, more experiential timescale, thus making *Abhidhamma* a helpful meditative aid. The simple practice of mindfulness is supposed to help the practitioner to notice and be aware, but not necessarily to judge, these responses, so that in time the mind becomes more stable and settled, able to be aware of each sense as it impinges on the mind. Through the application of mindfulness, impressions cease to be so engulfing or confusing and it is possible to notice habits of minds more closely, without attachment or hatred. This freedom from overload also allows the *kusala* mind to arise in response to the world around.

BASIC REALITIES

Citta mind: this is constantly changing its nature. Each moment of *citta* lasts for an infinitesimal period of time.

Cetasika mental states: these are the factors that accompany different moments of mind. In unskilful consciousness there may be hatred or conceit or one other of the unskilful *cetasikas*. In skilful consciousness mental factors such as mindfulness and wisdom are present. Some of these factors, such as joy, concentration and energy can occur in either skilful or unskilful *cittas*. Others, such as mindfulness, loving-kindness and wisdom, only occur where there is skilful consciousness.

Rūpa matter: in essence the four great primaries of extension (earth), cohesion (water), energy (fire) and movement (air). It is of a longer timespan than consciousness, but changes very rapidly.

Nibbāna: the unconditioned.

For the purposes of observation, the interactions between mind, mental states and matter may be observed on an 'experiential' timescale, in the stages by which the mind, for instance, notices a piece of fruit, decides to eat it and enjoy it.

BHAVAṄGA

In Southern schools of Buddhism, the mind at rest between moments of consciousness, and in deepest sleep, is called the *bhavaṅga* consciousness. In most humans this is the result of past skilfulness and usually, though not always, is accompanied by wisdom too. When the mind feels refreshed after a deep sleep, this means, according to the theory, that it has been resting in its natural, passive radiance. While this may be overlaid by other things, this is the proper quality of mind for a human being. In sleep and, momentarily, between thought processes, however, it is at rest and 'passive' (*vipāka*). In waking consciousness, active thought processes occur which may or may not be skilful or *kusala*: these are active (*kamma/karma*) and create the conditions for future passive states and events that occur in the world around. A famous image compares the thought process in each moment to a man asleep under a mango tree. A mango falls and his sleep is disturbed. He notices the fruit, picks it up and then eats it. If it is enjoyed with mindfulness and alertness, the active part of the process will have good consequences, producing good *kamma/karma*. If he gobbles it greedily, without awareness and beset by hindrances, then the result will not be so good.

THE THIRTY-TWO ATTRIBUTES OF THE FIRST SKILFUL CONSCIOUSNESS (*CITTA*), ASSOCIATED WITH JOY AND KNOWLEDGE

The philosophical system of *Abhidhamma* posits a phenomenological description of experience that describes the skilful mind, the unskilful mind and the nature of the way these relate to sense-impressions received from the realm of matter. It describes and lists the way the mind, its mental states and physical experience can be classified on a moment-to-moment basis. The *Dhammasaṅgaṇi*, the first book of the Pāli *Abhidhamma*, opens with a list of attributes or mental factors (*cetasika*) that are present both in the skilful mind and in the first *jhāna*. So in daily life, when there is mindfulness, full attention and enjoyment, the skilful mind may be present: when playing tennis, for instance, if it is enjoyed, or doing something like gardening, with care and alert attention. The body and mind are engaged, there is flexibility, strength and other features described in the 'skilful' mind. Such a state may also arise at a moment of generosity or kindness, which transforms body and mind. These factors are present, in a weaker, passive form in deepest sleep and between thought moments. When developed in daily life, in an active form, they produce good *kamma/karma* for the future. According to the *Abhidhamma*, the practice of mindfulness and meditation will also produce *kusala citta*, which becomes stable and takes the mind then to *jhāna*. The alert attention and focus associated with this *citta* becomes steady, and the mind becomes completely absorbed upon the object. It should be noted that while *jhāna* is a state of *samādhi*, it also has to contain mindfulness and wisdom to be the *jhāna* of the eightfold path. If it is to be called a trance, it is a lucid, awake one.

1–7: Seven Universals, present in all consciousness

Contact, feeling, perception, volition, one-pointedness, psychic life, and attention

8–13: Six particulars, present in all skilful consciousness and some unskilful consciousness

Initial thought, sustained thought, release onto the object, effort, joy, willingness

14–19: Six 'beautiful' factors, present only in skilful consciousness

Faith, mindfulness, moral integrity, concern for consequences, non-greed (generosity), non-hatred (loving-kindness, or one of the other divine abidings of compassion or sympathetic joy)

20–31: The Six pairs

Tranquillity of body and mind, lightness of body and mind, softness of body and mind, manageability of body and mind, health of body and mind, straightness of body and mind

32: Wisdom

(Adaptation of the first list in the Dhammasaṅgaṇi, made, as the text suggests, by conflating all the qualities associated with one factor: so wisdom includes right view (sammādiṭṭhi), the faculty of wisdom, the power of wisdom and the absence of dullness.)

In Sanskrit *Abhidharma* systems, the doctrine of the radiant mind as a constant presence in all forms of consciousness is more fully developed. So in the *Abhidharmakośa*, the universal factors, neutral in Pāli Buddhism, contain positive features, which are overlaid when unskilful *citta* arises.

THE PRACTICE OF LOVING-KINDNESS AND THE LAY LIFE

The human birth and the heaven realms are considered the natural home of the skilful *citta*. This is sometimes given expression through the idea of the Universal Monarch, the king who rules through justice and kindness, not force. Although he seems to represent a typological model for an exemplary lay life rather than a genuine political figure in early Indian history, the Universal Monarch provided an early exemplar of lay kingship which was deeply influential in Indian thought and attitudes to royalty in Buddhist countries. Indeed such an ideal probably animated much of the work of the third century BCE ruler in India, Aśoka. Struck by severe remorse after massacres in which he was involved, he initiated a series of reforms that were implemented throughout his empire. These edicts were recorded on rocks and pillars, covering a territory ranging from Kandahar in the North West, Taxila in the North, the area now known as Mysore in the South and Orissa in the East. Many of these are still in existence, and enjoin the protection of animals, the alleviation of severe punishment, ecological measures, and, strikingly, the abolition of the death penalty. These recommendations, their use of the language of non-harm and an emphasis on *dhamma*, echo the measures of Universal Monarch in *suttas* and gave inspiration to much subsequent Buddhist royal practice.

To the ancient Indian, being a monarch represented the best kind of human rebirth, and for the Buddhist, in its possibilities of acting with generosity and justice, the highest expression of the lay life. A king, for instance, is addressed as 'god' or 'illustrious one' (*deva*). In a polytheistic society, this appellation, while denoting high authority, would not have quite the same connotations as it would have done historically in the West. In the twenty-first century some people find it difficult to see the role of monarch as being positive or desirable. Indeed many Buddhist stories, in particular the *Mūgapakkha Jātaka* (*Jātaka* 539), where the Bodhisatta tries to avoid the terrible karmic consequences of kingship, demonstrate that is not always so. For the most part, however, ancient Indians would have regarded being a monarch as an immensely positive and happy station in life, to which much good *kamma/karma* must have contributed. As modern readers we can 'unpack' stories involving kingship as descriptive of a sense of enjoyment, authority and of some control over events around. As in many ancient cultures, regal office symbolizes good fortune, a sense of being in charge of one's surroundings and finding a 'throne' in one's dealings.

The realm the Universal Monarch lives in, and his palace, is described with the same kind of paradisical vocabulary and language elements that come to be associated with much of the Pure-Land tradition and the heavenly realms of Northern Buddhism. His city is like a *maṇḍala*: it has four gates, made of different gems. His palace is as at the centre of that; his private meditation room at the centre of that. As with these 'imaginary' realms, the underlying implication of such *suttas* is not only that they represent the happiness possible after death for the practitioner of *bhāvanā*, but that the mind that is happy and peaceful in meditation can lie at the centre of a human life too. These realms, it is hinted, are expressions of some of the possibilities of seeing oneself and one's surroundings differently when there is *sīla*, *dāna*, mindfulness and loving-kindness in daily practice – the world of the city, where the monarch works for the happiness of others. They may also surround an inner world too, the inner rooms of the monarch, where meditation can be practised.

The *Mahāsudassana-Sutta* differs from accounts of other Buddhist heaven realms in that the world described is a human one, albeit a mythologized one, with vastly long lifespans, palaces made of the seven kinds of gems and lotus ponds provided by the king for his subjects to bathe in. The humanity of the realm is significant, and firmly distinguishes this and other early Buddhist *suttas* and stories describing monarchs of this kind from the sense-sphere heavens and the paradises of Eastern Buddhism. The universal monarch is a man: he is fully aware of the approach of death and, in accordance with the world view of the *Jātaka* story literature, is always intent on continuance in the realm of suffering beings to enact his Bodhisatta vow. The extract below shows the Bodhisatta, or Buddha in an earlier life, practising the four *jhānas* and the divine abidings as such a king, just before death. It gives an example of the occasional use in *suttas* and *Jātaka*, or story literature, of a lay practitioner undertaking *bhāvanā* in an explicitly meditative context. Such monarchs also usually end their lives practising meditation, an echo of the ancient Indian custom of the *sannyāsin*, who, in the last stage of life, leaves the householder's existence for spiritual practice. The Buddha tells the story of his earlier life as the great king when he arrives at a run-down shanty town called Kusinārā, close to death, perhaps at this point wishing to align himself with the most glorious of his earlier lives as a layman. His attendant, Ānanda, tries to prevent him from dying in such a decrepit location; the Buddha then enjoins him not to dismiss this spot. He tells him of the great kingdom that had once existed there 'in the past', but which has now completely passed out of sight.

THE KING SITS IN MEDITATION

And then, Ānanda, this thought occurred to the Great King of Glory.
   'Of what action is this the fruit? Of what action is this the result, that I am of such great power and have so much influence?' Then, Ānanda, the great king thought this:
   'Of three qualities this is the fruit, of three this is the result, that I am of such great power and have so much influence. Generosity, restraint and self-control.'
   Now the Great King of Glory, Ānanda, entered into the upper room of the great palace. Standing at the door, he spoke with great feeling:
   'Stay here, thoughts of lust! Stay here, thoughts of hatred! Stay here, thoughts of cruelty!
   'No further, thoughts of lust! No further, thoughts of hatred! No further, thoughts of cruelty!'
   And when, Ānanda, the Great King of Glory had entered the upper room of the Great Palace, he sat down on a golden couch and, quite secluded from sense desires and secluded from unskilful states, he entered into and remained in the first *jhāna*, which is accompanied by initial and sustained thought, filled with the joy and happiness born of seclusion. With the stilling of initial and sustained thought, he entered and remained in the second *jhāna*, which is accompanied by internal

peace, confidence and unification of the mind. Furthermore, with the fading away of joy, equanimous, mindful and clearly comprehending, he experienced that happiness in the body about which the noble ones declare, 'The one who is equanimous and mindful abides in happiness' and entered into the third jhāna. With the abandoning of happiness and pain and the disappearance of the earlier pleasant and unpleasant feeling, the monk enters into and abides in the fourth jhāna, that is beyond pleasure and pain, and is purified by equanimity and mindfulness.

And then, Ānanda, the Great King of Glory left the upper room of the Great Palace, and entered into a golden room and sat down on a silver couch. Sitting cross-legged he pervaded one direction with a mind filled with loving kindness. Then the second direction, then the third, then the fourth. And in this way, the whole universe, above, below, all around and everywhere, he continued to pervade with a mind filled with loving kindness, far-reaching, grown great, boundless, free from the slightest trace of hatred or cruelty.

Then he pervaded one direction with a mind filled with compassion. Then the second direction, then the third, then the fourth. And in this way, the whole universe, above, below, all around and everywhere, he continued to pervade with a mind filled with compassion, far-reaching, grown great, boundless, free from the slightest trace of hatred or cruelty.

Then he pervaded one direction with a mind filled with sympathetic joy. Then the second direction, then the third, then the fourth. And in this way, the whole universe, above, below, all around and everywhere, he continued to pervade with a mind filled with sympathetic joy, far-reaching, grown great, boundless, free from the slightest trace of hatred or cruelty.

Then he pervaded one direction with a mind filled with equanimity. Then the second direction, then the third, then the fourth. And in this way, the whole universe, above, below, all around and everywhere, he continued to pervade with a mind filled with equanimity, far-reaching, grown great, boundless, free from the slightest trace of hatred or cruelty.

D II 185–6

LOVING-KINDNESS AS A MEDITATION PRACTICE

Loving-kindness, like all the divine abidings, is said to be possible in daily life from moment to moment, directed towards different beings and in different situations. Pursued as a sitting practice, however, in seclusion, as described in this extract from the *Mahāsudassana-Sutta*, it is intended to strengthen concentration (*samādhi*) and leads to *jhāna*. The way the king pursues the exercise is in a format that is broadly comparable to the pattern in which these practices are described in *suttas*. The meditator extends loving-kindness to all beings in one direction, usually the East, then to each one of the four directions in turn. He then moves on to direct loving-kindness to all beings above, and then all beings below, before considering beings in all of these six directions and extending loving-kindness towards them all. The extract is useful not only as an illustration of the way that such a meditation is perceived as the natural fulfilment of the human condition, but also as a basic introduction to the practice of the divine abidings. These are considered indispensable in most Buddhist schools. It is noteworthy that, as so often in Buddhist texts, before the introduction of a meditation in early Buddhist texts an element of good behaviour in the world (*sīla*) is also suggested at the outset, by the recollection of earlier acts by the king. The question with which he introduces this also demonstrates that the 'the great king of glory' was not attached to his role, and fully aware of its impermanence. Indeed he seems to want to understand his present condition as a result (*vipāka*), one in a number of stages involving many different 'selves', conditioned by action (*kamma*) that has taken place in the past.

DEVA AND BRAHMA REALMS

A disinterested wish for the happiness of all beings, that can be developed to become loving-kindness, is considered to be one of the roots that lead to a human rebirth. The Universal Monarch is doing a practice which is a 'brahma-abiding', and so can lead to a heavenly birth. The *Mettā-sutta* is the most famous text on the practice of loving-kindness. It brings a heaven realm to the human: 'This abiding, they say, is Brahma'.

The innate health of the human mind, as understood in early Buddhism, is integral to understanding many of the passages that delineate the problems and hindrances that can undermine the meditator. It is a constant, implied presence in all Buddhist schools, though more greatly emphasized in Northern and Eastern Buddhism. Buddhism considers a human rebirth as a positive and lucky achievement. It represents an opportunity that is very

METTĀ-SUTTA: THE DISCOURSE ON LOVING-KINDNESS

He who is skilled in welfare, who wishes to attain that calm state
(nibbāna), should act in this way: he should be able, upright, perfectly
upright, of noble speech, gentle and humble.

Contented, easily supported, with few duties, of simple livelihood,
with senses calmed, discreet, not impudent, he should not be greedily
attached to families.

He should not pursue the slightest thing for which other wise men
might blame him. May all beings be happy and secure, may their
hearts be wholesome!

Whatever living beings there be: feeble or strong, tall, stout or
medium, short, small or large, without exception; seen or unseen,
those dwelling far or near, those who are born or those who are yet to
be born, may all beings be happy!

Let one not deceive another, nor despise any person, whatsoever,
in any place. Let him not wish any harm to another out of anger or
ill-will.

Just as a mother would protect her only child at the risk of her own
life, even so, let him cultivate a boundless heart towards all beings.

Let his thoughts of boundless love pervade the whole world: above,
below and across without any obstruction, without any hatred, without
any enmity.

Whether he stands, walks, sits or lies down, as long as he is
awake, he should develop this mindfulness. This abiding, they say, is
Brahma.

Not falling into wrong views, being virtuous and endowed with
insight, by discarding attachment to sense desires, he never again
knows rebirth.

(Sn 143–52)

rare in the circle of *saṃsāra*, as the best of all rebirths to achieve knowledge
and to practise meditation. The many heaven realms – and early Buddhism
describes twenty-six of these, most of which correspond to meditational
states which may be achieved in this lifetime – are filled with beings whose
minds have undergone some sort of purification and have lessened the hold

of the hindrances. Whether through generosity, kindness, self-restraint, or meditation, these devas and brahmas are seen by many modern Buddhists as embodiments of possibilities open to anyone who has taken a human rebirth. Although regarded as literal rebirths, they are also now regarded as metaphoric enactments of states of mind accessible to humans. We can feel ourselves, literally, descending into a hell realm that seems to last for aeons; likewise in an experience of profound happiness, aeons of time seem to pass on a different scale from the usual experience of 'humans'. In Pāli texts it should be noted, however, that they refer only and specifically to rebirths that occur after death. The level of different realms, however, does correspond precisely to meditative attainments and the effects of acts of generosity, good actions and meditation in this world.

According to early Buddhism, volition (*cetanā*) produces action, and action produces future results. Just as the rebirth of any human must be positive for that body to have been acquired, so actions and volitions of the present moment produce rebirths of various kinds, in different realms, according to their nature. For beings of deva realms, the radiance of the mind informs the body too – the word devas, or gods or goddesses, is derived from the verb *div* 'to shine'. Like the many gods and goddesses of Greek mythology, these beings are said to like contact with humans – despite what is for them our distasteful smell! – and are invoked as protectors, guardians and guides in chants and blessings. They represent the highest rebirths possible on the basis of *sīla*, liberality, restraint and faith and, from the evidence of their depiction on early Buddhist temples, tend to be having fun most of the time. Their bodily forms enact the beauty, sensuousness and freedom from anxiety, supposed possible through keeping the basic precepts and being generous. Above them are the usually invisible beings of Brahmā realms, whose bodies can fill expanses of the universe, and who spend many aeons enjoying the restorative happiness and bliss of meditative states.

Many early Buddhist stories concern men and women reborn in the Heaven of the Thirty-Three for a simple act of generosity. It is difficult for most of them to gain enlightenment, however.

The unhappy destinies include animals, many ghosts and spirits, jealous gods and those in hells of various kinds. According to traditional texts, these are literal rebirths and are treated as such in modern Southern Buddhist countries, where chants and amulets are considered helpful ways of protecting oneself from any malignity. More importantly, such beings are considered objects of compassion. Spirits are propitiated in the building of houses and hotels, and good wishes and loving-kindness are extended to unfortunate beings to help them to find a better rebirth.

THIRTY-ONE REALMS OF EXISTENCE

Formless sphere
Obtained by practice of the sphere of:
Neither identification nor non-identification
No-thingness
Infinite consciousness
Infinite space (lifespan from 20,000 to 84,000 aeons)

Form world
Obtained by practice of the fourth *jhāna*:
The Eldest, the Clear-Sighted, the Lovely, the Serene, the Durable; Without mind, Great Reward

Obtained by practice of the third *jhāna*:
The Utterly Beautiful, Boundless Beauty, Limited Beauty

Obtained by practice of the second *jhāna*:
Streaming with Radiance, Boundless Radiance, Limited Radiance

Obtained by practice of the first *jhāna*:
Great Brahmā, Brahmā's high priests, Brahmā's retinue

Sense sphere
Happy states: devas with mastery over Others' Creations, who Delight in Creating, who are Delighted, who are Happy, the Thirty-Three gods and the People of the Four Great Kings.
The Human.

Unhappy states: jealous gods, unhappy ghosts, animals, hells.

A last abiding, *nibbāna*/*nirvāṇa*, could be added to the list to make thirty-two. This is existence that has transcended rebirth, and is accessible to those who are enlightened: it is regarded as the goal of the Buddhist meditative path.

> There is, monks, a non-born, a non-brought-into-being, a non-made and a non-conditioned. If, monks, there was no non-born, non-brought into being, non-made and non-conditioned, no escape would be discerned from what is born, brought to being, made, conditioned. But since there is a non-born, a non-brought into being, a non-made and a non-conditioned, therefore an escape is discerned from what is born, brought-to-being, made, conditioned.
>
> (Ud 80–1)

THE HUMAN REALM AND BODY

According to early Buddhist philosophy, heavenly rebirths, wonderful and enduring as they are, do not offer the 'grit' of suffering we have in the human realm upon which it is possible to practise the spiritual path, and achieve freedom from rebirth. Beings of the animal, ghost, and hell realms have suffering that may also be seen as representations of what happens to the human mind when it sinks and becomes filled with greed, hatred or delusion. These realms are very difficult to leave. A mental state that allows jealousy, greed or envy to dominate the mind is difficult to relinquish. So it is also very hard for such beings, worthy though they may be of our compassion, and, in the case of animals, delight, to practise a spiritual path. It is not considered possible for a being in a lower realm to practise meditation or to obtain enlightenment in that body. The human realm is the natural home for a Buddha, who, with a fully awakened mind, is said to know all these realms and can teach beings release from their suffering. It also, according to early Buddhism, provides the kind of body most suited to the practice of meditation and the development of wisdom. Humans are able to experience and touch on all realms, but for much of the time, except in very unfortunate circumstances, exist in a balanced environment where change and progress are possible.

DEPENDENT ORIGINATION

According to the Buddhist tradition, however, all realms of existence are impermanent, unsatisfactory and cannot be 'owned' or rightly seen as self.

One doctrinal feature that characterizes all schools is that of dependent origination (*paṭiccasamupāda/pratityasamupāda*), or dependent arising, as it is sometimes known. This cycle of causal links seems to have emerged as a full list at some time during the Buddha's period of teaching. It describes the continuous round of rebirth, which we are all said to experience from lifetime to lifetime and, in our perception and reaction to objects, from moment to moment. This process, whereby dependent on one feature of our experience another arises, is said to be going on all the time. Traditionally it is thought that the chain may be broken at two points where the mind has the chance to be free. The first is between ignorance and the arising of formations, a process associated with the purification of views and insight meditation (*vipassanā*). This happens when bad habits are seen clearly as they arise and are hence discarded. The second is between feeling and craving, a process associated with the purification of emotion and calm (*samatha*). So, in eating an apple, if the good feeling that arises is appreciated with mindfulness and does not move on to craving, there is some freedom from the cycle and the mind is restored to 'skilfulness'. This is likely to make the practitioner less attached to the idea of 'apples': when presented with one again there is a chance to be free from the formations – karmic activities fed by past tendencies – associated with being too greedy about them. If there is too much greed or muddle, this leads to the mind going to proliferation and becoming clouded. Of course many such processes are going on in our mental habits, and schools of meditation do not suggest that people try and change them all at once, but that the process is observed sometimes with mindfulness.

THE TWELVE LINKS OF DEPENDENT ORIGINATION
1 Ignorance
2 Formations, volitional activities
3 Consciousness
4 Name and form
5 Six sense bases (the mind is included as a sense in Buddhism)
6 Contact
7 Feeling
8 Thirst, craving
9 Clinging
10 Becoming
11 Birth
12 Death

According to the *Vinaya*, dependent origination is the doctrine that the Buddha considered after his enlightenment, when he reflected upon its twelve links, backwards and forwards. Indeed to this day, considering its links, both forwards and backwards, is regarded as a meditation practice in some Buddhist traditions. Importance is attached as much to the sense of *process* as to each link in itself: the mind becomes free by considering each link in turn. An understanding of dependent origination is supposed to work on 'views' so that an experiential middle way, free from views, is found. This lies between the annihilationist view, that everything ceases at death, and the eternalist view, that something permanent and unchanging continues after death. The doctrine moves the question away from the 'person' to the sense of process. In Myanmar, the Moguk school, which has three hundred branches and is as popular there as the more widely known Mahasi Sayadaw method, teaches dependent origination before and as part of the meditation practice. Practitioners are encouraged to consider each link in turn, reflect on it and see how it applies to the rise and fall of their own mental states. As with so many Buddhist lists of this kind, flexibility and freedom from fixity are supposed to characterize this investigation.

Dependent origination is regarded differently by different schools. The Sarvāstivādins compared each stage to a process in the life-cycle, from the formation of the embryo, at the third link, consciousness, through the growth, maturity and decay of a living being. In some it is associated with the doctrine of emptiness (*śūnyatā*). The Madhyamaka school, for instance, saw the process as illustrating the middle way between things being taken as mere illusions and them being taken as substantially and eternally existing. One second-century Indian philosopher, Nāgārjuna, is associated with the doctrine of *śunyatā*, or emptiness, meant not as a lack, or a non-existence (*abhava*) but rather the absence of independent existence (*nihsvabhava*). He made the doctrine of dependent origination a special study. In its various links, he said, we can see not only the interdependence of the arising of the factors contributing to the specificity of any self at a particular time, but also its interconnectedness. The 'identity' of a being depends upon many events and causes, for the period of time in which it exists. At death, many of these causes change, but some contribute to the formation of the next identity, not only at the moment of conception but in the volitional formations that may be carried on to influence the next 'being' and the conditions associated with it. The same applies to the processes making up a being and the world.

THE PADDY FIELD

The description below comes from Upatissa's manual *The Path of Freedom* (*Vimuttimagga*). We do not know much about the author. His work reaches us through a Chinese translation, from what was either Sanskrit or Pāli in the original. He does, however, seem to be a practitioner and the recorder of an early form of Buddhism, perhaps around the fourth century CE. His approach is slightly less technical, sometimes more approachable and seems more based on experiential meditative examination than the more famous, and possibly later commentator Buddhaghosa. He, like his counterpart, enjoys similes to explain meditative practice and doctrine, as in the following description.

According to one's deeds one is born in various states. Therefore there is rebirth, and through birth, decay and death. Thus, conditioned by birth, there is decay and death.

As paddy-seeds are conditioned by the paddy plant, so conditioned by ignorance the formations arise.

Conditioned by the seed is the bud, so is the arising of consciousness, by the formations.

Conditioned by the bud is the leaf; so is the arising of name-form, by consciousness.

Conditioned by the leaf is the branch; so is the arising of the six-sphered sense, by name-form.

Conditioned by the branch is the plant; so is the arising of contact, by the six-sphered sense.

Conditioned by the plant is the flower; so is the arising of feeling, by contact.

Conditioned by the flower is the nectar; so is the arising of craving, by feeling.

Conditioned by the nectar is the ear of rice; so is the arising of clinging, by craving.

Conditioned by the ear of rice is the seed; so is the arising of becoming, by clinging.

Conditioned by the seed is the bud, so is the arising of birth, by becoming.

Thus the several successions come to be. Thus one cannot know the past or the future. Thus birth succeeds beginning with the causal condition of ignorance. Of it the past or the future cannot be known.

Ehara (1977: 260)

Although Upatissa describes dependent origination as twelvefold, he does not include the link of 'death' in this list, which occurs after becoming: it is, however, implied by the imagery of a plant that goes to maturation and then dies. There is also a positive process, known as positive dependent origination. The twelve links of this lead gradually to liberation.

A MODERN VIEW

The twelve links of *paticcasamupāda* apply, whether we are considering a single moment of time or a whole lifetime. It will probably be less confusing for the Western reader if we present here a possible interpretation of this doctrine as it operates within a stretch of time neither as short as a moment nor as long as a lifetime. It must be stressed that this is only one suggested interpretation of *paticcasamupāda*... The only way we can hope to understand this 'subtle *paticcasamupāda*' is by pondering it constantly and conscientiously until we begin to comprehend its labyrinthine ways. At times it will seem very clear to us, and beautifully logical; then again our vision will be temporarily clouded over as we begin to penetrate to another layer of meaning.

Saddhatissa (1971: 40)

BUDDHIST THEORY

Later traditions of Buddhism, though highly differentiated, also often exploit many basic distinctions described in Pāli texts: the creative tension between concentration and mindfulness and calm and insight constantly resurfaces throughout most forms of Buddhism, with a different phraseology and application. Many doctrinal elements can be found in all schools of Buddhism: the importance of mindfulness, the twelve links of dependent origination – and indeed an eightfold path, though this is again sometimes formulated with different emphases in subsequent traditions. The idea that hindrances or defilements block or hinder the natural state of the mind is also developed further.

Certain features emerge subsequently, however, which are not stated or suggested in early forms of Buddhism. These include such notions as the idea of the *Tathāgatagarbha*, the seedbed of the Buddha mind, which develop the idea of the radiant mind. There is, in some schools, a far greater emphasis on the Bodhisattva path as a goal for everyone. There is an increased focus in all forms of Buddhism on the Buddha and, sometimes, certain deities to be worshipped as a means of cultivating the qualities needed for enlightenment. It is as if these deities come to personify and embody qualities of the skilful and awakened mind. A greater use of mantric meditations also arises in some of the other schools, and indeed in Southern Buddhism in subsequent centuries. Such ideas and practices bring – or indeed may be introduced by – innovations and different forms of meditation. Many of these forms we can trace back as developments of ancient, pre-existing ones, such as older Vedic mantric meditations, or applications of traditional theory in new context, as in many schools that explore the relationship between a 'radiant' mind and the obstructions which hinder it. Some very new developments occurred in local contexts. As Buddhism moved and evolved, it sometimes incorporated elements which either were not explored in early Buddhism, or represented some new departures in arousing mindfulness, concentration and wisdom.

The Pāli canon, the formulation of the Southern schools, contains many elements that are developed in other localities, and perhaps subsequent schools, to a greater or lesser extent. Features such as the inherent radiance of the mind, a predisposition towards mindfulness, an appreciation of the power of the recollection of the Buddha and the evocation of earlier Buddhas as embodiments and teachers of these factors are all present. In this regard the importance of the divine abidings, loving-kindness, compassion, sympathetic joy and equanimity should be stressed. According to the Pāli canon it is not possible to attain enlightenment or awakening without the fulfilment of these: there is no enlightenment without love. This is brought down to earth by the specificity of the Buddha's teaching when dealing with individuals who come to challenge him or ask for help.

CONCLUSION

As this brief summary of some key ideas and methods of teaching meditation in early Buddhism demonstrates, early Buddhist texts and subsequent Buddhist practice in Southern Buddhist countries depends upon a balance. This lies between the perception of an innate knowledge in the human mind, sometimes described in terms of radiance and brightness, and an acknowledgement of the problems that can beset it, which can be overcome by developing calm and insight. The human psyche is perceived as possessing some innate predisposition towards health and wisdom, but lives and acts within deeply ingrained latent tendencies and habitual mental patterns, which need to be addressed according to temperament. These are summarized in a theory common to all Buddhist schools, that of dependent origination. This cycle, which leads to continued rebirth and suffering, can be seen operating on a moment-to-moment basis, on a day-to-day basis, and in the time-scheme of one lifetime to another. While the features described here are often also described in other schools of Buddhism, variations in the underlying theory of the mind and the personal aspiration of the meditator lead, in some forms of Buddhism, to some changes in practice and the way that meditation is viewed.

FURTHER READING

Chah, Ajahn (2006) *Talks on Meditation: A Collection of Talks on Cultivating the Mind*, Kandy: BPS.

Ehara, N.R.M., Soma Thera and Kheminda Thera trans. (1977) *The Path of Freedom by Arahant Upatissa*, Kandy: BPS.

Gethin, R. (1998) *The Foundations of Buddhism*, Oxford: OUP, 112–59, 202–18.

Hamilton, S. (2001) *Indian Philosophy: A Short Introduction*, Oxford and New York: OUP.

Harvey, P. (1990) *Introduction to Buddhism: Teachings, History and Practices*, Cambridge: CUP, 73–94.

Norman, K.R. (1992) *The Group of Discourses (Sutta-Nipāta)*, 2, revised trans., Oxford: Pali Text Society, 177 (for comment on v 151 of *Mettā-Sutta*).

Saddhatissa, Ven. H. (1971) *The Buddha's Way*, London: George, Allen and Unwin.

Buddhaghosa and the forty objects of meditation

Four

Because his words were deep (*ghosa*) like that of the Awakened One (Buddha)
they called him Buddhaghosa.

Cūlavamsa

One of the reasons why Southern Buddhism has been able to sustain a
thriving meditative tradition has been because of the work of one man, the
early commentator on Buddhist meditation, Buddhaghosa. Not a great deal
of biographical detail is known about him except that he was a brilliant
brahmin scholar, was born in Magadha in India, moved to Sri Lanka and
stayed for some time at the great temple, Mahāvihāra, at Anurādhapura. He
composed his manual of meditation, *The Path of Purification (Visuddhimagga)*, in
the fifth century CE, after extensive study of Sinhalese commentaries on the
Pāli canon. Many legends have accreted around him. One says that he wrote
his manual in one day, but it was borrowed by Sakka, the king of the gods,
that evening. Noticing this, he wrote it again – but that text was also borrowed
overnight. Finally, he wrote the third copy at dawn, and then found the other
two returned to him. When he showed them to the head of the monastic
order, all three copies were identical. Whatever the 'truth' of this story it
provides us with an effective illustration of the great punctiliousness, care
and internal consistency for which his writings are justly renowned. Indeed
most myths about Buddhaghosa concern the written word. On his arrival in
Sri Lanka, for instance, it is said he recorded a violent conversation between
two women at the harbour: it became the first written evidence to be used
in courts there. That so many stories about him involve the use of writing
is an indicator of his pre-eminence in this field. His output was prodigious.
Other manuals, such as Upatissa's *Path of Freedom*, may have preceded him, but
it is his advice, preserved on manuscripts, which has been passed down in
Southern Buddhist countries as the great authority on the theory, practice
and daily problems associated with taking up a meditation subject. *The Path
of Purification*, along with other commentaries, rightly or wrongly attributed
to him, is clearly derived from extensive consultation and, perhaps, personal

Figure 4.1 ***Stūpa*** **in Sri Lanka, where Buddhaghosa wrote his manual for meditation**

practice. It gives thorough and detailed guidance as well as doctrinal background to the meditations recommended by the Buddha.

One of Buddhaghosa's principal achievements was his rigorous systematization. He called a meditation object a 'basis for work' or 'field of operation' (*kammaṭṭhāna*), a post-canonical term, and he designated forty of these from the Pāli canon. The word 'object' has been used, but the list includes states of mind and collections of attributes as well. His advice ranges from precise doctrinal analysis, to anecdotes about arahats, to practical tips, all collected into a highly formal exposition. It has provided a compendium of instruction that is consulted to this day in Southern Buddhist countries: his manual is often cited where canonical texts are neglected, although he quotes extensively from these. Indeed he gives us much information that could only have been derived by an 'on-the-spot' observer. Some texts, such as the canonical *Vibhaṅga* and the *Paṭisambhidāmagga*, give practical information that supplements earlier canonical sources. Without his descriptions of, however, the construction of the *kasiṇa*, step-by-step details on how to pursue the practice of the 'divine abidings' and the techniques for practising formless meditation, we would have little textual account of how these meditations were undertaken in the centuries after the time of the Buddha. Moreover, his commentaries have governed the way Pāli texts are viewed and studied to this day.

Buddhaghosa's forty objects are intended primarily for the cultivation of calm (*samatha*) but many, such as the meditation on the stages of the decomposition of the body, breathing mindfulness and the defining of the four elements, may also be used as insight (*vipassanā*). Many other traditions of Buddhism make much greater use of features that he does not describe, although he occasionally suggests them. His school, perhaps already self-conscious in its polarization with what came later to be known as Mahāyāna, does not mention mantric meditation, visualizations, or some of the devotional practices that become central to other schools. His classification of meditation subjects, however, is probably the most authoritative of those in all the traditions. In this chapter we look at his classification and explore a little how these meditations have traditionally been conducted.

THE FORTY MEDITATION OBJECTS

1–10: ten devices (*kasiṇa*):
earth, water, fire, air, dark blue/black, yellow, red, white, light, limited space

11–20: ten 'foul' meditations (*asubha*):
bloated corpse, blue-black corpse, festering corpse, corpse-with-cracked-skin, corpse-gnawn-and-mangled, corpse-cut-to-pieces, corpse-mutilated-and-cut-to-pieces, bloody corpse, corpse-infested-with-worms and the skeleton

21–30: ten recollections (*anussati*):
Buddha, *dhamma*, *saṅgha*, good conduct (*sīla*), generosity, *devas*, mindfulness of death, mindfulness of body, breathing mindfulness and the recollection of peace

31–34: four divine abidings (*brahma-vihārā*), immeasurables (*appamāṇā*):
loving-kindness, compassion, sympathetic joy and equanimity

35–38: four formless spheres (*arūpa*):
sphere of infinite space, sphere of infinite consciousness, sphere of no-thingness and sphere of neither identification nor non-identification

39: the perception of loathsomeness in food (*āhāre paṭikkūlasaññā*)

40: the defining of the four elements (catudhātuvavatthānam) that occur within the body: earth, water, fire and air.

TAKING REFUGE AND BEHAVIOUR

Before describing meditation, Buddhaghosa starts his work with injunctions concerning behaviour. As has been discussed in earlier chapters, for Asians, both in ancient and modern times, keeping the moral precepts and generosity are usually the first starting point for meditation, accompanied by devotional practices to the Triple Gem. These are classified by Buddhaghosa as the twenty-first to twenty-third elements of *samatha* meditation and are used as a preliminary to most other meditations. They should not be underestimated for their intent, both for their arousal of a sense of reassurance and happiness for the meditator who starts a practice and for their action as a subconscious reminder for behaviour in the world afterwards. The taking of refuge in the Triple Gem is considered important as a good start to dispel internal and external 'ghosts' or any other kind of hindrances that may leave a bad aftertaste from the day's events. The offering of flowers, candles and butterlamps to a shrine are also intended to arouse cheerfulness and peace before the practice begins. After this, the meditator takes up an object, in a Western context often the breath (29 in Buddhaghosa's list). The meditator learns instructions from the 'good friend', a teacher of meditation, who gives basic guidance and whom the meditator feels is trustworthy. After a while the mental image (*nimitta*) may arise in the mind's eye for a *samatha* practitioner. This gives the basis for the further development of the five factors of *jhāna*, initial thought, sustained thought, joy, happiness and one-pointedness, which are cultivated until they become 'limbs', able to support the mind for the first *jhāna*.

THE FIVE *JHĀNA* FACTORS

Buddhaghosa makes a clear distinction between each:

Vitakka (initial thought): compared by Buddhaghosa to a bee that notes and aims for a flower, or the hand that holds a dish for polishing.

Vicāra (sustained thought): compared by Buddhaghosa to the circling of the bee around the flower, or the hand polishing the dish held by *vitakka*.

Pīti (joy): when the attention comes to rest upon the image and confidence, effort, concentration, mindfulness, and wisdom are developing, the mind may start to experience a rush of joy. Buddhaghosa says this is of five kinds:

1   minor, which can lift even just a single hair on the body
2   momentary, like flashes of lightning
3   showering, like waves breaking on the sea-shore
4   uplifting, which can literally lift the body
5   pervading, so that the body and mind are filled like a pig's bladder with water, or a flooded rock-cavern. Eventually, when joy has reached its highest level, mind and body become settled.

Sukha: happiness is the feeling that arises when joy is tranquillized and still. Joy is compared in the Pāli canon to an exhausted man who sees a pool in a desert; happiness occurs when he drinks from the pool and sits in the shade beside it.

Ekaggatā: the mind is completely unified and 'gone to oneness'.

All of these factors are described as coming together for the first *jhāna*. The mental image becomes settled, and the mind becomes unified. Each one of the five factors is said by Buddhaghosa to suppress a particular hindrance. The application of the mind through initial thought suppresses sloth and torpor, the exploratory qualities of sustained thought suppress doubt, joy suppresses ill-will, happiness or contentment suppresses agitation and worry, and one-pointedness, he says, suppresses sense-desire. This means in practice that particular care would be placed in arousing the appropriate antidote: exploring the object, say the breath, if there is an excess of doubt, or allowing the mind to rest in contentment of the breath if there is worry. In jhāna the five faculties of faith, effort, mindfulness, concentration and wisdom are also said to come into balance.

GUARDING THE SIGN

Buddhaghosa compares the development of the mental image (nimitta), in samatha meditation, to a child learning to walk. At first the child stands for a moment and makes one step; then he tumbles; then he tries again – and tumbles, until the supporting factors are strong enough for him to walk unaided. Buddhaghosa describes this momentary access to jhānic meditation as access (upacāra) concentration, a non-canonical term that denotes a 'half-way' house, before the jhāna factors are fully developed, to the complete settling of the mind. Sometimes the movement to jhāna will happen soon, if the factors are strong, but more often the nimitta needs 'guarding', by carefully attending to activities in daily life and noticing where energy and mindfulness are lost or drained. This process, Buddhaghosa says, needs to be undertaken with the same care that a mother carrying a future universal monarch in her womb would protect her growing embryo. Buddhaghosa's advice is geared for the monastic orders, but the list is used now, with some modifications for lay practitioners too.

The process of 'guarding the nimitta' involves seven factors. The meditator should in each respect cultivate what is suitable and leave what is unsuitable.

1   Lodgings: these are suitable if, while staying there, a mental image arises, or the one that has already arisen flourishes. If it is difficult to get a nimitta when living somewhere, one should move on. He suggests moving from one lodging to another, if that is possible. He cites the example of a particular cave in Sri Lanka, where five hundred monks became arahats, that is particularly suited to meditation practice.
2   Resort: the general environs of the monastery. A village should be neither too far or too close, so that it can be visited for food each day but does not impinge too much on the activities of the meditator.
3   Speech: Buddhaghosa cites thirty-two kinds of directionless talk which lead to loss of the nimitta when one comes to practise again. There is suitable talk, such as dhamma discussion, though even this should be practised with moderation.

4   *Person:* one should mix with the type of person who helps the practice of concentration, and does not scatter it with directionless chat or excessive concern about his own bodily needs. This type creates disturbances, like muddy water added to clear.

5   *Food:* one sort of food suits one person, another sort suits another; some find sweet better, some sour.

6   *Climate:* a cool climate suits some people's meditation practice, a hot climate suits others.

7   *Postures:* walking suits one, standing, sitting, or lying down another: he should try each for three days and see which works best.

In a modern context this list is taught within the practicalities of the monastic and lay life. For instance it may not be good to meditate in room that is too cold, as the mind does not relax properly, but if the room is too warm, the meditator may become sleepy. It is advised to notice just how much food is needed and helpful, and of what kind, a balance which may differ from person to person. In effect the list is advising the meditator to be aware of what helps the development of the *nimitta*, and to cultivate the conditions which foster it: moving house, for instance, may not be possible, but modern teachers recommend moving room or furniture to make a better place for practice.

The 29th object – the breath – has already been discussed in Chapter 2, and forms the basis of most Buddhist meditative systems. The other subjects, described here, also feature to a greater or lesser degree in most other Buddhist systems, but are sometimes conducted quite differently in those from the way Buddhaghosa describes them.

Once *jhāna* has been obtained, the meditator may go on to further meditations. Throughout, following the spirit of canonical texts, the meditator is instructed to retain mindfulness and clear comprehension. He is instructed to practise the five 'masteries' of meditation: the ability to advert, to enter, to sustain, to emerge and, finally, to remember any meditative state. The one who does these, Buddhaghosa says, will have the ability to enter states at will and leave them at will. He also observes the defects of the meditation states, and practises insight.

Each of the forty objects is a meditation, so it is worth looking at these in greater detail.

BUDDHAGHOSA'S FORTY OBJECTS

1–10. *Kasiṇa*: the beautiful object

The first ten meditation objects are considered 'beautiful' (*subha*) by the commentaries, and are intended to arouse concentration (*samādhi*), away from the activities of the day. A *kasiṇa* is a meditation device, usually a disc, which is used as a means of focusing the mind for the attainment of *jhāna*. The word is derived from the Sanskrit word for entire or whole: the object becomes the centre of the visual field and occupies the full attention of the meditator, whose mind is 'brought to oneness' (*ekaggatā*). The commentators suggest that the meditator should make his own device, under a teacher's guidance, and then follow a certain series of procedures. First he or she washes and, after reciting the homage to the Triple Gem, takes the object and brings attention to it repeatedly, saying the word that describes it to him or herself, e.g. 'earth, earth'. Then the meditator shuts the eyes and waits for an eidetic after-image to arise in the mind's eye on the basis of the external one, all the while repeating the words, 'earth, earth'. This process is repeated until eventually another, stable image arises that can be used as the basis for meditation. With continued mindfulness the five *jhāna* factors develop and gradually the mind is freed from the hindrances of sense desire, ill-will, sloth and torpor, restlessness and worry and vacillating doubt. Once purified, the mind enters *jhāna*.

The practice is usually taught under special conditions. The meditator needs to keep the mind balanced and alert while conducting the exercise, and, as it requires time and patience, it is generally taught in secluded or forest-monasteries in Thailand, Myanmar and Sri Lanka. Buddhaghosa and subsequent teachers often place some emphasis on the construction of the device as a preparatory exercise to undertaking the meditation. Many monasteries however have *kasiṇa* discs that have already been constructed and are hung in the shrine halls for meditators to use when instructed. Although Buddhaghosa was cautious in describing the use of devices taken from natural surroundings, some modern teachers in the Thai forest traditions suggest taking a spontaneously seen example of the object – say light from sunshine, or space between trees, as the initial object.

11–20. The 'foul' meditations

The next ten meditation objects, the stages of decomposition of a corpse, are termed 'foul' or 'unlovely' (*asubha*) but are also considered ways of bringing the mind to concentration and jhāna. Because of their unpleasant nature, but, more specifically, the complexity of their subject matter, they are not considered objects that can develop further jhānas, unless one element is made the object. Whereas there is an inherent simplicity to the image obtained through an element or a colour, the decomposing body has many attributes, and so the mind does not come to one-pointedness so easily. They are recommended particularly to meditators predisposed towards greed: to this day, however, their usage is strictly limited and they tend only to be given under very special conditions. Monks in Bangkok, for instance, may be taken to the mortuary of a hospital as a group, under supervision, and the practice would not now be conducted alone or in the context in which it was described. Charnel-grounds were located in inauspicious sites, outside the city walls, and attendants who worked there would be of the lowest castes. For brahmins, the dead body was perceived as polluting and ritual purifications were needed for all members of a family where someone had died or where there had been contact with death. Poor or abandoned people, where there was no money for cremation and ceremony, would simply be consigned to the charnel-ground and left to decompose. For their association with the inauspicious, the Buddhist exercises then would have been deeply shocking. Despite this social taboo, however, at the time of the Buddha the dead body would probably be a much more familiar sight than it is now in the West. Life expectation was low, death would be familiar to all households and the corpse would be seen at home and at cremations. The Buddha, for his own order of monks, ignored societal strictures concerning death, and monks' robes were supposed to be sewn together from shrouds, washed and cut into patches. The Buddha recommended that the practitioner went to the charnel-ground and viewed the corpse in one of the stages of decomposition, taking it as his meditation object in the same way as the kasiṇa. He would also remind himself of the mark of not-self: that his body will one day become like that. Buddhaghosa, with the careful psychological precision that characterizes much of the commentarial tradition, says that the practice should arouse saṃvega – a sense of urgency and the consequent vitality it arouses – but should not lead to vipphandana, the prurient 'shaking' and excitement we associate now with seeing horror films. Some of his guidelines seem designed to protect the meditator from becoming disoriented or excessively terrified. He should tell his friends where he is going when he goes to conduct this meditation, he should always answer queries if he meets someone who asks him the way, even if it means forgetting his meditation subject, and he should memorize clearly the directions back to his monastery. Presumably then, as now, meditators could get 'spooked out' by what they had seen.

We do not know if the Buddha invented these practices, although there are no descriptions that pre-date him, but early sources suggest that they come to be associated with Buddhist practitioners. In India, other traditions, such as the Śaivite, also developed some corpse meditations, and the practice is associated with *Tantra*: to do what is taboo can arouse power. Interestingly, in the Pāli canon, the words 'it is as if' (*seyyathāpi*) introduce the exercise, suggesting it could also be a visualization, not requiring an actual dead body. Although Buddhaghosa does not pursue this option, such a possibility is described in a fifth-century meditation text known as the *Yogalehrbuch*, found in China. In this the corpse is visualized through all stages of decomposition: this suggests a development that may have been more suitable in a culture where cremation and the abandonment of bodies in a charnel-ground was not the norm. Tibetan Buddhism also includes variations of this kind (see Chapter 8).

THE TEN RECOLLECTIONS

21–23. The recollection of the Buddha, dhamma and saṅgha
This employs the iti pi so formula, discussed more fully in Chapter 6 as a popular Southern lay practice.

24–26. The recollection of *sīla* (good behaviour), generosity and of the devas
These meditations, on remembering acts of good behaviour and generosity in the world, culminate in reminding oneself of the beings described as inhabiting the sense-sphere heavens described in Chapter 3, up to the lowest level of the Brahma heavens, a realm associated more specifically with the practice of *samatha* meditation. The meditator notes that he has also performed such acts of generosity, kindness and restraint, and will be reborn there too. These recollections are often neglected in modern accounts of meditative practice, but are considered of prime importance within the canon, Buddhaghosa's manual and subsequent practice in Southern Buddhist countries. By remembering that one has kept the five precepts and moments where there has been an act of generosity, one starts to see one's own proximity to the beings who have taken rebirth in heavenly realms on the basis of such activity. The depiction of the devas invests temple art throughout India and

South Asia with a life, vitality and grace that is associated with the happines of simple hospitality and restraint in daily life, particularly in the support of the monastic orders. These often sensuous pictures act as a demonstration of what the practitioner can become, through faith, generosity and conduct. The fact that the last of these meditations touches the base of the 'pure' meditative realms gives an indication of the way that the area of *sīla* and generosity is regarded as an essential grounding for meditative practice. Although these meditations do not, according to Buddhaghosa, enable the practitioner to attain *jhāna*, they are considered as necessary in daily life for calming the mind in preparation for practice. In canonical texts, the Buddha often assigns them for daily business and to the laity and to those who have already attained the first stage of path, stream-entry.

27. Mindfulness of death

This meditation is often given by the Buddha in Pāli texts, though some care seems to have been associated with its assignation. For those apparently needing a shock, like an assembly of Nādika, who are given a particularly gruesome account of its sudden and unexpected power, the awesome and terrifying chance of one's own body being attacked, by any means, is stressed. For some practitioners, such as the kindly and assiduous layman Mahānāma, reassurance is given that death, when it comes in time, will bring him rebirth in a heavenly realm. As a chronicler rather than a teacher, Buddhaghosa cannot emulate this specificity, but places the Buddha's varied advice on this meditation from a number of sources, in a number of categories that suggest ways of practice. Unlike the Buddha, who varies his advice as to whether it should be practised first with regard to oneself or others, Buddhaghosa makes what seems now to be a sensible accommodation to a tradition that has, of necessity, become systematized. He stresses that it should be practised with regard to others first, then oneself, and warns against its recollection where the object may cause distress or fear, as in the death of a loved one, or relief, as in the death of an enemy. The practice should arouse urgency (*samvega*), which can then be stilled in meditation.

Death can be recollected in eight aspects, as:

1   appearing like a murderer, taking one by surprise
2   ruining all happiness and success
3   showing that even great men die
4   ensuring that one's body is shared by many, when eaten by worms
5   reminding us of the fragility of health and life
6   being signless, giving no indication of when it will occur
7   reminding us of the limitedness of any lifespan
8   demonstrating that any one life is, from a larger point of view, as short as a moment.

Different aspects are recommended for different types of people, in ways that the meditation teacher will discern. The practice should not be applied to consideration of one either dearly loved or hated.

28. Mindfulness of body

Some variations on this meditation, regarded in all traditions of Buddhism as the cornerstone of meditative practice, have already been discussed in Chapter 2. In the context of calm meditation, Buddhaghosa takes it to be the use of the focusing upon one aspect of bodily experience as the basis for *jhāna*. The body is divided into thirty-two parts, a canonical system to which Buddhaghosa adds the brain as the 32nd feature. As in the canon, each is assigned to a different element, from earth, water, fire and air. So the bony and hard parts of the body may be used as the basis for meditation on the earth *kasiṇa*. The watery parts of the body, represented by blood, mucus, saliva and phlegm, may be used as the basis for meditation on water. The warmth of the body may be used as the basis for fire meditation. The airy 'winds' in the body, such as the breath and the bodily airs supposed to reinforce the circulation, can form the basis of air meditation. As an insight practice, the relationship between name and form is examined. Manifestations of the elements may be seen for their impermanence, unsatisfactorinees and as 'non-self'.

29. Mindfulness of breathing

STAGES OF BREATHING MINDFULNESS

1 *Counting*: compared to herdsman counting cattle
2 *Following*: following the breath as it enters and leaves body
3 *Touching*: concentration at the tip of the nose, compared to the gatekeeper, or a saw cutting wood
4 *Settling*: settling on the image
5 *Observing*: becoming familiar with the *jhāna* and developing skills with regard to it
6 *Turning away*: insight into *nāma* (name) and *rūpa* (form)
7 *Purification*: purification of the defilements of insight, in succession
8 *Looking back*: development of skills in recollection.

This meditation was briefly discussed in Chapter 2. Buddhaghosa describes four stages of its practice: counting, following, touching and settling, which together help the practitioner to attain jhāna. These are practised in succession. First the breaths are counted, and then the movement of the breath in and out of the body is followed. For the touching, the point where the breath enters and leaves the body, usually the tip of the nose, is used as the object of concentration, while mindfulness is aware of the movement of the breath as it comes and goes. Buddhaghosa uses the image of the gatekeeper, watching all those who enter and leave a city, or someone who is aware of the point of contact of a saw, but is also mindful of the movement of the whole. He also recommends various ways that the practice may be tranquillized if it becomes over-excited or disturbed, or energized if the mind becomes slack and listless.

He gives some indication as to how to recognize the mental image (*nimitta*) when it arises. The practice of breathing mindfulness is compared to the striking of a gong: just as the sounds become more subtle after the gong is struck, so the object of the practice becomes more refined. Buddhaghosa gives several descriptions of the mental image as it appears differently to various people. The list includes a cluster of pearls, the touch of cotton or silk, the rough touch of a cotton seed, or a wreath of flowers, or a puff of smoke, or a stretched-out cobweb, or a lotus flower or the disc of the sun or the moon. The meditator can sometimes think he has lost the object, but just has to imagine the image there until it returns: the settling, or establishing, is the fourth stage, where the image becomes settled and the mind can enter jhāna. A fine, patient craft is needed for the watching of the breath: it is compared to the careful attention needed to work on a piece of needlework with a fine, sharp needle, or a herdsman waiting at a drinking place for his oxen to arrive.

Four further stages are added after the meditation has been obtained. These are observing, turning away, purification and 'looking back'. The practitioner needs to develop the jhāna and become familiar and skilled with the masteries of adverting to it, entering it, sustaining it, leaving it and remembering it afterwards. He should then investigate it with regard to 'name' (nāma) and 'form' (rūpa), distinguishing between the mind and mental states as 'name', and the material, the breath and the body, as 'form'. Having made this distinction, he investigates the causes of mind and the material, and sees in them the three signs or marks of existence: that they are impermanent, unsatisfactory and non-self. After going through ten purifications of insight, he abandons the wish for various states and experiences 'equanimity about formations'. Greed fades away and he is liberated from formations altogether. Finally, as an arahat, an awakened being, he develops skill in recollection and is ready 'to receive the highest gifts of the world and with its devas'.

30. Mindfulness of peace

This practice, sometimes mentioned, evoked and more often just elicited in the canonical material by the repetitive rhythm of a verse or the phrasing of a sutta, is never described there. Buddhaghosa recommends bringing to mind the qualities of nibbāna. Another commentator, Upatissa, and some modern teachers, recommend bringing to mind any moment of peace in meditation and reminding oneself of it, to reintroduce that quality.

31–34. The four divine abidings

In the canon, as we saw in Chapter 3, there are some descriptions of the practice of loving-kindness and the other divine abidings, compassion, sympathetic joy and equanimity, described pervading each direction in turn and then all directions, including above and below. According to Buddhaghosa, when the meditator does this, or moves from considering a neutral person, to a someone dearly loved or to an enemy, and then all beings, the divine abiding eventually becomes limitless, including all beings, in all directions. The mind is freed from the constriction of the sense-sphere and, on the basis of the sign of manifold beings, enters *jhāna*. The method can then be refined to include further *jhānas*, dependent on the appropriate purification of feeling. Buddhaghosa recommends that one should wish for one's own happiness first, for instance, and develop loving-kindness to oneself, before moving out from that object to other beings. He also indicates that one should take great care when practising the divine abiding of compassion, that one does not fall prey to the 'near enemy' of compassion, grief or sorrow.

From the psychological point of view these sections are amongst the most interesting and helpful pieces within the manual. Whether they are simply the articulation of recommendations of his own tradition, or contributions based on his own observation, we cannot know. His reticence in putting forward his own opinion elsewhere suggests that he is recording what were, by this stage, long-established guidelines. We are, however, indebted to him for his record of this shrewd advice and of potential pitfalls even of these practices, where danger can lie as much in excessive sentimentality or grief as in the direct opposite of the quality being described.

THE DIVINE ABIDINGS: *BRAHMAVIHĀRA*

31. Loving-kindness (*mettā*): the practice of loving-kindness is considered essential to much Buddhist practice, and to this day this *samatha* practice is taught also in insight schools. In the canon it is said to promote wellbeing, health, long life and, on a day-to-day level, a good night's sleep. Buddhaghosa compares it to a mother's feeling for a dearly loved child. Its near enemy is attached affection, for that too sees virtues, but is linked to desire, and so is compared to an adversary who 'stays near one's side'. Its far enemy is hatred, 'like an enemy lying in wait in a wilderness'. When someone hates they become miserable and tormented: it is not possible, as Buddhaghosa notes, to feel loving-kindness and hatred at the same moment. The highest level of loving-kindness is liberation by the 'beautiful'.

32. Compassion (*karuṇā*): the practice of compassion allays suffering, and is compared to a mother's feeling for a child who is in pain. Its near enemy is grief, because that too perceives failure, and its far enemy is cruelty, which cannot survive where there is compassion present. Its highest level is the sphere of infinite space, the fifth *jhāna* in the eightfold system.

33. Sympathetic joy (*mudita*): the practice of sympathetic joy is characterized by gladness or happiness at the success of others. It is compared to a mother's feeling for a child who is happy; its function is to be free from envy. Buddhaghosa says it can still be developed for someone who is unhappy, by considering their past and future good fortune. It is caused by seeing another's success and eliminates boredom. Its highest level is the sphere of infinite consciousness, the sixth *jhāna* in the eightfold system.

34. Equanimity (*upekkhā*): Buddhaghosa says this is neutral, in that it sees all beings with the same regard. It is compared to the attitude of a mother whose child has made an independent life. It is said to quieten both resentment and approval. It succeeds when it accompanies the perception that all beings inherit their own *kamma*; it fails when it becomes indifference. Its highest level is the sphere of no-thingness, the seventh *jhāna* in the eightfold system.

Each of these divine abidings may be developed in daily life on a moment-by-moment basis in one's usual dealings, or as meditations to be practised in seclusion, where they can lead to *jhāna*.

(see *The Path of Purification*, Chapter IX)

35–38. The formless spheres

The advice given by Buddhaghosa and the other commentators is particularly informative for the procedures it gives for the meditations on formlessness. The Buddha gives only sparse comment on these, perhaps assuming that they can be learnt elsewhere, or perhaps not wishing to dwell on the detail of a practice which he felt should be learnt from a teacher. Buddhaghosa, as always, examines and explains, providing simple analogies from daily experience and some painstakingly delineated detail as regards procedure. These meditations are distinguished from the others in that they are treated as both objects and states of mind. They seem to stand in a different dimension. The mind that perceives, and even the perception of this too, start to become as important an area for investigation as the observation of a preliminary object. So while many states are possible on the basis of most of the other meditation objects, these states are defined solely by the nature of the mind with which the object is known and understood.

BUDDHAGHOSA'S TREATMENT OF THE FORMLESS REALMS

35. The sphere of infinite space

Bearing in mind that there are subtle disturbances in any kind of meditation based on materiality, the meditator considers infinite space, internally saying to himself 'space, space'. He does not 'fold up' the physical object as someone would a mat, or prise it away from his attention as someone taking a cake out of a tin. Rather, he moves his attention away from it to the space it leaves: as someone who has stopped a hole in a cart, sack or pot with a scrunched up, coloured rag might consider the space left behind if wind blows the rag away.

36. The sphere of infinite consciousness

Seeing that attention even to this object is not as peaceful as considering consciousness itself, the meditator moves the attention away from the infinite object to the mind that pervades that object, and lets that become infinite, repeating to himself 'consciousness, consciousness'.

37. The sphere of no-thingness

The meditator sees that there is still something yet more peaceful. 'There is not, there is not' or 'no-thingness, no-thingness'. If a man has been in a meditation hall with a number of monks and returns when it is empty, he does not consider where each one has gone, but just stands at the doorway and sees that it is now empty: that is like this state. Such a meditator is said to 'own' nothing.

38. The sphere of neither perception nor non-perception

Seeing that even that act of perceiving could be more peaceful, the meditator finds the state where there is neither perception nor non-perception. A number of images are employed to explain this. It is, he says, as if a novice smeared a bowl with oil and put it aside. When asked to bring the bowl so that his teacher could drink rice-water, the novice said, 'But it has oil in it'. When asked to bring the bowl so that his teacher could fill a tube with it, he said, 'But there is no oil'. The great peace of this sphere is compared to a king, riding splendidly and in pomp on an elephant, who proceeds through a busy town. He notices craftsmen on the streets, covered in dust, working on skills such as ivory carving. He admires and is pleased, but does not wish to join them. So the meditator enjoys great peace, but does not wish to turn his mind to this or that meditative attainment, or to any of the skills connected with practising meditation.

It seems from the simple yet expressive analogies used by Buddhaghosa that the formless spheres describe a kind of freedom whereby the mind does not 'own' its meditative attainments, and does not have specific attachments or views concerning them. Although not essential for enlightenment, as pursuits in themselves, and as correctives perhaps to attachment to the more obviously 'pleasant' jhānas, they seem to be an integral element in the Buddha's meditative system and are taught to this day to very advanced practitioners in Northeast Thailand and Myanmar. Few modern or ancient manuals discuss them, however, and they seem intended for those with considerable prior experience, taught under conditions of some confidentiality. Pursued properly, they are said allow freedom for the meditator from many attachments, though they are not essential to the goal.

Two of the formless meditations, on no-thingness and neither perception nor non-perception, were practices previously rejected by the Buddha, as not leading to peace. It is possible that the early jhānas, now always taught before them, were introduced by the Buddha to give the basis of calm and happiness to the mind, which he felt were needed for insight and for the beneficial use of these meditations. Buddhaghosa, along with the Pāli canon, says that the meditator needs a firm basis in each jhāna before moving on to the next, or he or she will 'slip' like a foolish calf that has wandered too far up a mountain. Modern meditation teachers make the point, which the Buddha does by implication by his rejection of his first teachers and the way he places these realms after other jhānas, that the meditator might need to return repeatedly to earlier jhānas. This is to reassure and refresh the mind with the happiness and joyfulness of a simple and more easily grasped meditation object. Certainly these realms occupy a special place in the canon and in subsequent commentaries: in a Buddhist context they need earlier *jhānas* as a basis, and, it is suggested by the Buddha's life story, perhaps do not lead to *nibbāna* if pursued without them.

39. Recollection of the repulsiveness of food

One feature that characterizes many Buddhist traditions at the present time is a decidedly earthy and sometimes humorous stress on the need to return to the world and awareness of some very basic features of human bodily experience after meditation. Perhaps we should bear this attitude in mind when considering this object, discussed by Buddhaghosa immediately after the most rarefied of practices, the formless spheres. It is intended to loosen attachment, not to arouse disgust. He describes in some detail the passage of food as it goes through the body and is then expelled, recommending the meditator notes each stage for himself or herself. This practice is mentioned a few times within the canon, though always in conjunction with other meditations which appear to balance it; it seems to have been tailored specifically for monastic practitioners. More commonly in the canon moderation in eating and simple mindfulness of the sense doors is advised for daily life and practice.

40. The one defining: the four elements

According to the Indian world-view, and early Buddhist texts, matter is made up of four elements, earth, water, fire and air, sometimes with a fifth, space, included. Each of these may be discerned in one's own body in the hardness of bones, the wateriness of blood and phlegm, the airiness in the winds that circulate through the body and fieriness in the warmth and vitality of the physical organism. This practice discerns each of the elements in the practitioner's body, either in a general sense, or, more specifically, by going through each of the bodily parts or aspects of bodily experience according to the elements in turn. Unlike corpse meditations, this meditation cannot be conducted on another body: it involves the practitioner becoming aware of the balance and relationship of each within his or her own bodily form. This practice seems to have occupied a central position in Southern Buddhism, both as a means of calming the mind, as indicated here by Buddhaghosa, and as a means of discerning the three signs of phenomena: as being impermanent, unsatisfactory and non-self. The monks' ordination ceremony involves each new monk being given the first five objects listed under the element of earth, hairs of the body, body hair, nails, teeth and skin as his first meditation in the monastic order. In one *sutta*, the Buddha's son is told to make his mind like each one of the elements in turn, able to withstand any adversity yet retain its own nature.

PSYCHIC POWERS AND THE OTHER DIRECT KNOWLEDGES

At this point mention should be made of the psychic powers, discussed extensively by the Buddha, Buddhaghosa and many other commentaries: whatever we might think now, they were perhaps historically one of the most attractive features of Buddhism as it spread north and eastwards outside its home terrain. These skills, which should, according to Buddhaghosa, be cultivated after attaining the fourth jhāna, involve mastery and freedom of movement in the use of kasiṇa practice and the attainment of different jhānas, sometimes in rapid succession, so that the practitioner can move freely from one meditation to another, and from one object to another. They are:

THE FIVEFOLD DIRECT KNOWLEDGES OF:

1　*The psychic powers:*
 a) being able to multiply oneself from one to being many, and from many becoming one again
 b) becoming visible or invisible at will
 c) passing through mountain walls, city enclosures and through mountains as if through space
 d) swimming up and down through the earth as if through water
 e) travelling over water as if over earth
 f) travelling through the sky cross-legged
 g) touching and stroking the sun and moon with the hand
 h) mastery over the body as far as the heaven world of Brahma.
These are compared to a skilled potter or goldsmith or his apprentice making any shape he wants.
2　*The divine ear:* being able to hear the subtlest of sounds of the gods and of humans, both near and far, in all directions.

3   *Knowing the minds of others*: discerning the quality of another's mind. So the practitioner knows that the heart of one who is joyful seems red, like banyan tree fruit, that the heart of one who is grief-stricken seems black, like rose-apple fruit, that the heart that is serene seems clear, like sesame oil.

4   *Recollecting past lives*: remembering past lives in succession, over several lives, rather than the dwelling upon a single existence. The practitioner who has attained the fourth *jhāna* starts by adverting to the most recent action he has performed that day, then, to the one before, and the one before that. Eventually he or she remembers much earlier events, and earlier lives, though this sequence is always maintained. This exercise requires that, with the equanimity of the fourth *jhāna*, no event should be allowed to become a sticking point, even one's own birth or death: the mind moves on to the event before that, and the one before that. Bluntness of memory is compared to the bluntness of chopping down a great tree: the practitioner returns repeatedly, always going to an earlier moment, despite the poor quality of the blade, until the tree eventually falls. As the practitioner sees an increasing amount of recollections, he or she comes to see process rather than individual events: whole past universes are experienced as coming into existence and passing away.

5   *The divine eye*: seeing the constant round of rebirths of others, as beings come into existence, continue for a while and pass away before taking rebirth again, according to their *kamma*.

In early Buddhism the psychic powers represent an exercise of the awake and skilful mind, like a proof or playful test of success. Some arahats are said not to possess these knowledges. Described so often, however, as the precursors to the final elimination of the defilements, they seem closely linked to the actual attainment of awakening, as if the mind at this refined stage becomes more flexible and less constrained when the defilements are loosened. The practitioner comes to step back and see, from a point of stability within the fourth *jhāna*, the whole process of universes coming into being, continuing and passing away. The perspective suggested evokes the encompassing awareness of the *maṇḍala* of deities and beings often depicted in Northern Buddhist art. It also seems analogous, in Western culture, to the visions of beings being born and dying, described in kabbalistic texts such as the thirteenth-century *Sephir Ha Bahir*, or the depictions of streams of beings moving from one realm to another painted and etched by William Blake.

With the heritage of mediaeval Christianity not forgotten, belief in the existence of psychic powers, let alone their active cultivation, is regarded in the modern West with some suspicion and unease. On the basis of canonical evidence, the Buddha also seems to have shown considerable caution, and indeed reprimands a brahmin youth, Kevaddha, for using them to show off to others, comparing this to a woman revealing her private parts in public. Stories abound, however, of his visiting suffering meditators after seeing with his Divine Eye that they are struggling, or of his recounting the past lives of some followers to elucidate their present situation. Many, if not all of these stories could be taken on a metaphorical level, as richly imaginative representations of different aspects of the psyche employed by a teacher sensitive to the emotional needs of his disciples. Certainly the texts would feel bowdlerized and anodyne without the colourful participation and presence of many beings and many realms, sometimes dismissed as irrelevant in more austere modern accounts of canonical texts. We might see them as wonderfully precise fictions of the imagination. At any event, in many modern Asian countries, stories of psychic intimations and miraculous abilities would be taken as literal truth. As part of a cosmology in which rebirth, the constant arising and passing away of existence and a world view in which the four elements underlying all material phenomena can be known and mastered by humans, they would be taken for granted. Throughout Buddhist Asia chants are offered to pass on merit to dead relatives and to reassure them in their new lives. Chants are also given for children who may be troubled by 'recollections' of past unhappiness. Whether such phenomena are 'true' or not, and whether such chants actually do what they say or not, as social mechanisms these methods seem to be restorative and healing in their intent and effect. Buddhaghosa, like the Buddha, treats the psychic powers as mental skills requiring great self-discipline and mastery over feeling, He also reserves discussion on their development until after the fourth *jhāna*, where equanimity has purified both the aversion or desire which might condition their inappropriate use. In the *Jātakas*, stories of the Buddha's past lives, the Bodhisatta, the Buddha's earlier self, does not use psychic powers to escape his *kamma*, when suffering persecution from others.

From the Buddhist perspective, the direct knowledges are not to be feared if they are part of the eightfold path. Early Buddhist texts repeatedly demonstrate that when there is good conduct (*sīla*), right intention, the calming of the mind and wisdom, they provide a means to be of use to others. Buddhaghosa goes through each one carefully in turn, after discussing all his meditation objects, describing how each may be cultivated and giving more information about method. The last is often described in the canon before the process of attaining enlightenment itself.

After this demonstration of what he regards as the full flowering of *samatha* meditation, Buddhaghosa then moves on to the stages of insight, to develop wisdom, as discussed briefly in earlier chapters.

TEN IMPEDIMENTS TO MEDITATION

Buddhaghosa lists all kinds of problems that might confront the practitioner, ranging from difficulties associated with excessive joy, the belief that a meditation state has brought enlightenment when it has not, to difficult neighbours and intrusive noise from building work. A good example of his advice on the logistics of sitting down to meditation is the list of 'ten impediments', which sometimes need to be set right before the meditator can practise, which catalogues various distractions to meditation. As Buddhaghosa points out, each one of the impediments may not trouble many meditators, but for some may cause difficulty. The examples he cites are primarily of those monks for whom each impediment in turn is *not* made into a problem: for one monk, who knew and could recite the whole of the canon, texts were not an impediment and he became an arahat. This pleasingly elliptic style is often found in Sri Lankan teaching monks to this day. The list is in Chapter 3 of Buddhaghosa's *The Path of Purification* and is sometimes adapted for a modern lay as well as monastic context.

1   Dwelling: someone may be troubled by lack of almsfood.
2   Family: supporters, family and friends may prove distracting.
3   A class of students: they can demand time and attention, in which case he should retreat to the forest.

4   Gain: people come to offer the meditator gifts and so take up time.
5   Building work: it provokes worry about materials, supplies, carpenters and joiners.
6   Travel: journeys are needed for almsfood or to give an ordination, in which case it should be completed before starting meditation.
7   Kin: fellow monks, preceptors, teachers and family members may get sick and need caring for. This impediment is got rid of by 'curing them by nursing'.
8   Illness: the meditator should wait until it goes, or after a few days declaring to himself, 'I will not be a slave to affliction!'
9   Texts: they can incur heavy responsibilities. Monks sometimes had to spend a lot of time on teaching and practising recitation; but they need not be a problem for some.
10 Psychic powers: as a product of *samādhi*, Buddhaghosa says they should not be a problem to one pursuing calm – but may become one to one pursuing insight.

BUDDHAGHOSA'S LEGACY

All of these practices analysed by Buddhaghosa are described within the Pāli canon, although no list within the canon follows this exact pattern. Canonical texts give inspiration, direct teaching and dramatic enactments of specific situations where meditations are taught. The commentarial tradition, as represented by Buddhaghosa, examines the detailed practical implications of the teachings.

It is for this that he is sometimes criticized. In Southern Buddhist countries, and indeed in the West, his very popularity and ease of consultation have made his manual read where canonical sources are not. It can be surprisingly difficult to find a book on Theravāda meditation in the West that does not immediately make assumptions on the basis of Buddhaghosa's analysis. In Myanmar, it is used as the principal text for the highly sophisticated monastic examination system, to the exclusion of the canonical *suttas* he himself prizes so highly.

Buddhaghosa's compendious and painstakingly careful manual on meditation seems, nonetheless, to have been largely instrumental in sustaining and shaping the course of the meditative tradition of Southern Buddhism. In practice, teachers in these meditative traditions do not seem

to be bound by him. Happy to use his basic limits and recommendatic
their teaching of both *samatha* and *vipassanā* is highly varied, often lo_ca_n,
differentiated, and exhibits extensive exploration and inventiveness in the
use of similes, application and method. Perhaps this is what one would
expect in a still very active meditative tradition.

CONCLUSION

This chapter delineates Buddhaghosa's forty objects for meditation. It has
discussed the nature of Buddhaghosa's legacy and attempted to suggest the
great impact his manual for meditation has made on meditative practice.

FURTHER READING

Gombrich, R.F. (1988) *Theravāda Buddhism; A Social History from Ancient Benares to Modern Colombo,*
London/New York: Routledge and Kegan Paul.
Gray, J. (1892) *Buddhaghosasuppatti, or, The historical romance of the rise and career of Buddhaghosa,* London:
Luzac.
Harvey, P. (1990) *Introduction to Buddhism: Teachings, History and Practices,* Cambridge: CUP, 246–57.
Nāṇamoli, Bhikkhu, trans. (1991) *The Path of Purification: Visuddhimagga: the Classic Manual of Buddhist
Doctrine and Meditation,* 5th edn., Kandy: BPS.

Chanting, Paying Respects and Devotional
Ritual
Five

Ekaṃ samayaṃ Bhagavā...

CHANTING

At this point it will be useful to examine Buddhist devotional practice, which takes many forms. Perhaps the most colourful, most locally differentiated and most exploratory of these is chanting. Chanting has historically formed the core practice of most Buddhists, both in a lay and monastic setting. Little documented in historical accounts and seldom discussed under a separate heading in dictionaries of Buddhism, the diversity of its methods and content nonetheless gives an indication of the way Buddhism has adapted and evolved in different cultural, linguistic and social conditions. In this chapter we will explore a few features of chanting, when it is conducted, and some ways in which it contributes to Buddhist meditative practice.

The purposes of chanting are specific to the time, place, person or people involved and the occasion. There are, however, a few categories which are helpful to bear in mind.

1   Taking refuge in the Triple Gem, the Buddha, *dhamma* and *saṅgha*: this activity, both communal and solitary, is performed by the monastic orders and the laity as a part of daily practice in most schools of Buddhism, with variation in content and method according to school.
2   Monastic *pāṭimokkha*: this communal chant of the monastic code of discipline for the ritual purification of the monastic order is conducted on a monthly basis.
3   Textual preservation: chanting conducted for the repetition of the *sūtras/ suttas* and to sustain the basic texts by the monastic orders.
4   Generally magical and protective: chanting practised for blessings and protection at festivals and ceremonies, both in the home and in the temple. It is usually conducted by monks and nuns, but lay practitioners

usually know some chants and in some countries there are strong traditions of lay chanting.

5   Meditative: the repetition of a mantra or collection of attributes for the purposes of private meditation. While secluded meditative practices of this kind are often conducted largely by the monks and nuns, such forms of chanting have historically provided a route for many lay practitioners, particularly in Tibet, China, Korea and Japan, to undertake activities regarded as salvific in themselves.

The boundaries between these categories are not always easy or desirable to define.

What is chanting?

Nowadays even those who have never encountered Buddhism in practice will have heard some of the different kinds of chanting on television, the radio, the internet or, more atmospherically, pouring out from a temple in an Asian country. Chanting, whether of long texts or short repetitive mantras, as a preliminary to meditation or as a meditation in itself, is one of the most fundamental features of Buddhist practice, both at a personal level and at a public, ceremonial level. Methods and techniques within each of these kinds of chanting vary considerably.

But before we consider distinct forms of chanting, we should ask a rather difficult question – what is it exactly? How does it differ from, say, singing songs, a practice which seems also to have characterized Buddhist practice since the inception of the tradition? Oddly enough, the Buddhist world does not really have a common generic term for 'chanting', except the English one, though everyone would recognize it. The Oxford English Dictionary (Compact Edn 378) classifies chanting with singing but also terms it a 'measured monotonous song, the musical recitation of words'. It has also been called a halfway point between singing and speech. These are certainly close definitions of how it appears, but do not tell us what it is and what it means for practising Buddhists – or indeed those that practise chanting in other traditions, such as Gregorian chant. There are, for instance, other forms of enunciation, such as sprechgesang, or the narrative parts of some oratorios, that also lie halfway between speech and song. These are, however, usually explanatory linking devices, albeit beautiful ones, that are not considered by those taking part to be quite the same as chant.

Rhythm and a fairly limited range of pitch do seem to be key factors in what we recognize as chanting. At any rate those who practise chanting in a Buddhist and, from what I gather, a Christian context too, see it as involving the active refining of the production of the sound itself within the body, outside the parameters of either singing or speaking. Discursive thought is either simplified greatly, as in the recollection of a very few simple attributes, or largely eliminated. Nonetheless, great attentiveness is enjoined for its proper development: there are usually elements, such as a slightly non-mechanical repetition, an awareness of the breath and the area in the body from which each sound emanates, which ensure that the chant does not involve a lack of mindfulness or clear comprehension. It is important to maintain awareness, along with what can sometimes be great passion, and to keep alert to the variations in the often simple, repetitive rhythm and subtleties of tone. Successful chanting also includes awareness of bodily posture and awareness of the sounds of others, if in a group context. Buddhist practitioners say of their chanting that it encompasses mindfulness of feeling and, in keeping awareness of the sometimes complex verbal content of the chants, mindfulness of the mind itself. More generally, chanting is also supposed to be fun, a comment often made by those in other kinds of religious traditions and something that does not always come across when a piece of text is given on the printed page! Indeed those that practise it say that it arouses all five factors of jhāna.

All these features have aligned the various forms of chants, in most Buddhist schools, to meditation practice.

How chanting is conducted

The audibility and the mode of enunciating varies greatly according to purpose. Where its purpose is public, as in the preservation of traditional texts, for blessings and protection, it is given with full voice, and is considered a collective meditative exercise. The chanting of the pāṭimokkha, the formal recitation of the monastic rules undertaken by all monks within their own community on a monthly basis, comes into this category. Those participating first confess and are freed from any minor faults they may have committed and so are communally ready to renew their life together. Another form of public chanting with full voice is the formal recitation of texts for their preservation, usually conducted in a fairly rapid monotone without great variation of pitch. Where its purpose is to start a meditation – often also conducted in groups – the chanting may also be in full voice, but may, as in the taking of the refuges and precepts, be soft and under the fully enunciated voice, with individuals saying each precept in their own time and without adhering to a group momentum. For private meditation, chanting in the form of mantras and the recollection of, for instance, the attributes of the Buddha, it may be half-murmured as a soft stream of sound, barely audible to anyone else, or chanted internally, to oneself.

Indeed within Buddhist countries its practice is often regarded as a lifetime work requiring considerable skill and care. Many monks make acquiring chanting skills their principal monastic duty and spiritual practice; different effects are intended through a variety of chanting methods. In Sri Lanka, chanting seems to have been greatly influenced by the mellifluous, rounded notes of Sanskrit *gāthā* recitation. The overall effect is of lilting waves of sound. Lay groups are also occasionally set up and have developed methods of their own, with, for instance, the assembly dividing itself into two parts, one starting slightly later than the other, so that one wave of sound meets the other, which starts before the first has finished. This seems in part to have been influenced by the musical range of Sinhala as a language. In Thailand, where language is tonal, chanting has also been influenced by the customary patterns made between the several pitches used normally in speech. In Myanmar, monastic chant is more vigorous and sharp, with an abrasive, awakening quality. But even within one monastery chanting methods can vary. At Wat Mahāthat, the royal monastery in Bangkok in Thailand, chanting has become a speciality: the same chant may be enunciated in a different way for a specific purpose, such as a funeral. Some chants can be recited in a minor or a major key, radically changing their effect. At funerals, for instance, a list of features of the *Abhidhamma*, which would usually take only a short time to chant, is intoned in a minor key for the benefit of the deceased person and his or her relatives. What looks on paper a short summary of technical terms is enunciated with protracted and slow resonance, making far greater use of melisma, the use of excursions around notes of a greater variety of pitch, up to a fourth or a fifth, to enunciate each syllable. Many practitioners find this the most moving of chanting styles. It appears that these diverse chanting methods, where one text may be recited in quite different ways in different localities and for different purposes, have emerged over a long period of time, presumably in accordance with local taste and what seems to work best. It has been argued that the variety of ways of chanting evolve to suit the temperaments and dispositions of the practitioners in the areas involved. There is certainly an immense variety of colour, tone and style from country to country. To appreciate this fully it is best to hear chants within their own context 'live', preferably at a ceremony where people are actively engaged in a ritual specific to the chant. Many, however, may now be heard on the internet for those who would like to listen to them: references to sites are given at the end of this chapter.

1. TAKING REFUGE

Most forms of Buddhism recommend some taking of refuge and the five precepts as a preliminary to meditation and also sometimes as a practice in itself, for arousing a sense of stability and confidence in where one stands. On a visit to a temple, a practitioner will take off their shoes – customary anyway on entering houses in most parts of Asia – and kneels or prostrates in front of a shrine to pay respects to the Buddha. Flowers, incense, butterlamps or candles may then be offered, with styles of offering varying from country to country. The importance of these practices, which vary from simple gestures of respect to full prostrations followed by extensive chanting as a means of settling the mind and paying homage to the Buddha, cannot be overestimated. They often form the core daily spiritual exercise of many practitioners, both in the lay and monastic life and, from the evidence of the earliest texts, have always been considered purificatory in themselves. The Pāli canon, for instance, takes what has become the formula for the chanting of the qualities of the Triple Gem as the primary means of practising the recollection of the Buddha, the *dhamma* and the *saṅgha*. These are Buddhaghosa's twenty-first, twenty-second and twenty-third meditation objects. While these practices are not said to lead to *jhāna*, or to establish mindfulness and concentration to the same degree as the usual kind of sitting practice, they are frequently recommended. They are said to bring into being a sense of peace and cheerfulness, to make memorable a moment of confidence and stillness so that it can be brought to mind at a later time and to act as a preliminary to the practice of most sitting meditations. The boundaries between such rituals and meditation itself are not necessarily well defined. In Tibet and Eastern Buddhist countries a fourth refuge is sometimes taken, in the teacher.

Chant in honour of the Triple Gem

To the Buddha, the reference point of the one who knows, to the teaching (dhamma), which shows the release from suffering, and the saṅgha, the

community of those who have practised the teaching in the past and do so
now.

Homage

Namo tassa bhagavato arahato sammā sambuddhassa
Namo tassa bhagavato arahato sammā sambuddhassa
Namo tassa bhagavato arahato sammā sambuddhassa
Buddhaṃ saranaṃ gacchāmi
Dhammaṃ saranaṃ gacchāmi
Sanghaṃ saranaṃ gacchāmi
Dutiyaṃ pi Buddham saranaṃ gacchāmi
Dutiyaṃ pi dhammam saranaṃ gacchāmi
Dutiyaṃ pi sangham saranaṃ gacchāmi
Tatiyaṃ pi Buddham saranaṃ gacchāmi
Tatiyaṃ pi dhammam saranaṃ gacchāmi
Tatiyaṃ pi sangham saranaṃ gacchāmi

Precepts

These are five undertakings, to abstain from taking life, stealing, sexual
conduct which harms oneself and others, lying and becoming intoxicated.
They form the basis of Buddhist ethical practice and the phrasing of each,
though simple, is considered important: the practitioner undertakes the rule
of training to abstain from each of these activities in turn. If one has been
broken, the appropriate precept is taken again. This does not release the
practitioner from the karmic results of any wrong action, but is felt to help
in making a new start. The keeping of each of the five precepts is considered
to have an active, positive effect on the world around, acting as a protection
for the person, those around him or her and the world in general. Early
Buddhist stories abound in incidents of the Buddha in an earlier life, or one
of his associates, finding good luck or freedom from harm through having
kept the precepts. From the point of view of the meditator, chanting them is
considered helpful to put aside some of the worry or restlessness connected
with events during the day, and to dispel 'demons', both inner and outer. As
undertakings, the precepts are sometimes recited rather than chanted.

Pāṇātipāta veramaṇi sikkhāpadaṃ samādiyāmi
Adinnādānā veramaṇi sikkhāpadaṃ samādiyāmi
Kāmesu micchācārā veramaṇi sikkhāpadaṃ samādiyāmi

Musāvāda veramaṇi sikkhāpadaṃ samādiyāmi

Sura meraya majja pamādaṭṭhāna veramaṇi sikkhāpadaṃ samādiyāmi

This may be chanted every day before meditation. Sometimes flowers, incense and lights are offered as well.

Paying homage

In this context some further explanation should also be given of the physical act of paying respects to the Buddha, associated with the practice of chanting for protection and refuge. One common feature is to make an añjali, the usual gesture of greeting in many Asian countries, where the hands are pressed together in front of the chest. This is thought to have developed from an ancient Indian custom of offering water in the hands as a gesture of friendship and reassurance of non-harm. It does not denote 'praying' but is rather a gesture of greeting and honour. Sometimes in addition to this there is some form of bowing to the shrine, usually, although not always, accompanied by kneeling. Sometimes prostrations are made, a practice for showing respect that is shared by many other Indian religions, which may involve the practitioner also making eight points of contact with the ground, or five. This is usually done in Southern traditions while standing or kneeling. In some traditions, a full prostration is made, lying face downwards on the ground, with the hands held in an añjali, also on the ground, before the head. The point is sometimes made to Westerners, alarmed by such practices, that the action is intended primarily for the benefit of the practitioner and is said to effect an opening of the heart. The movement from standing, to kneeling, to making the full prostration and then getting up again is taught as a continuous flow, and becomes a graceful series of postures that engages the whole body in one unified meditative exercise. The practice is particularly associated with the repentance practices of Eastern forms of Buddhism, and is intended to clear the effects of actions which have made them unhappy. In Tiantai, prostrations and repentance practice were conducted as one of the main meditations to be undertaken, linked to other practices, over a period of ninety days as part of an extended meditative retreat. A Tibetan practice of this kind involves taking of a vow to make several hundred thousand full prostrations, which usually takes years, with perhaps fifty or a hundred a day. When undertaken with this sort of physical and emotional commitment, prostration as a practice can be arduous and very demanding, but those that undertake it find it productive of great strength (viriya) and stamina as well as confidence (*saddhā*). It is adopted sometimes when visiting sacred sites in Tibet, or indeed for some pilgrimages, with the intention to travel, usually when making a pilgrimage.

Such prostrations are one example of a characteristic that recurs throughout all forms of Buddhism, whereby a single element in the basic devotional procedure is developed into a full meditation practice. It is then regarded as having a beneficial and, when practised in conjunction with other practices, eventually a salvific effect on the mind. In Thailand it is customary at the end of the day for many people to visit the larger temple *stūpas*, or outside shrines, such as at Sanam Leung in Bangkok. As darkness falls, often quite suddenly, they circumambulate the shrine holding a lit candle, incense-stick and flower which they intend to offer. People circle the shrine three times. For the first circling, the first part of the *iti pi so* chant, the recollection of the attributes of the Buddha is continously chanted or murmured. For the second, the recollection of the attributes of the teaching is similarly chanted and for the third, the recollection of the qualities of the *saṅgha*. When they have finished, people offer the flowers, incense and lights on various tables, candle-holders and jars of sand, and perhaps make more offerings or do some more chanting before moving on. Sometimes a small film of gold-leaf is tied around the incense-stick, flower and candle that can be bought cheaply as you enter the temple. This can then be rubbed onto smaller shrines around the larger central *stūpa* or shrine, an action also intended to bring merit. These recollections are not thought to bring all the effects of a meditation practice in terms of arousing mindfulness, concentration and wisdom, but they make a tranquil finish to a day's work. The act of walking around the shrine, the smell of incense, the sight of the lights and flowers in the darkness around the *stūpa*, the sound of the continued chants, and the physical act of rubbing the gold onto the human figure of the Buddha, all help a serene transition from ritual to a sense of *samatha*.

Recollection of qualities of the Triple Gem

Itipi so bhagavā araham sammāsambuddho vijjācaraṇasampanno sugato lokāvidū anuttaro purisadamma–sārathi satthā devamanussānam buddho bhagavā ti.

By this reason the Exalted One is an arahat, fully awakened, perfect in knowledge and conduct, well gone, the knower of worlds, incomparable leader of people to be tamed, teacher of gods and humans, a Buddha, the Exalted One.

Svākkhāto bhagavatā dhammo sandiṭṭhiko akāliko ehipassiko opanayiko paccattam veditabbo viññūhī ti.

The *dhamma* is well taught by the Exalted One, visible here and now, immediate, inviting inspection, leading onwards, to be experienced by the wise for themselves.

Supaṭipanno bhagavato sāvakasaṅgho uju paṭipanno bhagavato sāvakasaṅgho ñāyapaṭipanno bhagavato sāvakasaṅgho sāmīci paṭipanno bhagavato sāvakasaṅgho yadidam cattāri purisayugāni aṭṭha purisapuggalā esa bhagavato sāvakasaṅgho āhuneyyo pāhuneyyo dakkhiṇeyyo añjalikaraṇiyo anuttaram puññakkhettam lokassā ti.

The *saṅgha* of the Exalted One's disciples is practising the good way, practising the straight way, practising the true way, practising the proper way, that is, the four pairs of people, the eight types of individuals; this *saṅgha* of the Exalted One's disciples is worthy of gifts, worthy of hospitality, worthy of offerings, worthy of añjalis, the unsurpassed field of merit for the world.

Figure 5.1 **Monks chanting in formal dress in Thailand**

Within the monastic tradition, two forms of chanting are considered primarily the province of the monastic orders.

2. MONASTIC IDENTITY

The first is the chanting for the purificatory ceremony mentioned above, the Pāṭimokkha. Philologically, this word has associations with literal purgatives used to clear the body, a startling metaphor that is nonetheless helpful in considering its function! The chanting is conducted in different ways by the monastic orders of many schools of Eastern as well as Southern Buddhism, usually on a monthly basis, and is considered to be a way of clearing bad feeling, remorse or irritability from the community. As the assembly chants the rules, their identity and purpose is reaffirmed so that they can resume their collective life.

3. THE PRESERVATION OF THE TEXTS

For hundreds of years, before the advent of writing, Buddhist texts were handed down by the bhāṇakas, groups of monks dedicated to preserving the canon. Each group maintained a different section of the three 'baskets' (tipiṭika): the texts given on specific occasions (suttas/sūtras), and the code for the monastic discipline (Vinaya) and the higher teaching (Abhidhamma/Abhidharma). In practice this meant that an enormous body of texts were preserved for centuries. The texts acquired many features of oral traditions that are found in many bardic poems around the world: redundancy, assonance, and, in some cases, poetic rhythms, in order to be memorized better. We do not know at what point chanting styles started to develop but the practice of chanting these texts is very old. The verses of the iti pi so chant are today sounded with the early Sanskritic and Pāli rhythms, suggesting that the way it is done now is ancient. Pāli commentaries, written in the centuries after the Buddha's death, say that he recited the Ratana-Sutta, an auspicious text chanted at special occasions to this day, to the people of Vesāli to dispel plagues and famine. Chanting this and other suttas continues in many countries, for the merit it brings, and as a means of retaining in the memory a corpus of texts that provide the backbone of monastic doctrinal debate and investigation: all contribute to the continuation of dhamma/dharma. The word 'sajjhāya', usually translated as repetition, rehearsal or study, has connotations of all of these activities and would have always involved what we now call 'chanting' (see A III 22).

The *bhāṇaka* tradition is no longer extant, but some groups of monks still preserve many features with which it is associated. In Vietnam, for instance, monks who take this form of training spend twenty or thirty years learning a particular body of texts according to set procedures. There are still a few monks in South Asian countries that have memorized the whole of the *tipiṭika*: in Myanmar there are at present seven such accredited chanters, whose skills are tested every ten years. The way this is intoned will tend to be fairly monochrome, if euphonious, involving only a narrow range of 'notes': the intention is not so much the production of a varied sound but simple preservation and recitation. In many Southern Buddhist countries the whole of the 'three baskets' of texts, the *Vinaya*, the *Suttas* and the *Abhidhamma*, is chanted over a period of several months by groups of monks to commemorate special events. Novice monks are required to learn and recite sections of the *Vessantara-Jātaka* for their parents, in order to demonstrate their chanting skills and to acquire merit for the family. In Myanmar and Thailand monks need to train extensively in the recitation of texts such as the *Mahāsamaya-sutta* or the *Vessantara-Jātaka*, in case there is an occasion or ceremony for which these particularly auspicious recitations are considered suitable. The chanting style for narrative texts for such purposes requires a rich and dramatic range of method, tempo, pitch and tone, dependent in part on subject matter and the magical effect each section may be thought to possess.

4. BLESSINGS AND PROTECTION

The most popular form of chanting and recitation, however, is *paritta*, for the purposes of blessing and protection. Such chanting is frequently undertaken by the laity too, either in the presence of the monastic orders or on their own. All Southern Buddhist monks, whether their specialism is chanting or not, will know, for instance, the discourse on loving kindness, the *Mettā-sutta* (see Chapter 3), and the texts on the blessings of the Triple Gem, the *Ratana-sutta* and the *Maṅgala-sutta*. These will be chanted on occasions where blessings are given to the laity. Other specific chants known by most Theravāda monks and many of the laity include talismanic *suttas* to recite before going to sleep, and blessings for the conclusion of any ceremony.

The most frequent and prevalent use of such chanting is before and after the offering of a meal by members of the laity, a *dāna* to the monks. In the Southern tradition monks are not supposed to cook for themselves, but rather receive food from lay offerers, who trust that in giving a meal to the monks merit and its consequent good *kamma/karma* will accrue to their family. The meals are offered either in the monastery or at the lay followers' homes. A home *dāna* may well be associated with a specific event, such as moving into a new house, or a birthday. This is considered a form of generosity which is thought to bring great good luck: the act of giving is felt to benefit all concerned in the ceremony and merit and good wishes are shared with all relatives and beings around. Specific chants and ways of chanting are associated with these events.

A whole world-view accompanies the recitation of such texts: they are thought to dispel evil spirits, bring happiness and wellbeing for the family, neighbours and friends, transfer merit to departed relatives and help to ensure a happy rebirth in the future. It is customary, for instance, for these to be chanted on welcoming a new baby into a family, inaugurating a new hotel or house, or bringing good luck for exams.

5. MANTRA OR REPETITIVE CHANTING MEDITATION

All of these kinds of chanting come under the category of what we would call *bhāvanā*, cultivation of the mind. The active witnessing of generosity, the transference of merit to other beings, the preservation of the teachings in their correct form and the purificatory effect of chanting the *Pāṭimokkha* for monks are all considered essential in different ways both for the teaching to continue and, in some cases, as a path for personal spiritual development. The recollection of a moment of generosity, for instance, made memorable by being witnessed by gods and family, is considered a complete meditative exercise, bringing freedom from fear and peace of mind. In some early texts the Buddha specifically enjoins such recollections as a means of calming the mind for those who as lay people are too busy to practise much sitting meditation. They are also strongly recommended as preliminary to meditation in all contexts by early commentators such as Buddhaghosa and Upatissa. In modern Buddhist contexts, in a practice recorded since the earliest texts, a dying person is specifically reminded of formal acts of generosity as a means of allowing the mind to be free from fear and guilt at the approach of death. *Cāga*, the word that describes the mental state associated with generosity, has connotations of 'letting go' and a freely undertaken renunciation.

There are some forms of chanting, however, which have become practices in themselves and are either an important element or the central feature of a specific meditative system. From Vedic times, the recitation of particular syllables, or groups of words, in a mantra, was considered a spiritual practice which, through both the meaning and the sound itself, allowed the practitioner to participate in the divine. This was manifest primarily through what was considered the highest sense, that of hearing. Aurally based meditation objects, rather than visual objects, are central to many Indic spiritual traditions and to Western developments around them, such as Transcendental Meditation. Early Buddhism, as described in the Pāli canonical and commentarial tradition, does not seem to have followed the route of taking one sound or simple mantra as a meditation. The practice of internal repetition of a single word is present in early descriptions of a practice like the kasiṇa practice, where the word 'fire' is spoken externally and internally. The actual words themselves, however, are not considered sacred as they are in a Hindu context, or in the mantras of some later Buddhist practice. Mantra-based meditations do, however, evolve in Southern Buddhism from, apparently, the first centuries CE. The recitation of the word 'Buddho', for instance, is linked to many meditative systems in Southern Buddhism today. This is now sometimes accompanied by a breathing practice linked to the syllables, with the syllable Bu accompanying, say, an inbreath, and the syllable Ddho accompanying an outbreath. Other forms of chanting a single name, mantra or a protective, auspicious chant known as a dhāraṇī, are a possibly later development within Buddhism. By the eighth century there were literally hundreds of different dhāraṇīs, associated with different meditative practices, either as preliminaries, the main body of a meditation practice or as a protection at the completion of a given meditation. These were particularly popular in Vietnam and Tibet. Many are still used today in Buddhist countries.

As Buddhism was developed by the Northern and Eastern schools, the chanting of mantras and syllables invested with esoteric meaning is developed in a number of ways. These vary from the highly formalized repetitions of 'seed' syllables and mantras associated with particular deities, to the more simple repetition of a name of a Buddha or a Bodhisattva. This could be conducted either with a rosary, usually of 108 beads, or within a temple context, when using a prayer wheel. Simpler forms of such chanting may also be used as an accompaniment to activities in daily life. As this process occurs, the idea that the name of a god, goddess, Buddha or Bodhisattva can itself be imbued with significance, through the power of what it denotes, again resurfaces, acquiring features previously associated with Vedic and

Brahminic ritual. Pure-Land Buddhism takes mantras associated with the name of the Amitābha Buddha, for instance, to be potent precisely because of the nature of the being named as much the effect of the sounding of the chant. In Japan, practices of this kind are particularly developed within the Nichiren schools.

In Pure-Land and Nichiren schools, practitioners employ such chanting as the main form of spiritual practice. While there is sometimes a worldly appeal in Nichiren schools, whereby the chants are used for immediate granting of wishes, there is also a deeply devotional element. Some meditative traditions of these schools see such aims as the first rung on a kind of ladder, leading in time to a number of possible levels of refinement. The chant is thought capable of taking the practitioner from the most obvious and manifest levels of efficacy − chanting to pass an exam or avert disaster for instance − to become, in some cases, what is regarded as a complete salvific meditative practice. The voice, body, feelings and mind of the person that chants become calmed, and are watched over a long period with an awareness that is gradually refined. This awareness is itself in time allowed to become an object for discernment and investigation to produce wisdom (paññā/prajñā). As the sound, the voice that produces it and the mind that engages with the chant are all seen as objects of meditation, so the relationship between knower and known, subject and object, and self and other, is explored through the continued mediation of the chant itself. At this level, calm and insight are both said to become developed. This element of gradual development does not always seem to have been taught or encouraged historically, and does not always seem to an outsider to be a feature of some chanting schools. At certain times, however, it has been formulated and, presumably, practised too. The Korean monk, Jinul, for instance, argued that chanting of this kind could lead the practitioner eventually to the source of sound and then, what is known as the dharmadhātu: a term used by Nāgārjuna and employed in many forms of Buddhism to describe the innately radiant mind, a transcendent state beyond dualities such as 'real' or 'unreal'. Until recently, it seems, in Korea exercises associated with developing chanting tend to be confined to the monastic orders and are not taught generally to the lay public.

Within many traditions of Buddhism, in particular in the Nichiren schools, the titles of sūtras are felt to be endowed with the attributes of the whole texts. Their protective and auspicious qualities are communicated to the practitioner through the act of chanting the name of the text or, sometimes, even the first syllable of the name. Such features are prominent within some Southern traditions too. In Myanmar, the chanting of the twenty-four features of the *Paṭṭhāna*, the seventh and, in that region, the most highly revered book of the *Abhidhamma*, is felt to bring good luck through instilling an intuitive understanding of the *paccayas*, the 'conditions' the texts describe. In Khmer regions, the chanting of, for instance, the first syllables of the titles of the seven books of the *Abhidhamma*, *Sam Vi Dha Pu Ka Ya Pa*, are also felt to be auspicious through their evocation of the whole system of *Abhidhamma*. The *Abhidhamma* is actively studied, learnt for chanting and applied in connection with meditation practices to this day, particularly in Myanmar, both in a monastic and also sometimes in a lay context. It perhaps appear to some, however, forbiddingly difficult. The chanting of the names of all the books then enables the practitioner to have some sympathetic attunement to a system that they may feel unable to study themselves. In such contexts, esoteric practices are also associated with chanting such syllables in a sequence. The syllables Na Mo Bu Ddha Ya, used as denoters of the five *aṅgas* or limbs of meditative practice, seem to be linked in Cambodia, Laos and Thailand to a rich and flourishing system of meditative ritual and symbology. This includes *yantras* – diagrams said to embody and teach meditative understanding through the relationship between the lines and

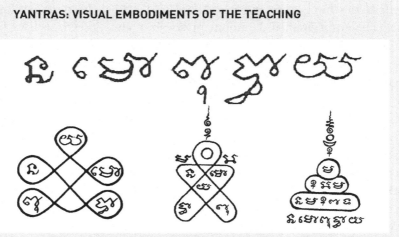

YANTRAS: VISUAL EMBODIMENTS OF THE TEACHING

Figure 5.2 **The chanted syllables Na Mo Bu Ddha Ya are linked to breathing practices in Thailand, Laos and Cambodia, and often shown on diagrams known as yantras**

AMULETS

A complex system of ritual, using methods that appear to be ancient, is sometimes linked to chants, so that they are employed alongside the more well-known verses, to empower amulets, charms and Buddha images. Countless amulets inscribed with protective yantras are sold at the amulet market in Bangkok and around Wat Maha That temple: most Buddhist taxi drivers in Thailand will have an amulet in their car, which, it has to be said, often feels much needed! The *Iti pi so* chant, widespread throughout Southern Buddhist countries as the canonical recollection of the attributes of the *Buddha, dhamma* and *saṅgha* is also sometimes incorporated and inscribed in a distilled form on amulets.

Figure 5.3 **Amulets such as these, from Thailand, are often empowered through chants and inscribed with yantras on the back**

shapes. These are described in Cambodian and Laotian texts, dating from the nineteenth century, and are linked to breathing practices.

CHANTING STYLES IN KOREA AND TIBET

The focus of this chapter has been on Southern Buddhist practice, but there are equally rich traditions in other areas too, which will be looked at in later chapters. The Chan/Seon/Zen practitioner, for instance, takes the sound as itself an object to be viewed by the mind. In the Tibetan traditions, mantras feature as accompaniments to visualizations; chants accompany empowerments, initiation and indeed most areas of life. Below are two quotes that give some sense of the diversity of theory and technique that comes to be associated with chant styles.

Zen chanting

Chanting meditation means keeping a not-moving mind and perceiving the sound of your own voice. Perceiving your voice means perceiving your true self or true nature. Then you and the sound are never separate, which means that you and the whole universe are never separate. Thus, to perceive our true nature is to perceive universal substance. With regular chanting, our sense of being centred gets stronger and stronger. When we are strongly centered, we can control our feelings, and thus our condition and situation.

In our Zen centers, people live together and practice together. At first, people come with strong opinions, strong likes and dislikes. For many people, chanting meditation is not easy: much confused thinking, many likes, many dislikes and so on. However, when we do chanting meditation correctly, perceiving the sound of our own voice and the voices all around us, our minds become clear. In clear mind, there is no like or dislike, only the sound of the voice. Ultimately, we learn that chanting meditation is not for our personal pleasure, to give us good feeling, but to make our direction clear. Our direction is to become clear and get enlightened, in order to save beings from suffering.

Perceiving sound means everything is universal sound: birds singing, thunder, dogs barking – all this is universal sound. If you have no mind, everything will be perceived just as it is. Therefore, when you are chanting with no mind it is also universal sound. If you have 'I' then it is 'my' sound. But with a mind clear like space, sometimes even the sound of a dog barking or a car horn honking will bring enlightenment, because at that moment you and the sound become one. When you and the sound become one, you don't hear the sound, you are the sound.

Sahn (1996)

The one voice chord: Tibetan and Mongolian chanting

According to the Tibetan tradition the Gyuto Tantric college was founded after one monk. Je Tzong Sherab Senge, had a strange dream in 1433 CE, in which he heard the sound of the bull at the same time as the sound of a high pure voice. He woke up and realised he had been hearing his own voice, producing two sounds. He then sat down to practise and found he could do it again. So he developed a system of chanting the 'one voice chord', with

Figure 5.4 **Wooden figurine from Myanmar/Burma of chanting figures**

three notes, representing male, female and a transforming force, and set up a school to teach it.

What is throat singing?

In the western world Throat singing is also called overtone singing, harmonic singing, or harmonic chant. The most known Throat singing is the Tibetan and Mongolian chanting but also many other regions in the World are practicing a similar type of singing, that manipulates the harmonics resonance's created as air travels through the human vocal folds and out the lips.

The harmonic frequencies created by the human vocal apparatus are harnessed in throat singing to select overtones by tuning the resonance in the mouth. The result of tuning allows the singer to create more than one pitch at the same time, with the capability of creating six pitches at once. Generally the sounds created by throat singing are low droning hums and high pitched flutelike melodies.

Hightower (2004)

CONCLUSION

This chapter can only give some hints of details of chanting and its associated customs and meditative practices. These are often highly localized, perhaps growing over centuries through a kind of maturation process within the soil of local meditation practice, language, rituals and customs. Chants are various and highly precise in their function and intent: those that pursue chanting regard the form as a particular, specialized skill. While not usually regarded as the whole of the meditative way, chanting often, in practice, colours, enlivens and strengthens feeling for meditative practice as well as making a space in any group of people or assembly to be free from obvious hindrances and practise meditation.

FURTHER READING

Bizot, F. (1976) *Le Figuier à Cinq Branches: Recherche sur le Bouddhism Khmer*, Paris: Publications de l'École Francaise de l'Extreme Orient.

Buddhavihara Temple (2001) *Morning and Evening Chanting*, Birmingham.

Harvey, P. (1990) *Introduction to Buddhism: Teachings, History and Practices*, Cambridge: CUP, 172–95.

Hightower, T.V. (2004) 'The One Voice Chord': http://home3.inet.tele.dk/hitower/voice.html

Sahn, S. (1996) 'Chanting with English translations and Temple rules, the Kwan Um school of Zen, Cumberland': http://www.kwanumzen.com/pdf/chantbk.pdf

Studholme, A. (2002) *The Origins of Oṃ Maṇipadme Hūṃ: A study of the Kāraṇḍavyūha Sūtra*, New York: State University of New York Press.

Tanabe, G.T. (2004) 'Chanting', Robert Buswell Jnr. (ed.), *Encyclopedia of Buddhism*, 2 vols., New York: Macmillan, 1, 137–9.

WEBSITES

A library of chants:

Buddha Net Audio chants: http://www.buddhanet.net/audio-chant.htm

'The prayer wheel: spiritual technology from Tibet' (2004) Dharma Haven: http://www.dharma-haven.org/tibetan/prayer-wheel.htm#Mani

Meditation and Southern Buddhism
Six

There is a mountain in Sri Lanka which has become a place of pilgrimage for Buddhists. At dawn the reflection of Adam's Peak can be seen in the clouds in the distance, one of very few places in the world where solitary geographical positioning makes such a mysterious event possible. It also has another natural quirk: a yard-long slight indentation in the ground on the summit is in the shape of a smooth, flat and evenly planted footprint. It is said to be the place where the Buddha Gotama first visited the island, stepping over from India. Pilgrims make the long climb up on the night of the full moon to pay homage to the footprint, an ancient practice described by Marco Polo, and to watch the mountain's triangular shadow appear on the clouds in the distance as the sun rises behind and then gradually disappear. This arduous, meditative walk, made with the accompaniment of chants, breaks for 'plain tea' and chat, has made the place a central feature of the Sri Lankan sacred and psychological map as well as the obviously geographical one. Everyone should climb the peak once in their life (down-to-earth Sri Lankans joke that doing it twice is a bit extreme). The *genius loci* also ensures that it is at least one spot on the island where other traditions and beings feel welcome, as evinced in its several names. The footprint is said by the Moslem community to be that of the Biblical Adam, Hindus call it Sri Pada, to denote the arrival of Śiva, and its other name, Samanalakande, was coined from Sinhala as the place where butterflies are said to go to die.

The story is a demonstration of the way that the advent of Buddhism in a particular region comes to be steeped in legends, local custom, environment and even geological setting. In this chapter we will look at the way Buddhist meditation has developed in the countries of what has become called Southern Buddhism: Sri Lanka, Thailand, Cambodia, Myanmar and Laos. Because traditions of practice have such an ancient ancestry, the cultures of these regions often exhibit features that link closely to and support the practice of meditation, so this chapter will also focus on some of these.

SRI LANKA
The first home for Buddhism outside India does seem to have been Sri Lanka, introduced through a mission sent by Emperor Aśoka under his son,

Mahinda. King Devanampiya Tissa (r. 250–210 BCE), after his conversion, undertook extensive building of the temple, the Thūpārāma Dagoba at the then capital in Anurādhapura. The now lost Brazen Palace Temple was also built there which had, according to an ancient Sinhalese chronicle, the Mahavaṃsa, nine storeys and housed one of the great early temples of Buddhism, the Mahāvihāra. It was here that Buddhaghosa supposedly stayed when he was writing his manual of meditation. A cutting from the bodhi tree under which the Buddha gained enlightenment was supposedly brought over by Princess Sanghamittā, King Aśoka's daughter, and one has been growing at that spot in Anurādhapura ever since. Every year pilgrims still come and bathe the tree in milk.

Four deities are said to guard the island, who have acquired Buddhist connotations. The rich sacred geography of the island is also enacted by the frequency of the depiction of the sixteen stūpas dotted around it. The Mahavaṃsa lists these, and all of them are frequently honoured by their depiction on temples throughout the island. The Sinhalese perceived themselves, from the earliest times, as following the way of the Buddha. There seems to have been, as in Southeast Asia, a distinction between forest monks, who practised a great deal of meditation, and followed more the model of the Indian ascetic, and those of the village, whose Buddhist teaching was linked to education and pastoral care but who would practise some, if less meditation too. This polarity dates back at least to the sixth century. In the early days it seems that monasteries such as the Mahāvihāra were active meditative centres as well as places of intellectual and textual inquiry. Their traditions in all these fields have persisted with some breaks throughout Sri Lankan history. Certainly differences of approach seem to have been live issues. The Abhayagiri monastery, for instance, seems to have been much more in sympathy with meditative trends that were issuing from India which gave rise to what came to be known as the Mahāyāna schools. There seem to have been three schools or nikāyas in Sri Lanka in the early days, perhaps in part separated by different attitudes towards practice. In the twelfth century, under the auspices of King Parakkamabāhu, the system became more homogeneous, and the tradition came to be known as 'Theravāda', broadly following the guidelines of the old Mahāvihāra. At this time this name came to be used by Buddhist traditions in Southeast Asia, perhaps primarily because of the Sri Lankan model's ability to accommodate the presence of local and state interests.

Figure 6.1 **Reclining stone Buddha at Gal Vihara, Polonnaruwa**

The laity

The extent to which the laity in Sri Lanka practised meditation in the past is not clear. In the first part of the twentieth century there was a widespread idea that sitting meditation was for 'too difficult' for lay people – in some contrast to the popular understanding in, say, Thailand. As monks ordain for life, there is little movement in and out of the *saṅgha*, so few ex-monks around who may have had opportunities to practise it. Historically, however, Sri Lanka has always been a country steeped in vibrant and emotional rituals, such as the *paritta*, or blessings ceremonies, lay chanting and domestic ritual at home. These tend to be Buddhist, but with strong local elements, such as offerings to local gods, deities, and the spirits of various woods, lakes and mountains.

This has given local practice what we might call a multi-layered feel, where a small amount of sitting meditation is interspersed with ritual, blessings, chant and a touch of insight practice. Beings all around are remembered. For instance, a ceremony for a life event, at home or in the temple, involves providing food to the monks, chanting and blessings. The laity will make the offerings and join in at certain times with the chants. There will probably also be a few minutes of loving-kindness practice, and, perhaps, a short meditation on the breath. A talk may follow, about some aspect of the path, and if the occasion is to mark a death or the anniversary of a death, there will be some element of insight practice in the reminder of the future state of the bodies of all beings. This mixture of listening, chanting, calm (*samatha*) and insight (*vipassanā*) is also rooted in a sense of place and beings all around. The merit from the event is usually 'shared', in a ceremony involving pouring water, as the wish is made that any benefit will go to the dead, and to all beings around and in the locality who may delight in the event or who may be unhappy and needing help. Sri Lankan monks – like those in many other Southern Buddhist traditions – tend to lead their guidance of the practice of loving-kindness for the laity with specific reference to known local places and areas. 'May all beings in x or y be well and happy' is a wish translated through ritual, and they, hope practice, into the participants' daily life and own surroundings. This practice is particularly favoured in Sri Lanka.

As so often in Buddhist settings, a simple ritual for a life event will have an earthiness, applicability and a sense of the festive all knitted in with other features of the teaching. Anyone who has attended many such events – on festival days, the anniversaries of the death of a relative or a friend – will be *bahusuto*, someone who has 'heard much', a complimentary epithet often employed by the Buddha to describe his followers. He or she will also be keyed in to many aspects of the teaching and basic meditative practice. This they can pursue further at some time, perhaps when they are old, a period in life which, in Southern Asian countries, is regarded as especially suitable for the practice of meditation. At other times a sense of the possibilities of meditation is present. Short meditations are also taught in schools, usually in the form of a loving-kindness practice. The whole evening ritual of dropping by a temple on the way home after work, central also in many Southeast Asian countries, involves the recollection of the qualities of the Buddha, *dhamma* and *saṅgha*. These are practices recommended by the Buddha and by Buddhaghosa under the heading of *samatha*. On full-moon day festivals the laity wear white, take precepts and spend a day at the temple. At these there are always many old people, particularly women, chanting and making offerings. The devotion and grace of this kind of *bhāvanā* is self-evident.

> There are four times. And what are they? Hearing *dhamma* at the right time, discussion of *dhamma* at the right time, *samatha* at the right time, *vipassanā* at the right time.
>
> A II 141

FLOWER OFFERINGS

In Sri Lanka, flower offerings are made with particular care. The heads are taken of lotuses, frangipani and jasmine flowers and piled up in decorative arrangements on dishes, sprinkled with water and offered to the shrine with some ancient flower-offering verses. The person offering pays respects (pūja) with the colourful and scented flowers, and makes a wish that through the merit of offering there may be freedom; earthenware butterlamps are also lit, with twisted cotton wicks floating in coconut oil.

As these flowers are fading away, so this body of mine is moving towards dissolution.

The merit of the activity is then transferred to any gods, humans, animals or suffering spirits who may be nearby.
'Puppha pūja', http://www.buddhanet.net/audio-chant.htm

Buddhism in Sri Lanka has certainly suffered periods of decline. The island at times has not been a unified whole, and was divided, for instance, after thirteenth-century Tamil invasions. The ordination line for monks had to reintroduced from Thailand in the sixteenth century and was lost for nuns entirely. Southern Buddhist nuns now adopt a *Vinaya* based on early precepts, but without a direct lineage that can be traced back to early times, as it can by nuns in Taiwan. The last few years of Sri Lanka's history have also been deeply troubled, with conflict between the Tamil and Sinhalese population, and the devastation of the recent tsunami. Despite this, the island still retains a reputation for its spiritual tradition. The monastic orders are thriving and its meditative heritage seems to have been sustained, for both men and women. There are many women who cannot ordain as the ordination lineage has been lost, but are called nuns, living by extra precepts in communities. There is a continued formation of temples, such as the Island Hermitage near Galle, and a number of new meditation centres, often in the forest regions. Some of these are open to the laity and to Westerners to stay for extended periods of personal practice. At a lay level, meditation has become more obviously popular, perhaps influenced by the number of tourists who have visited the island in search of teaching and somewhere for

Figure 6.2 **Butter lamps in Sri Lanka: the wicks are made from twisted cotton, and dipped in coconut oil before lighting**

personal practice. Burmese insight methods have had some impact, as well as the trend for some Westerners interested in meditation to take monastic ordination. Despite setbacks, Buddhism is everywhere in Sri Lanka still. Wherever you go, from the earliest hours of the morning, Buddhist chants are heard continuously on radio; along major thoroughfares, alongside the fumes of petrol and roadside waste, you can always smell incense and burning coconut oil in butterlamp offerings at the many shrines on the way.

SOUTHEAST ASIA

Myanmar/Burma also has some legendary claims to an early Buddhist influence. Buddhism arrived in the very early part of the first millennium and still constitutes the major religion of the region. The ethnic groups are varied, and some, such as the Shan, have strong local practices linked to Buddhist ones. These include much-loved rituals such as the recitation of the *Vessantara-Jātaka*, a long festive event, where chant, listening and generosity (*dāna*) all contribute in various ways to what could be called local *bhāvanā*. The practice of meditation, despite the country's troubled political history, also seems to thrive there. The Burmese have a reputation for their *vipassanā* methods, although in practice there are many dedicated *samatha*

Figure 6.3 **Flooded temples at Inle Lake, Shan State, Myanmar/Burma**

practitioners too. A Buddhist nun from the region assured me she had a strong *vipassanā* interest – which she recommended to be done after extensive *jhāna* training. The authorities there are wary of some traditional Buddhist meditative traditions: this is in part because some magical Tantric practices conducted by a discredited monastic group brought other, unrelated, *samatha* practices into disrepute. Since the nineteenth century Myanmar has been the source of famous *vipassanā* teachings, such as those taught by U Ba Khin (1899–1971) and Mahasi Sayadaw (1904–82). They place less emphasis on *samatha*, although originally did not, as is commonly misunderstood, reject it. The effects of these methods were described by John Coleman, an ex-CIA agent taught by U Ba Khin. Through a painfully inexorable realization after a period of sustained practice, he saw bodily phenomena in their moving, ever-changing state. Recognizing that he cannot stop this, he 'lets go' and finds release:

> As the attention moves slowly and with utmost concentration from feet to legs to arms to head each bit comes under the most microscopic scrutiny. It is the awareness of the movement and change and friction of the *kalapas* [microscopic energy-fields] which go to make up the body tissue, bones and blood which gives rise to the intense sensation of burning and ultimate

Figure 6.4 **Face of the Buddha, Myanmar/Burma**

transcending of ordinary consciousness. It is this state, which ... holds the
promise of well-being and lifelong happiness.

Coleman (1971: 223–4)

The Buddha speaks of four effective routes to awakening, all of which
seem represented by various schools now: *samatha* before *vipassanā*, *vipassanā*
before *samatha*, the two yoked together and *dhamma*-excitement (A II 157).
Could this be an illustration of the methods of the last?

In Myanmar, *Abhidhamma*, one philosophical line of the Buddha's
teaching, is particularly revered, employed both as a meditative tool and
subject for animated debate. The many Burmese monks who visit the
West are highly trained in meditation, *Abhidhamma* and the *suttas*. Of these
countries, Myanmar has a strong representation amongst the laity of active
meditators, who do not regard arahatship as an impossible goal. In Laos and
Cambodia, also longstanding Buddhist countries, the influence of practices
described by Francois Bizot seems to be present. These involve ritual, an
alchemical understanding of meditation as the transmutation of the 'base' to
the refined, and meditation itself. Understanding derived from alchemy has
had a dramatic effect on the formulation of terminology for *samatha* practice
in particular. Local versions of *Jātakas* and post-canonical *Jātakas* are popular:
those in Laos are apparently particularly funny.

Figure 6.5 **Stone head of the Buddha, Cambodia**

YANTRAS

The idea of an innate Buddha nature is not anticipated in Pāli canonical texts, but the notion of a 'body' to be created through meditation practice does feature: the factors that produce *jhāna* are called 'jhāna limbs'. Perhaps influenced by Chinese Buddhism re-entering Laos, Cambodia and Thailand through waves of immigration from the twelfth century onwards, some later esoteric *samatha* schools suggest that the meditative process is like an alchemical one, or the development of an embryo. Khmer texts and rituals

Figure 6.6 **Young monk walking through a temple door, Laos**

concerned with these ideas seem to date from the fifteenth century. These are often accompanied by *yantras*, designs or patterns that embody knowledge, a form of expression that has always been popular throughout Southeast Asia. Thai *yantras* in intricately decorative patterns describe stages of meditative practice; they are commonly engraved on the back of protective amulets that can be bought in markets throughout Southeast Asia.

Na Yan: a modern explanation

The characters NA MO BU DDHA YĀ contain all that meaning [of the path], and can then themselves be drawn as yan, where the lines of the Khmer characters become the form of the yan, as in these two examples. NA *Golden Face* is also used as a symbol of *mettā*, or love:

To grasp the form of the yan is *samatha*, and to grasp the meaning is *vipassanā*. For the meditator, a yantra executed fluidly may indeed contain all that is symbolized by the form and the characters.

This is a non-linear, non-verbal process, and when language is
transcended in this way, when the meditator penetrates the illusion of
subject–object by 'letting go of the grammar', the limited self which
depends for its existence on the object is also transcended. When one-
pointedness arises in this way, *bhāvanā* is fulfilled. Whether the path-
moment or one of the stages of concentration arise is another matter,
depending on pre-conditions (or lack of conditions) in the meditator.
Paul Dennison (1997: 22–3), formerly Thanissaro Bhikkhu

In Thailand, Buddhism also has a long and eventful history. As in other
Southern Buddhist countries, the meditative tradition is rich and highly
differentiated. The forest centres of Northeastern Thailand in particular
have produced teachers such as Ajahn Mun (1870–1949), Ajahn Maha
Boowa (1913–) and Ajahn Chah (1919–92), who have had an enormous
impact in the West. Thai practitioners are also particularly noted for taking
samatha meditation to an advanced level. Ajahn Sudhiro, in common with
some other Thai teachers, gives guidance in forms of *samatha* practice that
are sometimes more fluid than those suggested by commentators such
as Buddhaghosa, though his guidelines are also sometimes followed.
Such methods teach, for those already experienced in meditation, *kasiṇa*
and space practices through the use of natural objects: a candle for fire,
the sky for blue, a pond for water, the space between trees for space,
and so on. The object is withdrawn for formless practice. The approach
varies, but such teaching encourages a relaxed movement in and out of
concentration, through the development of the masteries of adverting,
entering, sustaining, emerging and recollection. This also ensures that
the mind is flexible and joyful for the practice of insight. Variations in
different monasteries are rich and indicate that the commentarial material,
while often exploited, provides just one source for meditative practice.
Lay practice exhibits strong meditative interest. There are some highly
respected women teachers; some women live as nuns in communities
where meditation practice is popular. In Thailand most men become
monks for a short period as a kind of rite of passage. This means that a
large proportion of the population have experience of monastic life, and
some practise meditation. Boonman Poonyathiro, a monk for a number
of years, teaches a form of *samatha* breathing mindfulness which, for
experienced practitioners, links the breath in all four of Buddhaghosa's
stages of counting, following, touching and settling to the four divine

abidings of loving-kindness, compassion, sympathetic joy and equanimity respectively. Insight practice is conducted afterwards.

Southern Buddhist countries have a strong tradition of both *samatha* and *vipassanā* meditation. Broadly speaking, *samatha* meditation involves the use of joy, the third *jhāna* factor and a factor of awakening, as an agent of transformation within meditation practice. For *vipassanā* meditation the key feature is *nibbidā*, variously translated as 'turning away', 'dispassion' or 'disenchantment' with the world. As the following extract from the Thai teacher of *samatha* and *vipassanā*, Ajahn Chah explains, this is not weariness in the conventional mundane sense of boredom, based on attachment. Rather it is an active turning to the factors which will bring purification and awakening to the mind:

> The sense of world-weariness that grows with insight, however, leads to detachment, turning away and aloofness that comes naturally from investigating and seeing the truth of the way things are. It is free from attachment to the sense of self that attempts to control and force things to go according to its desires. The clarity of insight is so strong that you no longer experience any sense of a self that has to struggle against the flow of its desires or endure through attachment. The three fetters of personality view, doubt and blind attachment to rules can't delude you or cause you to make any serious mistakes in practice. This is the very beginning of the Path, the first clear insight into ultimate truth, and paves the way for further insight.
>
> Chah (2006: 107)

The famously ascetic and rigorous forest teacher, Mahā Boowa, for instance, employed a system whereby concentration was developed as a means to wisdom, but for some meditators he taught wisdom as a means to concentration:

> When wisdom has been nagging at those things to which the *citta* [mind] is firmly attached, what the *citta* knows about them cannot be superior to that which wisdom reveals, so the *citta* will then drop into a state of calm and attain *samādhi*.
>
> Boowa (1973: 15)

There are endless permutations on the interplay between these two elements in various schools.

Richard Gombrich writes of Buddhism's early dissemination,

The major factor has no doubt been the power and beauty of its thought.
It offered both a coherent universalist ethic and a way to salvation from
suffering.

Gombrich (1988: 151)

In the countries where Southern Buddhism took root, it seems to have
answered meditative as well as theoretical needs, which have continued as
exploratory strands of the living tradition.

THE RECOLLECTION OF THE BUDDHA, *DHAMMA* AND THE *SAṄGHA*

The distinctions between schools of Buddhism were not as clear-cut in the
early centuries as has sometimes been presented. Some elements that became
important in meditative practice seem to reflect a sea-change in a climate
of taste as much as a sectarian bias. One such feature, which emerged in
the centuries after the Buddha's death, is an element of devotion, emerging
at this time also in the Brahminical traditions. This did have a considerable
impact on the way the Buddha is regarded, recollected, and, in some later
schools worshipped, as he becoming increasingly an idealized and almost
godlike figure. Although this is occasionally suggested in the early Pāli texts,
it is not emphasized. Devotional and hagiographical elements later assumed
a far greater importance in all schools of Buddhism.

In Buddhist temples, the figure of the Buddha sits at the centre of a
richly various inhabited universe where all kinds of activities are going
on. Temples in Southern Buddhist countries are filled with pictures of the
Buddha's last lives, scenes where he is depicted renewing the Bodhisatta
vow and manifold different expressions of the Buddhist path. The temple
precincts also sometimes have other events going on. At festivals these may
include dances, recitations, and plays. Outside Southern Buddhist temples
there is often a shrine to local spirits and deities, who are honoured before
entering the temple itself. The figure of Guan Yin, the Chinese Buddhist
goddess of compassion, often has her own shrine in temples in Thailand.
At these, visitors can pay homage, throw yarrow stalk oracles and make
offerings before going into the shrine itself.

THE BUDDHA: AS HISTORICAL FIGURE AND OBJECT OF DEVOTIONAL PRACTICE

The life story of the Buddha has had a powerful impact on the psychological life of Southern Buddhists, so it is worth describing a little about the way this works. The death of the historical Buddha, in his eighties, appears to have occurred in 405 BCE. There is no biography of Gotama Buddha from his own lifetime, but the process of writing biographies seems to have started soon after his death, with the *Jātakanidāna*, a narrative that contains his vow to become a Bodhisatta/Bodhisattva, an aspirant Buddha, many lifetimes previously. The verses of this are canonical, and so date from the earliest strata of texts. In the twentieth century, scholars assembled a chronological sequence of key events of the Buddha's life, also including incidents recorded in the various earliest texts.

It seems that the Buddha Gotama was born as the son of a chieftain or local princeling. Protected from seeing suffering in his youth, because his parents were anxious to encourage him to become a universal monarch and so avoid following the path of Buddhahood, he is introduced to *dukkha* through four signs. These were seen on journeys out from the palace in his youth: old man, sick man, dead man and in the figure of a solitary renunciate, an apparently free man. He then leaves his wife and son — though he goes back to teach them after his enlightenment — to pursue meditative, and then ascetic practices. For several years he mortifies the body and mind with a group of five ascetics. Realizing this is not the middle way, he accepts food, eating some milk rice given by a woman, Sujātā, and remembers a simple experience he had as a child, described in Chapter 1. On the night of the enlightenment he practises all the *jhānas* and remembers innumerable past lives. Finally he becomes enlightened, free from rebirth. For the next forty-five years he teaches the 'middle way' and the 'eightfold path', a way of practice that integrates behaviour in the world, meditation and the practice of wisdom.

There are a number of 'biographical' accounts of the Buddha that date from his lifetime and the centuries after his death, which often incorporate mythical and symbolic material. These include accounts of his earlier lives, as the Bodhisatta, the being bound for, or destined for enlightenment (*bodhisakta*), who will be discussed in the next chapter. These narratives, of interspersed biography and autobiography, are known as *Jātakas*, the partly canonical stories of his lives spent in preparation to become a Buddha. Often supplemented and even supplanted by local, non-canonical tales of a similar type that have evolved throughout Southern Buddhist countries, they give a densely eventful imaginative landscape to the Bodhisatta vow and the quest for Buddhahood. Earlier rebirths as elephant, mouse, lion, horse, god, prince, priest or fisherman communicate a sense of the great diversity of experience necessary to teach others. Different registers or modes include the comic, the tragic, the melodramatic, the heroic, the farcical and the mundane, as the Bodhisatta is tested within a number of settings and different frames of reference, as if through interpenetrating leaves of understanding. Chronicles such as the Mahāvaṃsa and Dīpavāṃsa also relate mythological incidents, such as the Buddha visiting Sri Lanka, which validate the country's special link to the Buddhist tradition.

The extent to which such narratives, alongside the mythical content of material recorded in the suttas, such as his miraculous birth, are historically 'true' raises the same sort of questions we find being asked about sacred biography in other contexts. The Buddha's visit to Sri Lanka, for instance, could be compared to the kind of stories that developed about Christ, who is said in the Glastonbury Legends to have 'visited' England, an event suggested by William Blake's poem, 'Jerusalem'. The truth of such an incident is felt by Christians to reside in the experience of those that are inspired by the poem as a hymn of redemption and Glastonbury as a sacred site on an interior, Christian map. This is, perhaps, comparable to the position many modern Buddhists feel about the supernatural incidents or such late additions to the life story as the visit to Sri Lanka. The stories include many layers, including validation of the geographical, the political and the historical. While for many Asians much of this material is taken as literal truth, many Buddhists also appreciate such details and subsequent accretions as symbolic contributions to whatever the 'historical' life story may have been. We can all recognize or sense some psychological truth embedded in events, such as, in the life story, the routing of the armies of Māra on the night of the enlightenment, or, in later 'historical' myths, the Buddha's visit to various places. Likewise, when we read the accounts of the Buddha as the Bodhisatta spending earlier births 'in the past' either in the meditative heavens, or as a lion, cat or mouse in the animal realms, we can feel the range of sympathy and knowledge being suggested by what can also be seen on a metaphoric level. This applies both internally, to a knowledge of the levels of subtle experience possible for the human mind, and externally, to an understanding of the experiences of many other living beings, in all kinds of existence. The fully awakened mind demonstrated by the Buddha is said to 'know all worlds' and to be a teacher 'of gods and humans': he understands the relationship between self and other, knower and known. Such stories provide great evidence of the scope and inventiveness of this understanding. In temples in Thailand, *Jātakas* are painted in vivid colours against a dark forest-green, black and grey wilderness as a background, which seems to suggest the world of the other, the different and the mysterious as well as the mundane. Layers of meaning seem to accrete around stories, chants, and rituals associated with the basic facts of the Buddha's life. Despite all kinds of apparent contradictions, these endlessly renewable and renewed elements of the Buddha's biography seem to sit comfortably with literal, historical facts.

In Southern Buddhism, the Buddha is regarded as a special kind of human, whose contact with the highest heavenly realms of experience and knowledge of the unfortunate realms is represented through stories of his past lives, in other bodily forms and accounts of his meditative experiences and teachings in his own lifetime. Features of his appearance and body in his last life are said to bear the imprint of the mythical, the magical and the godlike: and are, perhaps, to be taken as symbolic. It is worthy of note, however, that there are several places in the canon, such as the *Dhātuvibhaṅga-Sutta* (M III 237–47), where he is either mistaken for another monk or needs pointing out: if he had a remarkable appearance, it was one he could easily drop to look ordinary. He lived with his order by the same rules that they did. He rebukes one follower, Vakkali, for 'clutching the hem of his robe' from excessive devotion to him. In the *Mahāparinibbāna-Sutta* he gives instructions for what is to happen to his body after death, as if to accommodate devotional impulses: he also stresses, however, that his teaching and *Vinaya* are what he has left behind for others.

What is meant by a 'Buddha' changes in different locations and schools of practice. However, finding ways in which the awakened mind may be aroused through meditation on his figure, either as an internalized 'knower', a guide or, in Eastern schools, as an expression of a pre-existent state that can be rediscovered within the meditator, is a feature of most schools of Buddhist meditation, in most traditions. After his death, the Buddha was regarded a little like a god as well as a human. The inheritance the Buddha left behind was of his teachings, some autobiographical material, some biographical information and detail, some stories, some myths and some reminders that practice of the teaching is the best way to follow the teacher. Interpreting all these levels and the texts associated with them is an ongoing challenge for those attempting to understand Buddhist practice and doctrine.

Figure 6.7 **Statues of the Buddha at teak wood factory, Chiang Mai**

THE THIRTY-TWO MARKS OF THE BUDDHA

Many legends and stories are associated with the birth of the Buddha. He was, for instance, said to have been born from his mother's side while she stood between two trees at Lumbīnī, now in Nepal, half way between her husband's and her parents' home. According to stories told in most schools of Buddhism, the baby displayed thirty-two marks or signs on his body. These attributes indicated to wise men and seers who examined him that he would one day become either a universal monarch, who would rule the world by *dhamma*, not force (see Chapter 3), or a Buddha, the teacher of gods and humans. Some of these mythical marks seem symbolic, such as the turban-crowned head, and some demonstrate participation in the divine. For instance, the Buddha is said to have a voice like Brahma, the king of the heavens where rebirth is obtained through the practice of meditation, and the golden skin of Sakka, the king of the sense-sphere heaven where beings are reborn for practising generosity and restraint. Some of the marks are conventionally heroic: he is said to have the very long arms and lionlike chest associated with royal warriors in Indian epic. Others seem experiential, or, to put it another way, features that could be produced by anyone in a certain relaxed and alert frame of mind, such as evenly rounded shoulders. Some seem to be almost internal descriptions of meditative states: the mark concerned with taste appears to be a subjective description, perhaps of meditative experience. Each mark is associated with a karmic action and result: for instance 'the golden skin' is the result of giving, and means that the person who possesses this characteristic will often be a recipient too. The whole list is used as an iconography for pictorial and sculptural depiction of the Buddha throughout Asia but also provides the basis for various meditative practices too. In Tibet it contributes to the visualization that creates an invoked and evoked form of the Bodhisattva within the mind's eye. In the *Pratyutpanna Sūtra* in India and derived Chinese Tiantai practices it comes to form part of a meditative walking and standing exercise. The practitioner imagines himself possessing each mark, as well as the Buddha, represented externally on the shrine, and then sees the impermanence of each, so using the mark both as an object for insight itself and as the basis from which to investigate the mind that perceives it.

The most mundane and 'grounded' mark is the first. The Buddha walks with an even tread, touching the ground with the whole of the foot. He possesses this mark because he has worked for the welfare of other beings, and, as a result of this, has a large following. The list demonstrates the way that the figure of the Buddha brings together attributes that indicate association with states of deep peace and bliss – his penultimate life was said to be in a meditative heaven – and those thoroughly down-to-earth and human. It is through all these attributes that he is said to be able to help other beings.

LAKKHAṆA SUTTA

The Thirty-Two marks of the Great Man

1 He has well-supported feet.
2 On the soles of his feet wheels arise, with a thousand spokes, with hub and with rim, complete in every way and well defined within.
3 He has projecting heels.
4 He has long fingers and toes.
5 He has soft and tender hands and feet.
6 He has net-like hands and feet.
7 He has raised ankles like conch shells.
8 The lower part of his leg is like an antelope's.

9 Standing, and without bending, he touches and rubs around his knees with both palms.

10 He is one in whom that part which should be concealed by garments, is covered by a bag.

11 He is gold-coloured, his skin shines like gold.

12 He is one who possesses subtle skin; owing to the subtlety of his skin, dirt and sweat do not stick to his body.

13 He is single-haired, so that on his body single hairs arise, one to each pore.

14 He has hair pointing upwards; dark upturned hairs arise, black in colour, turning in rings, turning auspiciously to the right.

15 He is straight of frame like Brahma.

16 He has seven outflows on his hands, on his feet, at the tips of his shoulders, and at the top of the back.

17 Lion-like is the upper part of his body.

18 Filled is the hollow between the shoulders.

19 He is proportioned like the sphere of the banyan tree: as long as his body, so is the span of his arms; as far as the span of the arms, so long is his body.

20 Evenly rounded are the shoulders.

21 He releases the highest of tastes.

22 He has a lion-like jaw.

23 He has forty teeth.

24 He has even teeth.

25 Undivided are his teeth.

26 Very white are his visible teeth.

27 He has a mighty tongue.

28 He has the voice of Brahma, resembling the song of a karavika bird.

29 Very blue are his eyes.

30 He has eyelashes like those of a cow.

31 The filament arising between the eyebrows is soft like white cotton.

32 The great man is turban-crowned.

The thirty-two marks of the Buddha have become part of the iconography of the Buddha and, subsequently, Bodhisattvas, in most traditions of Buddhist art and meditative practice.

MUDRĀ AND POSTURE

Throughout India, gesture has always been considered an important part of ritual, devotion and meditative practice. Ancient temple dance forms gesture becomes a kind of language, with the hands and the pose of the body expressing meaning in a way that would be understood by many present. Thai court temple dances also use mudrā to express, for instance, the qualities of the Triple Gem. The Buddha's life story also comes to be associated with different bodily postures and hand positions, which are translated into the physical form of Buddha images. The enlightenment is shown by the samādhi posture, with the hands cupped in the lap in meditation. The 'calling the earth to witness' gesture shows the Buddha touching the ground with the right hand. This posture is associated with adhiṭṭhāna, or resolve. After asking the goddess of the earth to testify by invoking his generosity to monks in past lives, he routs Māra, sees his own worth to sit in meditation and determines not to move until he has become enlightened. Murals of the stages of the Buddha's life are widespread throughout Southeast Asian temples: Etienne Lamotte also identified thirty-four episodes from the Buddha's life at Sāñcī, India, in bas-relief depictions that predate literary evidence. In Thailand the symbology of these postures was codified during the third reign of the Chakri dynasty (1824–51) into a list of forty poses. In practice there are even more postures in this composite visual biography, often also associated with events in the life of the Buddha and depicted on temple walls.

DAYS OF THE WEEK AND BUDDHIST THEORY

The assignation of postures to days of the week is a particular feature of Thai Buddhism (see Appendix B). The Thais, perhaps more than those of other Southeast Asian countries, have a great interest in astrology and such areas of symbolic correspondence. Birthdays are very important, and they will often make offerings to the saṅgha to mark them. Such interest constitutes what is, to them, a civilized and humane way in which any given person can feel part of a kind of Thai sacred folk calendar. The day of the week the person was born on, the month and the year of birth are all imbued with special import. The birth 'day', as well as the astrological configuration associated with the birthdate of any given person, lends people a separate identity – but also links them to a larger, universally applicable system of Buddhist correspondences. Those born on a Monday, like the present king, wear yellow on that day, as does anyone else on a Monday, or any occasion when people wish to mark allegiance to him. The wearer might also know the posture in the Buddha's life with which Monday is associated and, perhaps, the factor of awakening specially intended for Monday birthdays: the first, mindfulness. Such a person may feel a passionate and animated sense of loyalty to the 'self' associated with that, but will not be too grudging on those whose birthday happens to fall on a Tuesday or Wednesday, who participate in other features necessary to render the system whole. Chinese, Indian and Thai astrological methods and systems, while heterogeneous, all link to one another in various ways and contribute to such subterranean alliances between quite different social groups. There is, for instance, a *stūpa* that is 'lucky' to visit, dependent on one's Chinese year of birth, such as rat, dragon or sheep. This is not just a practical way of preventing traffic jams to one site, which it certainly is. As well as linking the symbolic language of one culture to another, it also encourages an awareness of the importance of manifold and diverse contributing elements in any given 'field'. Indeed it seems to become an expression of an inclusive Buddhist folk world system, that allows Indian, Thai and Chinese world views all to work together, and even support one another, transcending local and national identity. New elements and new lists can be incorporated all the time.

SEVEN FACTORS OF AWAKENING

In Thailand the factors of awakening are one of the most popular Buddhist canonical lists, for their applicability and for their capacity to arouse happiness in bhāvanā. As positive factors they are considered as antidotes to the hindrances. They are: mindfulness, investigation, effort, joy, tranquillity, concentration and equanimity. These may be developed at the beginning of the path and can be deepened at each stage. They can be aroused during daily life or, fully cultivated, can be employed to direct the mind to the meditation object and then to wisdom. All have to be aroused for the attainment of liberation. The list supplies the seeds of an understanding which can be taken just for fun but can also be used for specific development of factors within a meditative context. One canonical story recounts the factors being chanted for their healing power. Indeed it is thought that is particularly useful to work on the one for the day that it is at the moment, thus ensuring that the list is seen to provide continuously appropriate and renewable guidance for different situations. There is thought to be a special association with the factor that links to one's own birth day. It should be emphasized, of course, that meditation is taught on the basis of temperament (*carita*), rather than such associations!

Monday mindfulness: *sati* (yellow)
Tuesday investigation of *dhammas*: *dhammavicaya* (pink)
Wednesday effort: *viriya* (green)
Thursday joy: *pīti* (orange)
Friday tranquillity: *passadhi* (blue)
Saturday concentration: *samādhi* (purple)
Sunday equanimity: *upekkhā* (red)

From the point of view of meditation practice, the factors of awakening (*bojjhaṅga*) provide the practitioner with a list useful for the articulation of problems and for giving encouragement and direction within the practice. The elements can be seen together, as a process working through any one meditation practice, or in the maturation of the meditation over a period of time. For instance, when one starts a job, like digging the garden, there is awareness of a field, and mindfulness. Investigation is then aroused by the act of digging as the types of soil and the stoniness of the earth are assessed. This allows effort appropriate to the job to be applied. Joy in the job in hand can then arise and, as work continues, this sometimes deepens into tranquillity. Concentration, or stillness, focuses on the job's completion. At the end of the task, the whole is relinquished with a satisfying sense of equanimity. This is a simple simile, but contains the principles which are useful for meditation too: problems can occur at any stage, and the process may not continue well. In breathing mindfulness meditation, with which this list is often associated in the canon, joy may become restlessness for instance, and may need a fine awareness of the breath to allow tranquillity to arise. At other points there may be a need for more effort, in directions suggested by the exploratory nature of *dhammavicaya*, exploration of *dhammas*, which will indicate within the breath areas of 'knot' or strain to help soften and refine the way effort can be applied. At the level of insight the list is also important. Mindfulness provides a ground in which the relationship, say, between 'name' and 'form' can be investigated. Effort is applied, and joy arises when insight is obtained. This also needs to be tranquillized, stilled and brought to equanimity. The list of factors is frequently employed by the Buddha to describe supports to breathing mindfulness practice, to arouse both calm and wisdom, and by Buddhaghosa as a way of balancing the factors within meditation. As we shall see it features in most schools of Buddhism, as the penultimate grouping in the thirty-seven factors contributing to awakening, before the eightfold path (see Chapter 7). It is a good example of the way, in regions that have been Buddhist for some time, a key teaching comes to work on many interpenetrating levels. In this case this includes the theoretical, the meditative, 'folk-wisdom', the humorous, and, when applied to the days of the week, even the sartorial.

THE RECOLLECTION OF THE *SAṄGHA*

The arahats

The assembly of the Buddha's followers, who have attained stages of awakening, are known as the *saṅgha*. The external embodiment and representatives of these are the orders of monks and nuns. Some modern Buddhists take all practitioners as an example of the *saṅgha*. While this possibility is not stated in canonical texts, the recollection of good friends is in one *sutta* recommended to a devout layman, Nandiya, after the Buddha and the *dhamma*, presumably to suggest a sense of community to him too. These constitute a refuge because they provide support, encouragement and teaching to others.

The following protective chant, of unknown antiquity, is very popular in Thailand and Cambodia. It pays homage to eight arahats, who surround the Buddha in a directional *maṇḍala*. The arrangement varies slightly from area to area. They appear to represent meditative qualities that complement one another: the quick intuition of Kondañña in the East faces the slow, careful kindness of the Buddha's carer in the West, Ānanda, whose awakening is delayed until after the Buddha's death. The austerity of the ascetic Kassapa, in the Southeast, contrasts with the relaxed, latent power of Gavampati in the Northwest. The custodian of the *Vinaya*, the monastic rules, which have remained intact for centuries in Southern Buddhism, is in the Southwest. Opposite is Rāhula, the Buddha's son, the embodiment of the new, in the Northeast. The two great disciples, Moggallāna and Sāriputta, at North and South, are often shown on either side of the Buddha, representatives of the two great complementary strands of spiritual work, calm and insight.

According to the texts, the friendship that existed between various members of the group was deep, and in these they often congratulate one another on their different strengths. As a group they demonstrate a diversity of approaches to the Buddhist path. Those who have reached awakening or enlightenment are free from defilements and follow a teaching that is of 'one taste', yet exhibit different strengths and skills according to their *kamma* and disposition. In the chant they are all called Buddhas: *sāvaka* Buddhas rather than fully awakened ones.

BUDDHAMAṄGALAGĀTHĀ: THE BUDDHA'S BLESSING VERSES
Among two-footed beings, the Fully Enlightened One is the best, sitting in the centre.
Kondañña sits in front of the Buddha, Kassapa to the Southeast,
Sāriputta at the Buddha's right-hand, Upāli to the Southwest,
Ānanda behind the Buddha, Gavampati to the Northwest,
Moggallāna at the Buddha's left-hand, and Rahula to the Northeast.
These Buddhas are indeed auspicious, all well established here,
And we pay them homage and venerate them with offerings.
By their power may we always have security and happiness.
Thus, paying homage to that which is utterly worthy of homage,
The Triple Gem,
May I gain much fruit of good actions,
Overcoming by its power dangers and obstacles!

Key

Kondañña: the arahat who correctly predicted at Gotama's birth that he could only become a Buddha, and would not choose the option predicted by others that he might become a Universal Monarch. He became an ascetic and practised with the Buddha before his enlightenment. After the enlightenment he was amongst the five who heard the Buddha's first sermon and was first to understand its import.

(*Mahā*)*Kassapa*: an ascetic who, after practising severe austerities with no results for thirty years, meets a lay friend, Citta, a follower of the Buddha for thirty years. Despite not even being a monk, Citta had experienced great meditative bliss and peace in the four *jhānas*, and was a stream-enterer (the first stage of awakening). Kassapa, stunned that a layman could achieve so much when he, by rejecting the middle way, had achieved nothing, immediately became a Buddhist monk. Soon afterwards he became an arahat. He always retained his love of wild terrain, natural beauty and asceticism, even when enlightened, and after he has become an arahat composes eloquent verses on the subject (Th 1051–90).

Sāriputta: the Buddha's chief disciple, of golden skin. Many aeons before he had made a vow to become the chief of the Buddha's followers. Renowned for his kindness, lack of pride and meditative skill, he is primarily esteemed for his great insight, teaching ability and love of highly detailed exposition. He is the disciple described by the Buddha as the greatest in wisdom, and is often depicted seating on the right side of the Buddha.

Upāli: a low-caste barber, who became a monk, in the first instance, as he was scared he would be punished on his return home after some Sakyan princes he was accompanying were ordained. At their request, he is ordained before them, so he will always have pre-eminence over them. He became the custodian of the Vinaya, the monks' rules, and would be consulted on any issues of procedure or behaviour amongst the saṅgha.

Ānanda: the Buddha's attendant and carer in the last years of the Buddha's life. Although a stream-enterer, he never achieved enlightenment in the Buddha's lifetime, and, famously, cried bitterly before the death of the Buddha. He persuaded the Buddha to found the order of nuns, but also forgot to ask him to extend his lifespan. A loving but 'human' monk, he often did the wrong thing, and is rebuked by others for certain failings. He seems to voice the worries and concerns of the 'common man'. He achieved enlightenment, after giving up hope of doing so, on the night before the First Council after the Buddha's death, just as he was going to bed. He is described as pre-eminent by the Buddha in a number of aspects, but is primarily known for his prodigious memory, which enabled him to remember all the discourses of the Buddha.

Gavampati: famed for his daily visits to the Heaven of the Four Kings, where he had a special seat, he is said to have taken a restorative nap there each day. He was, however, capable of immense power. He is called upon by the Buddha to avert a flood with his psychic power when a river bursts its banks, while all the other monks are sleeping. He is sometimes associated with the four right efforts.

Moggallāna: a friend of Sāriputta, with whom he ordained. His skin was dark, like a blue lotus. He was famed for his great meditative mastery and is pre-eminent amongst the disciples for his psychic powers. He is associated too with great compassion, in his visits to beings in other, sometimes lower realms, whom he discerns with his Divine Eye. He is also renowned for a sense of mischief. By wiggling his big toe he causes a monastery full of backsliding monks to shake from the foundations, so terrifying them into good behaviour. He sits on the left-hand side of the Buddha, and is the second great disciple.

Rāhula: the Buddha's son, famed for his beauty, obedience and, until his enlightenment, some vanity. He is sent by his mother after the enlightenment to 'claim his inheritance'. He ordains as a monk, and after a short period becomes an arahat in his early twenties. The *Rāhulovāda Sutta* is given to him as a teaching by his father.

Women arahats

There were said to be many women amongst the arahats too. Nuns and lay women give teachings sanctioned by the Buddha. Verses recorded in the *Therīgāthā* are worth reading for their autobiographical material, almost unknown in India at this period, the aptness of their observation of the natural world, the creativity of their use of domestic and physical imagery, and for an underlying humour and humanity. These are amongst the earliest spiritual poems in the world composed by women. Arahatship, which is said to remove the defilements from the practitioner, does not seem to have diminished the character of these early meditators. One poem, for instance, by an ex-courtesan called Ambapālī, an elderly and enlightened nun, recalls her past beauty. In a long series of verses she works teasingly down her body, describing each aspect of her former glory, such as her hair, face and breasts, at first in lyrical terms suggestive of *kāvya*, an Indian poetic form – and then in its present ugly condition in old age. It is like a playful interchange between past and present, distilling the middle way neatly through the poetess' gracious and measured equipoise, that veers neither to attraction or disgust for her changing form.

A FEMALE BEGGAR

One autobiographical poem was composed by a woman called Candā. Reduced to beggary, she encountered the nun Paṭācārā and her followers, who took pity on her, welcomed her and provided her with food. Because of the nuns' kindness, she decided to follow their teaching too, so she approached the elder nun and learnt meditation from her. Because she had already developed so much insight in the past, she soon became enlightened, possessing three special knowledges: the recollection of past lives, the arising and falling away of beings and the exhaustion of the corruptions, defilements producing further rebirths. Freed from her sufferings, and at last tasting happiness, she composed the following verses, which testify to the warmth of friendship that must have existed in the early *saṅgha*, and to the meditative guidance she had experienced from another nun.

Before, I was in a very bad way: without husband, without children,
Without friends and without relatives, I did not find food or clothing.
I took a stick and a bowl, and begged for food from family to family.
Burnt by both heat and cold, I wandered for seven years.
And then I saw a nun. She had obtained food and drink.
So I went up to her and said, 'Please give me the going forth, and accept
    me into a homeless state!'
This woman, Paṭācārā, had compassion on me, and accepted me into the
    order of nuns.
She gave me teachings, and urged me to go for the very best goal.
I listened to what she had to say, and I did just what she told me.
This lady's instruction was not in vain; now, possessed with the three
    knowledges, I am freed from the corruptions.

(Thī 122–6)

The wife of the Buddha

It is important to mention that amongst the arahats and followers of the Buddha is the Buddha's wife, Rahulamātā, or Yasodharā, as she is known in some traditions. She too was on a long spiritual path, and had made a vow to be the support and spouse of the Bodhisattva as he makes his way to Buddhahood. They spent many lifetimes together, during which time she shows her loyalty and initiative, offering companionship towards him in

> **TWO VERSES FROM AMBAPĀLĪ'S EXTENDED POEM**
>
> Melodious was my call, like a cuckoo wandering around a thicket;
> Because of old age it stumbles about all over the place:
> What is said by the speaker of truth is not off the point!
>
> Once upon a time my throat looked lovely, like a well-polished,
>   exquisite conch shell;
> Because of old age it is clapped out and bowed-down:
> What is said by the speaker of truth is not off the point!
>
> (Thī 261–2)

the various trials depicted through many aeons. When her husband reaches his final goal, she decides to become a nun too, and also, after the practice of meditation, achieves awakening, as does their son. There is a large shrine to her in Nepal.

CONCLUSION

This chapter has considered some of the ways Buddhist meditative practice has evolved in Southern Buddhist countries. As with some other longstanding Buddhist regions, this has become highly varied, imbued with new theory, local ritual, folk understanding and custom in ways that highlight an interpenetration of levels of Buddhist teaching when it has been practised for a long time in a particular area.

TIMELINES

250–210 BCE	Sinhalese King Devanampiya Tissa converts to Buddhism
25 BCE	Pāli canon recorded on palm leaves by King Vaṭṭagāmiṇi in Sri Lanka
100 -	Sri Lankan monks go to Myanmar and Thailand
c.200	Chinese monks go to Vietnam
c.377–700	Period of flourishing of Buddhist monasteries in Anurādhapura, Sri Lanka
c.500	Indian monks go to Java, Sumatra and Borneo and establish Buddhism
788–820	Borobudar built in Java
850–1100	Temple construction in Angkor Wat, Cambodia

1057	King Anawartha of Pagan conquers neighbouring Thaton and establishes Buddhism there
1165	Sinhalese king Parakkamabāhu promotes Theravāda
c.1300	'Theravāda' becomes pre-eminent in Myanmar, Thailand and Cambodia, overlaying older elements
c.1500	Temple at Angkor Wat converted to be Buddhist centre
1520–47	Reign of King Phōtisālarāt, an active promoter of Buddhism, in Laos
1753	Monks from Thai court reinstate Buddhist line in Sri Lanka
1803	Sri Lankans ordained in Myanmar found Amarapura Nikāya in Sri Lanka
1829	Thai prince Mongkut founds Thammayut monastic school

FURTHER READING

Bechert, H. and Gombrich, R.F. (eds) (1991) *The World of Buddhism: Buddhist Monks and Nuns in Society and Culture*, London: Thames and Hudson.

Coleman, J. (1971) *The Quiet Mind*, London: Rider.

Dennison, P. in Callow, J. ed., (1996) 'Na Yan: an introduction', *Samatha: Insight from a Meditation Tradition*, Llangunllo, Wales: Samatha Trust, 2, 16–18.

Dennison, P. (1997) 'Na Yan Continued', *Samatha: Insight from a Meditation Tradition*, 3, 19–23.

Gombrich, R.F. (1971) *Precept and Practice, Traditional Buddhism in the Rural Highlands of Ceylon*, Oxford: Clarendon

Gombrich, R.F. (1988) *Theravāda Buddhism; A Social History from Ancient Benares to Modern Colombo*, London/New York: Routledge and Kegan Paul.

Holt, J.C. (1996) *The Religious World of Kīrti Śrī: Buddhism, Art and Politics in Late Medieval Sri Lanka*, Oxford/New York: OUP.

Lamotte, E., Webb-Boin S. trans. (1988) *History of Indian Buddhism*, Louvain-Paris: Peeters Press.

Matics, K.I. (2008) *Gestures of the Buddha*, 4th edn, Bangkok: Chulalongkorn University Press.

McDaniel, J. (2004) 'Laos', Robert Buswell Jnr. (ed.), *Encyclopedia of Buddhism*, 2 vols., New York: Macmillan, 2, 456–9.

McNab, U. and friends (1996) *The Suttanta on the Marks*, Llangunllo, Powys: Samatha Trust.

Nyanaponika Thera and Hecker, H., Bodhi, Bhikkhu ed., (2003) *The Great Disciples of the Buddha: Their Lives, Their Works, Their Legacy*, Boston/Kandy: Wisdom/BPS.

Skilling, P. (2000) 'The Arahats of the Eight Directions', *Fragile Palm Leaves for the Preservation of Buddhist Literature*, 6: 12, 22.

Strong, J.S. (2001) *The Buddha: a Short Biography*, Oxford: Oneworld.

Thomas, E.J. (1927) *The Life of the Buddha as Legend and History*, London: Routledge and Kegan Paul.

WEBSITES

'The recollections of Buddha, dhamma and saṅgha': http://www.buddhanet.net/audio-chant.htm

Developments in Early Indian Buddhism
Seven

For example a man endowed with sight when he is alone at night
Gets up at midnight, and in the clear sky
Sees many hundred thousand stars:
If he thinks of them mindfully he recalls them by day also.

Pratyutpanna Sūtra (Paul Harrison trans.)

At no time does Buddhism appear to have been a static or rigid system. Divergences in practice, questions being asked or thought important and doctrinal points seem to have developed from the earliest days of the tradition. Sometimes these would cut across divides of locality or school, as reflections of more widespread trends. Because of this, disentangling the very early schools of Buddhism in India is a challenging but still ongoing process, as scholars attempt to isolate layers of the tradition from texts only committed to writing in the early centuries CE. What does seem to be the case, however, is that some of the labels we have come to use now, like Mahāyāna and Theravāda, while certainly applicable to schools in subsequent centuries, were not clear-cut denoters of difference in the first centuries CE. During this period other texts and schools are recorded, some in what has become known as Buddhist Hybrid Sanskrit, a Sanskritized version of Middle Indian, and some in Sanskrit. These various schools share many common sources and, given that writing does not come in for a while it is not always clear which can be called 'early' and which 'late'. Monks tended to practise with the same sort of monastic discipline in all schools, and probably studied and meditated with those of other traditions as well.

These various approaches, however, reveal innovative formulations of Buddhist doctrine and often have quite a different style and emphasis. It would be impossible to do justice to the full richness of Indian thought during this extraordinary period of philosophical investigation. In this chapter we will look at just a few significant developments in theory and practice, which influenced the course of Buddhist history as it was exported to other countries and cultures. They represent only a small part of a larger, highly complex forum of intellectual and meditative debate on many fronts.

DEVOTIONAL PRACTICE

One of the most notable of these, discussed a little in the last chapter, is the evolution of a strong element of devotion. In the *Mahāparinibbāna-Sutta* the Buddha gives what is the only canonical instruction as to how his relics and ashes should be dispensed after death. These, he said, should be distributed and could become objects of veneration for those that wish. Some centuries after that, Indian religions in general seem to have moved towards a far greater emphasis on personal devotion as an important element of salvific practice, as evidenced in the eventual development in the Brahminical tradition of *bhakti*. *Stūpas*, housing relics of the Buddha, and the arahats were established throughout India and Sri Lanka. These were often built as embodiments of the teachings, with the thirty-seven factors contributing to awakening or enlightenment providing a basic structure that included the four foundations of mindfulness being symbolized by the lowest step, and the seven factors of awakening and the eightfold path as the peak. These thirty-seven factors, described in most schools of Buddhism, were felt to embody the whole path, and to provide a distillation of the entire teaching. The relics were placed deep inside, and the *stūpa*, perhaps near to a bodhi tree taken from the one where the Buddha gained enlightenment in Bodhgayā, became a sacred pilgrimage site. Merit — and hence help on one's spiritual path — came to the practitioner who visited these sites, circumambulated them and made offerings to them. The structure would then be part of the practitioner's mental landscape, perhaps an external embodiment of an interior 'map' in the heart for the person who practises meditation on his or her own. The thirty-seven factors contributing to awakening feature in many forms of Buddhism, in particular the Southern and the Northern schools.

THE THIRTY-SEVEN FACTORS CONTRIBUTING TO AWAKENING (BODHIPAKKHIYĀDHAMMA)

The four foundations of mindfulness: body, feeling, mind, dhamma
The four right efforts: averting bad states that have not arisen, abandoning bad states that have, cultivating good states that have not arisen, and maintaining good states that have arisen
The four bases of success: willingness, effort, mind, investigation
The five faculties: faith, effort, mindfulness, concentration and wisdom

The five powers: faith, effort, mindfulness, concentration and wisdom

The seven factors of awakening: mindfulness, investigation of dhamma, effort, joy, tranquillity, concentration and equanimity

The noble eightfold path: right view, right intention, right speech, right action, right livelihood, right effort, right mindfulness, right concentration

We do not know at what time the Buddha himself starts to be represented in art and sculpture, but in the early centuries CE, perhaps through Greek influence, representations of him become more common. The earliest known figurative depiction is on a Kuśan coin dated c.150 CE, now in the Ashmolean Museum, Oxford. Ceremonies and practices associated with the empowerment of Buddha images are recorded in early Indian texts and there are some legends of the Buddha himself visiting such images and requesting them to carry on the work that he had started himself. At any rate

Figure 7.1 **Wat Phra Sri Sampet, a *stūpa* in Ayutthaya, Thailand; such *stūpas* are considered embodiments of the thirty-seven factors contributing to awakening**

very early depictions of the Bodhisatta/Bodhisattva, a generic name for his previous 'selves' in earlier lives, are still extant in stone relief and paintings at Ajaṇṭā and Bhārhut. These date from the first or second century BCE. There may well have been early representations of the Buddha or the Bodhisatta that are lost now.

THE BODHISATTVA

As this trend towards devotion increased, so also did the idea of a Bodhisattva, a being destined for, or bound to, enlightenment. In the Pāli canon a series of 547 stories, the *Jātakas*, describes some of the past lives of the Buddha Gotama as he acquired the qualities that enabled him to find awakening himself and teach others. According to the introduction to these stories he saw an earlier Buddha, Dīpaṅkara, in a previous life, and took the vow in his presence to defer his own enlightenment as an arahat, possible at that time, to become a Buddha in a subsequent life. He is enjoined by Dīpaṅkara to practise ten 'perfections', which will take countless lives, in many different forms, to bring to fruition in his final life. The *Jātakas* describe his acquisition over many lifetimes of the perfections, and various other qualities, which will make him qualified as a 'teacher of gods and humans'.

PERFECTIONS

The Ten Perfections
1   Generosity (*dāna*)
2   Good conduct (*sīla*)
3   Renunciation (*nekkhamma*)
4   Wisdom (*paññā*)
5   Effort (*viriya*)
6   Acceptance (*khanti*)
7   Truth (*sacca*)
8   Resolve (*adhiṭṭhāna*)
9   Loving-kindness (*mettā*)
10 Equanimity (*upekkhā*)

In another, perhaps earlier formulation of the Perfections, used by Śāntideva and the Northern schools, the list differs so that six are given.

These are denoted by Sanskrit rather than Pāli. These six have become immensely popular and are also employed in China, Korea and Japan.

1   Generosity (*dāna*)
2   Good conduct (*śīla*)
3   Acceptance (*kṣānti*)
4   Effort (*vīrya*)
5   Meditation (*dhyāna*)
6   Wisdom (*prajñā*)

Many schools that emerged in India at this time place far greater emphasis on the Bodhisattva. Some introduce the revolutionary idea that all beings could, if they chose, become a Bodhisattva themselves, where previously it was considered a path only for a heroic minority. This teaching becomes increasingly associated with Northern and Eastern Buddhist schools. This

Figure 7.2 **Stone Buddha in Indian temple**

led in time to a differentiation between Mahāyana, 'the greater vehicle', and what these schools sometimes called the Hīnayāna, 'the lesser vehicle'. The latter term is understandably less favoured by scholars and practitioners of many forms of Buddhism today and is not used in the Southern schools and texts. The word Mahāyāna is certainly applicable, however, as a generic term used by, for instance, Tibetan Buddhists of themselves, just as the perhaps equally contentious term, Theravāda, 'teaching of the elders', is used by most modern Southern Buddhists to describe themselves. In practice, for many centuries the monastic disciplines were not much different and monks seem to have studied and practised with little demarcation between what became the Northern and Southern schools of practice. The principal feature of the Mahāyāna movement is a change in the Bodhisattva vow. In a tendency that started before the development of a self-conscious school, this vow of commitment to the welfare of all sentient beings, a longer path, starts to be extended and enjoined as a possibility for anyone.

The debate between Mahāyāna and the Southern schools of course is ancient and need not be discussed here in great detail. This is a book about meditation, so it should perhaps be noted that modern experienced teachers of neither of these traditions regard their own as having an exclusive hold on 'superior' human feeling. The texts of the Southern schools, in their emphasis on the Buddha's probity, encouragement of others to teach and an internal emphasis on compassion, generosity and respect could hardly be called less kind or dedicated to teaching than those of the Northern traditions. Moreover, it is argued, the specificity of teachings in the Pāli canon and matters such as the differentiation between one's own feelings and others – as described in Buddhaghosa's account of the divine abidings – demonstrate an acknowledgement of individual needs that resonates with much modern psychological understanding and plain common sense. It is important to wish for the happiness of all beings; but one should also remember to know the difference between what one wishes for oneself and what one might impose with views or rigidity on others. These elements of the commentary and canon suggest practicality and an avoidance of sentimentality when arousing feeling that indicate a highly sophisticated psychological as well as meditative system. The movements that culminated in the Mahāyāna, perhaps responding to needs they saw in the community of practitioners, particularly amongst the laity, saw that such feeling may need a formal expression within a vow or a commitment to enlightenment. In so doing, they provided a radical creativity in their understanding of compassion and its companion quality, 'skill in means', the way this compassion could be applied in practice. The vow that accompanied the Bodhisattva ideal, to dedicate oneself to all sentient beings, was one which could transform people's outlook on their lives, and all their daily experience. Indeed it could be argued that it was an undertaking whose formulation could well have been based as much on meditative experience as doctrinal difference. How can I help others? How can events in daily life contribute to this? As many commentators point out, the apparent split between Mahāyāna and other schools perhaps suggests a different kind of motivation, which may be present in any school, or a single individual, at different times.

The basis for a differentiation between them lay in part in a distinction found in the Pāli canon. In this there are thought to be three great paths to enlightenment.

1   The first is the path of the disciples (śrāvaka), as it is sometimes known, aimed at arahatship. This is the route taken by someone who is enlightened on hearing directly the words of a Buddha, or from practising a Buddha's teaching. Sāriputta and Moggallāna are arahats, for instance, and certainly teach others, often in greatly complex detail. While they may display miraculous powers such as great wisdom, the psychic powers or other excellences, they do not possess the full development of these exhibited by a Buddha, who is the one who rediscovers the 'forgotten path' to enlightenment and recreates the teaching afresh.

2   The second is the *pratyekabuddha*. The enigmatic roots of this word are the subject of great scholarly debate, but the term denotes a being who becomes enlightened through his own power, without hearing the words of the Buddha. He exhibits many of the great skills of the Buddha but he does not teach the full path to enlightenment to others. *Jātaka* stories are full of such beings, who represent the spiritual path at times when there is no Buddha to teach the way. But while they display miraculous abilities, such as the ability to fly through the air at will, and do indeed teach, through silence, actions or through elliptic riddles and utterances, they are not shown giving systematic teaching and guidance. For this they have sometimes been termed 'Silent Buddhas'.

3   The third path is that of the Bodhisattva, who has made a vow one day to become a Buddha, who finds the teaching anew when it has been lost and delivers it to others. According to the Pāli canon such beings are very rare: there have, it is said, been twenty-eight including the present Buddha over many past aeons. One Buddha does not exist at the same time as another, and a new one can emerge only when the teaching of the one before has died completely. The path to Buddhahood is initiated by the Bodhisatta/Bodhisattva vow, in which the being vows to bring enlightenment to other sentient beings as well as find it for himself.

In the first centuries of the first millenium many texts emerged, from schools we do not always identify, which explored these notions further. They placed great emphasis on visualization practices, mantras, and a strong element of devotion. Some of these espoused the idea that these three paths were open to all beings, and that the third, the Bodhisattva path, was an aspiration possible to everyone. All beings could attain Buddhahood, and in some instances the Bodhisattva vow was modified so that the practitioner made an undertaking to postpone his or her own Buddhahood until all sentient beings could become enlightened too.

Bodhisattva vow

As long as space abides and as long as the world abides, so long may I abide, destroying the sufferings of the world.

Bodhicaryāvatāra 10.55

The Supreme Worship

A feature which also became central to much of the devotional practice of the Northern and Eastern schools is that of the Supreme Worship. If we can go by versions of the *Ajātaśatru-kaukṛtyavinodana-sūtra*, found amongst translations in China in the second century CE, it is very ancient. The supreme worship had seven elements, though the composition of these seems to have varied.

1   Praise (*vandanā*)
2   Worship (*pūjanā*)
3   Confession of faults (*deśanā*)
4   Rejoicing in merit (*modanā*)

5   Requesting the teaching (*adhyeṣaṇā*)
6   Begging the Buddhas not to abandon beings (*yācanā*)
7   Dedication of merit (*nāmanā*)

Adapted from version in Bhadracaryā

Offered to the arising of the mind dedicated to Buddhahood, the Supreme Worship is recommended by the eighth-century writer, Śāntideva, for the accumulation of merit, to balance and support the wisdom needed for the fulfilment of the Bodhisattva vow. It is one of many such expressions of great devotion, commitment and prayer that come to form an important part of Buddhist meditation, particularly in the North, Central Asia and China.

PHILOSOPHICAL DEVELOPMENTS

Revolutionary ideas concerning the nature of time, developed in the first instance by one school of Buddhism, the Sarvāstivāda, reinforced the expansiveness of such theory and practice. The Sarvāstivādin school seems to have developed at first from an abstruse Abhidhammic question. In the thought processes through which moments of consciousness pass as each object is experienced, how can a momentary object be presented to the senses and yet still 'exist' at the moment of consciousness when it is received and investigated by the mind immediately afterwards? The Sarvāstivādins posited the notion that for such events to be possible all phenomena, of all times, past, present and future, must, to a certain extent, co-exist, and so they derived their name, which means 'all exist' (*sarvam asti*). The object, lasting for a moment, is received by the mind and investigated after it has lapsed, and so both times, past and present, must be present.

This paved the way for great extrapolations, for if this is the case, then the future could be said to exist as well. All Buddhas and indeed all enlightened beings exist now too. Indeed for the practitioner, his or her own enlightenment is a present fact that he or she just has to discover or develop for him or herself. The Sarvāstivādins went even further in the adventurousness of their thought. Why should causes operate only from past to present; could not a cause for a present event be in the future? This stellar explosion – for it could be called that – of creative formulation accompanied a trend for new texts themselves to be 'revealed' by the Buddha or other Buddhas or enlightened beings. A great symbolic application of the 'fully awakened mind', the imaginative possibility of 'new' or 'newly found' texts had enormous implications, as legends could be composed and circulated validating whole new treatises and *sūtras* many centuries after the death of the Buddha. New meditative teachings and intellectual arguments propounded by the Buddha, or other Buddhas, could be accessed by practitioners in the present, 'found' in texts hidden in caves, in dreams, or be received as inspired personal composition. The idea of Buddha 'fields' (*kṣetra*) started to be introduced, whereby Buddhas in numberless world systems inhabited glorious lands in part created by themselves: these were greatly influential in the subsequent development of Pure-Land Buddhism. Although many of these texts were anonymous, subsequent Buddhist traditions are indebted to the meditative and exploratory work of the *saṅgha* that composed so many texts on the basis of this psychological and metaphoric possibility. It is an important development in Buddhism: the introduction of such narrative framing devices provides great testament to the inherent balance of the tradition as it adjusted itself to changing conditions and found often inspired new formulation through meditation, theory and custom.

DHĀRAṆĪ

A *dhāraṇī* is a word derived from the Sanskrit, 'to hold' *dhā* or 'retain' means anything that helps one to retain or secure something. So it comes to be applied to a protective mantra that allows the practitioner to retain the teaching, or good luck, or a way of averting evil. Soon it comes to mean 'spell', with, in Chinese Buddhism, the idea that it in some way contains or holds the essence of some quality, like compassion or wisdom. In Tiantai Buddhism for instance, there is a *dhāraṇī* associated with liberating insight, which, if chanted frequently, will confer this quality upon the practitioner.

Emptiness (*Śūnyatā*)

The great ebullience and inspirational brilliance of Buddhist theory in these centuries demanded some counterweight. If the doctrines of the Bodhisattva, and indeed many Buddhas and Bodhisattvas, are seen as filling the universe in this way, the universe itself needs to be described in terms which allows the practitioner literally to empty his mind and give the mind's enjoyment of participation in this universe a chance to rest and restore itself. The doctrine of emptiness (*śūnyatā*) emerges as the insight element that balances this richness and proliferation of gods, bodhisattvas and enlightening beings. The doctrine of emptiness had different applications in varied settings and philosophies and is understood by different schools variously. Within a meditative context it is usually taught, however, as an emptiness which should not be frightening or intimidating. Rather it is seen as a non-substantial space from which events can arise and where they can dissolve when their purpose is completed. It seems to be like a kind of earth of the meditation practice, where the many events of a visualization, a constructed image (*nimitta*) or a chanted mantra, things formed and unformed, have a quieter place in which to settle, without becoming substantialized, and hence focuses of attachment.

According to the Southern system of *Abhidhamma*, there are four basic 'realities': consciousness (*citta*), mental state (*cetasika*), physical form (*rūpa*) and *nibbāna*. Nāgārjuna (c.150–250 CE) posited the idea that neither consciousness nor the flux of events could be considered as real; this paved the way, eventually, for the idea of what came later to be called the doctrine of interpenetration, whereby mind could work within matter. Two separate strands of Buddhist philosophy emerged in the second and third centuries. The Madhyamaka school, in their fine analysis and exposition, were weighted more towards the active cultivation of wisdom (*paññā/prajñā*), and an approach that encouraged seeing the emptiness of all phenomena. The Yogācāra school posited a different view of reality: the storage consciousness (*ālaya-vijñāna*) contains the 'seeds' (*bīja*) of proliferations and defilements. Through the practice of concentration (*samādhi*) the underlying stratum of the Buddha mind, both empty and radiant, would be found. Both schools saw themselves as following the middle way between nihilism and realism, though with different emphases. This slight shift in orientation between schools that are more analytical, or *vipassanā* based, and those that are primarily meditative and *samatha* based, persists in subsequent developments of Buddhist meditative practice.

Śāntideva

Perhaps the most eloquent exponent of the Bodhisattva ideal was Śāntideva (c.685–763), whose *Bodhicaryāvatāra* has inspired generations of practitioners, in all traditions of Buddhism as well as the Northern, with which he is most associated. His life-story is surrounded by legends, myths and wonderful miracles. According to the stories, which contain little of what we might call 'historical biography', his childhood, perhaps like the Buddha's, was as a prince in the court of a king in Saurāṣṭra. After his father's death, Mañjuśrī,

the Bodhisattva who most embodied the Buddha's wisdom, is said to have
come to him in a vision, occupied the royal throne and pronounced himself
as Śāntideva's good friend in the teaching, his spiritual guide. The female
Bodhisattva of compassion, Tārā, also appeared to him, and declared herself
his mother.

Considering himself initiated and metaphorically protected in this way
by both the principles of wisdom and compassion, Śāntideva became a
minister to a king. Eventually he attached himself to the famous Buddhist
monastery and university at Nālandā, where, to the distaste of the other
students, he lounged around, ate too much and apparently did no work at
all. Forced to defend his learning by his fellow students, he displayed his
memory of the university's own 'set texts' and added one of his own – the
Bodhicaryāvatāra. Immediately acknowledged by his fellows, he then taught
and wrote extensively. The following extract indicates the way that a now
popular devotional element has been fused with daily mindfulness practice,
emphasizing awareness at all times.

From the *Bodhicaryāvatāra*

5. 23 I make this salutation with my hands to those who wish to guard the
mind. With all your effort, guard both mindfulness and awareness.

24. Just as a man weak with illness is not fit for any work, so a mind
distracted from these two is not fit for any work.

25. What is heard, reflected upon, or cultivated in meditation, like water
in a leaky jar, does not stay in the memory of a mind that lacks awareness.

26. Many, though learned, possessing faith, and though absorbed in
effort, are befouled by offences due to the fault of lacking awareness.

27. Though they have amassed meritorious deeds, they end up in an evil
realm, plundered by the thief, lack of awareness, who comes after the theft
of mindfulness.

28. This band of robbers, the defilements, seeks out a point of access.
When it has found one, it plunders and destroys life in a good realm.

29. Therefore mindfulness should never be taken from the door to the
mind, and, if it does go, it should be reinstated, remembering the torment of
hell.

30. Mindfulness comes easily to those fortunate people who practise
wholeheartedly, through the instruction of their preceptor, because they live
with their teacher, and out of fear.

31. The Buddhas and Bodhisattvas have unobstructed vision in all directions. Every single thing is before them. Before them I stand.

32. Meditating thus, one should remain possessed of shame, respect and fear. One should recollect the Buddha in this way at every moment.

Crosby and Skilton (1996: 36–7)

THE EMERGENCE OF MAHĀYĀNA TRENDS

The early centuries of the first millenium are proving a challenging time for scholars to consider and the way that Buddhism evolved in India at that time is a continued source of debate and discussion. It has been posited that elements that contributed to what subsequently became known as Mahāyāna emerged from an increased emphasis on lay practice and the emergence of the cult of *stūpas*, often held by powerful lay groups outside the monastic hierarchy. Others have argued that some texts represented an attempt to validate new doctrines and implement a more socially egalitarian religious movement. Yet others have posited that these trends emerged from reformist forest monks. It is possible that some features of practice, possibly ancient, emerged from a rejection of a 'closed' canon and a commentarial tradition represented by for instance, Buddhaghosa and the Mahāvihāra in Sri Lanka. A growing consensus is emerging that there were probably many different kinds of ideas and schools around, with key notions that overlapped with one another, as in a large pattern of interlocking circles. Some of these features were to a certain extent anticipated in early Buddhism as it is represented in the Pāli canon, and simply became more popular generally. The ideal of the Bodhisattva, the presence of practices involving, for instance, the thirty-two marks of the Buddha and the encouragement of the eidetic faculty through visualization, as in the *Mahāsamāya-Sutta* and the *Mahāsudassana-Sutta*, are all elements that occur in Pāli Buddhist texts, considered to represent at least one strand of the earliest Buddhist schools.

In the first centuries of the millenium, however, these are supplemented or developed by features which seem to surface in a number of different texts. Whatever we might call this process, a profound evolutionary change transformed the form and content of Buddhist *sūtras*, theory and practice. This in consequence affected attitudes to the practice of meditation. New ideas either permitted, or perhaps were even the result of, new forms for meditation practices. These share many features of earlier ones, but are quite distinct in their content and practice.

Some of the features which influence emergent forms of meditation practice are:

- The idea of the Bodhisattva, that is extended and amplified
- The practice of visualization, which becomes increasingly associated with meditation
- New texts that create imagined worlds, with Buddhas or Bodhisattvas in their own 'fields' as an imaginative exercise
- The idea of emptiness
- The idea of interpenetration and of the inter-relatedness of phenomena
- A greater emphasis on Tantra, a system employed within India from the eighth century, whereby the practitioner derives union with a god, goddess or Bodhisattva, representing a quality such as enlightenment, wisdom or compassion. This usually involves esoteric teaching
- The idea of the *Tathāgatagarbha*, the seed of Buddhahood, said to be latent in all beings.

In varying degrees, one or some of these elements accompany Buddhism as it moves to other areas outside India. The idea of the *Tathagatāgarbha*, based on a now lost second-century Indian text, resonated with Chinese alchemical interests, and while it never seems to have been strongly promulgated in India, gave rise to new forms of meditative practice in the East. The notion of the underlying Buddha nature and the 'storehouse' was espoused by the Tiantai schools in China and, subsequently, by chanting traditions in Japan. An important meditative text influencing practice in Tiantai, the *Pratyutpanna-Sūtra*, teaching concentration on manifold Buddhas encountered 'face-to-face', is developed as a walking practice with visualization, and, in China, accompanies insight elements. The notion of 'Buddha-fields' contributed to the development of Pure-Land meditations in China and Japan. The emergence of *Tantra* in India, prominent in the eighth century, also accompanied the concurrent spread of Buddhism to Tibet, and proved particularly popular there, as did other practices popular in India in the centuries in which Buddhism became established in Tibet. The eighth-century Yogācāra–Madhyamaka text, the *Bhāvanākrama*, by Kamalaśīla, written in Tibet but in Sanskrit, formed the basis of subsequent Tibetan schools of meditation. India was the home not only of the Buddha, but also of a deeply creative and exploratory system of meditation, which constantly interacted with philosophical formulation. It provided, with each new wave of its development, new impetus for the movement of Buddhism to other contexts, so that elements which may even have been marginal or fleeting in their appeal in their initial context became catalysts for new meditations and formulations of meditative doctrine elsewhere.

TANTRA

Thought by some to derive from the word for 'loom', or weaving, Tantra is a way of practice based on the union of disparate elements. In Buddhist tantric forms of ritual, gesture and visualization are considered a means of allowing the practitioner a relationship with the deity or emanation of the Bodhisattva or Buddha involved. First, external offerings are made to the physical representation of the Buddha or the appropriate emanation on a shrine. Then they are made internally, within the mind of the meditator. Through performing a series of gestures, the placing of the hands (mudrā) becomes an active means of engaging with the deity, in accompaniment to a visualization exercise. In this the god or emanation of the Buddha is worshipped internally in the heart of the practitioner, in the invoked form, and externally, in the visual sphere, as an evoked form. The practitioner makes offerings symbolizing all of the senses and attempts to link the externally visualized form to the internal. At some point in the exercise the gods, bodhisattvas and teachers who provide protection to the meditator, as well as depth, animation and variation to the meditation, are all dismissed, and the mind of the practitioner enters on emptiness. A mantra to the god or emanation of the Buddha is murmured or recited several hundred times with the eyes shut while the practitioners counts out the times on a rosary of 108 beads. After this the practice is dedicated to the enlightenment and happiness of all sentient beings, and the meditator makes a clean return to the 'normal' world of the everyday senses.

Tantra is sometimes associated with an understanding derived through erotic and sexual imagery. There was a precedent for this in the Pāli canon, in the story of Nanda, who is encouraged by the Buddha to carry on with his meditation by a vision of beautiful heavenly maidens that would be his if he succeeded (Nanda in fact becomes enlightened and needs them no more!). By and large, however, the use of the overtly sexual in meditation objects is not a feature of Southern Buddhism. It was, however, by this time central in many traditions of India: the antinomian, the taboo and the erotic were felt to arouse great power and energy, which, if harnessed, could provide a kind of homeopathic medicine in meditation, freeing the mind from associated defilements. Such practices needed preliminary training and care: they were usually only taught after requisite initiations and ceremonies protected the meditator from loss of control or from being 'possessed' by energies they could not handle. Practised widely in India in other traditions, Tantra proved particularly popular in the transmission of Buddhism to Tibet, espoused in Vajrayāna traditions. It is to Tibetan Buddhism that we need to go for modern exponents of the tradition.

In India, however, Buddhism started to go into some decline. From the fifth to the eighth centuries Chinese pilgrims commented on this with regard to the monastic orders. Other Indian traditions seemed to be acquiring pre-eminence. By the twelfth century, with the Mogul invasions, Buddhism was in a sharp decline from which it never really recovered. Apart from the one pocket of the Newars in Nepal, and areas that came to be influenced by Tibet, such as Ladakh, Sikkim and Bhutan, for nearly a thousand years there was little Buddhist activity in the Indian sub-continent. In the twentieth century the situation changed. There has been a growth of interest in a number of different areas: the Ambedkar movement and its popularity amongst the Dalits, the lowest castes, has made millions of converts. It must represent one of the largest growing communities of Buddhist practitioners in the world, but it is early days to see the way this group evolves. There has been a growth of interest in some *vipassanā* traditions amongst the middle classes. As the homeland of the Buddha, India experiences a great influx of tourists to its sacred sites. How these factors will work in the long term is not yet clear.

SURVIVING FORMS OF INDIAN BUDDHISM IN NEPAL

While discussing India something should be said about Newar Buddhism, the last surviving remnant of Indian Buddhism in India and the only place in the world where the Buddhist tradition still uses Sanskrit texts. Indeed Nepal gives us an example of odd and striking parallels between Buddhist traditions that may not have had contact with one another for up to a thousand years. The *siddhaṃ* script used in mantras in Japan is virtually the same as that used here, though contact between these two countries has only recently been revived. In the 1930s there was a considerable Theravāda Buddhist input in Nepal, which has co-existed with more ancient forms and is sometimes critical of what is perceived as the slightly decadent adaptation to local cults that characterizes Newar practice, which include, for instance, shrines to the smallpox goddess.

Another important element in defining Nepalese Buddhism has been the impact of easier travel on Lumbīnī, the birthplace of the Buddha, which has become a pilgrimage site for Buddhists from all over the world. Japanese Buddhist influence is now particularly evident in the

Figure 7.3 **Prayer wheels in at the Swayabhunath Temple, Kathmandu, Nepal**

form of lodging houses and temples in this area. The influx of the Tibetan diaspora has meant the introduction of prayer-wheels. More generally, the advent of the 'backpacking' generation from abroad has introduced a spirit of inquiry and appreciation of Buddhism within the region. Historically this has been a troubled area: while the effect remains to be seen of the recent input from a number of Buddhist schools, longstanding 'hybrids' of practice still ensure the survival of the oldest strata of the tradition. The Newars are a good example of ancient forms of Buddhism in some way mixing with more recent forms, over a long period of time. In the twentieth century a number of other Buddhist countries developed a Buddhism which to some extent has accommodated movements from outside, so that several strands co-exist together.

TIMELINES

c.400 BCE	Death of Gotama Buddha
c.268–232 BCE	King Aśoka
100 BCE	Sāñcī stūpa
c.200	Nāgārjuna
c.320–90	Asaṅga, founder of Yogācāra school
c.500	Buddhist university at Nālandā
c.1200	Destruction of monastic universities
2007	50,000 Dalits convert to Buddhism in mass ceremony

FURTHER READING

Cousins, L.S. (1985) 'Buddhism', in Hinnells, J.R. (ed.) *A Handbook of Living Religions*, Harmondsworth, Middx: Penguin.

Crosby, K. and Skilton, A. (eds), Williams, P. intro., (1996) *Śāntideva:The Bodhicaryāvatāra*, Oxford/New York: OUP.

Hamilton, S. (2001) *Indian Philosophy: A Very Short Introduction*, Oxford: OUP.

Harrison, P. (1978) 'Buddhānusmṛti in the *Pratyutpanna-Buddhasaṃmukhāvasthitasamādhisūtra*', *Journal of Indian Philosophy*, 6: 35–57.

Harvey, P. (1984) 'The Symbolism of the Early Stūpa', *Jornal of the International Association of Buddhist Studies*, Vol.7, No. 2: 67–93.

Harvey, P. (1990) *Introduction to Buddhism: Teachings, History and Practices*, Cambridge: CUP, 73–138.

LeVine, S., and Gellner, D.N. (2005) *Rebuilding Buddhism: The Theravada Movement in Twentieth Century Nepal*, Cambridge, MA/London: Harvard University Press.

Lusthaus, D. (2004) 'Yogācāra School', Robert Buswell Jnr. (ed.), *Encyclopedia of Buddhism*, 2 vols., New York: Macmillan, 2, 914–24.

Seyfort Ruegg, D. (1989) *Buddha-nature, Mind and the Problem of Gradualism in a Comparative Perspective: on the Transmission and Reception of Buddhism in India and Tibet*, London: SOAS University of London.

Skilton, A. (1994) *A Concise History of Buddhism*, Birmingham: Windrush, 1994.

Williams, P. (1989) *Mahāyāna Buddhism*, London/New York: Routledge.

Williams, P. with Tribe, A. (2000) *Buddhist Thought: a Complete Introduction to the Buddhist Tradition*, London/New York: Routledge.

Buddhist Meditation Traditions in Tibet

The Union of the Three Vehicles, a Tibetan perspective

(Chapter written by Georgios Halkias)

Eight

The advent of Buddhism in Tibet in the seventh and eighth centuries CE gave rise to one of the greatest Buddhist civilizations Asia has ever known. Tibetan Buddhism flourished in the Tibetan plateau and across the culturally Tibetan regions of India, Nepal, Bhutan, Mongolia, Russia and Northeastern China. It came to be represented by four major schools, each emphasizing particular scriptures, meditative traditions and master-based lineages. All four schools hold equal claim to possessing complete training systems to enlightenment. Tibetans at large are adherents of Mahāyāna Buddhism. Traditionally they are also initiates of esoteric practices of the Tantric variety found within a large Tibetan collection of Vajrayāna texts, encompassing translations from Sanskrit and indigenous Tibetan compositions.

Mahāyāna, not unlike Southern Buddhism, attaches vital importance to disciplining one's mind, stressing both the cultivation of great compassion

Figure 8.1 **Temple in Tibet**

for all suffering sentient beings and the view of the inherent emptiness of all phenomena. The primary motivation of Mahāyānists is devoting, without self-gain, their life to liberate all living beings from the bondage of *saṃsāra*, the mind's compulsive grasping at a supposed inherent self and an equally rigid external reality. The altruistic commitment takes the form of a series of vows as outlined in the *Bodhicaryāvatāra* (*Engaging in the Bodhisattva's Way*), an Indian Buddhist classic written by scholar and mystic Śāntideva, destined to become a Tibetan Buddhist favourite. Śāntideva encapsulates the aspiration of the Mahāyāna journey when he writes:

> For as long as space endures, and for as long as living beings remain,
> Until then may I too abide to dispel the misery of the world.

In order to be of benefit to others, a Bodhisattva-aspirant abandons his delusional habits and strives to refashion himself through the cultivation of six perfections, namely: generosity, good conduct, acceptance, effort, meditation and wisdom, the supreme insight that realizes the dependent nature of all phenomena. Practitioners of the six perfections are on the vehicle of the Bodhisattvas, the Bodhisattvayāna (another term for Mahāyāna), in which they grow accustomed in the thirty-seven aspects of awakening and, in five stages, traverse ten levels of spiritual perfection.

The ideal of a Bodhisattva finds its ultimate vindication in the worship of Avalokiteśvara. Translated as Chenrezig in Tibetan, he is the Bodhisattva embodiment of the compassion of all Buddhas. In this capacity he is revered most of all deities in countries where Mahāyāna flourished. His voice, encapsulated in the mantra Oṃ maṇi padme hūṃ (Hail to the Jewel on the Lotus), is known by every Tibetan who recites it in order to accumulate merit and spiritual strength. Where else is there to turn but to the progenitor and patron-saint of the Tibetans, Avalokiteśvara, who, according to local histories, came to Tibet in the form of a monkey and mated with an indigenous flesh-eating ogress to prevent her, out of compassion, from causing further harm? No credit is accorded to Darwin; from their offspring evolved the race of the Tibetan people. A large number of Tibetan religious scriptures are devoted to Avalokiteśvara and the line of the Dalai Lamas is held to be an emanation of his immeasurable compassion recurring in Tibet.

Tibetan Buddhist literature, in all its diversity, is often arranged in a scheme of three vehicles. Each vehicle (Skt. yāna) corresponds to a major turning of the 'wheel of *dharma*', according to which Buddha Śākyamuni is said to have imparted three seminal instructions to his disciples as seen fit with their mental capacities:

1   at Sarnath, he granted the 'Hīnayāna' teachings, centring on the four noble truths and the eightfold path
2   at Vulture Peak Mountain, near Rājagṛha, he revealed the Mahāyāna cycle of instruction, teaching emptiness as the supreme wisdom
3   at Śrāvastī, he secretly bestowed the Vajrayāna teachings focusing on the concept of inherent Buddha-nature (Skt. *tathāgatagarbha*) residing in all beings endowed with sentience.

According to this threefold scheme of the Tibetan doxographical tradition, Buddhist practice consists of abiding in the conduct and ethos of Hīnayāna, maintaining the Bodhisattva's altruistic motivation, and training in the esoteric teachings of the expedient vehicle of the *vajra* (lit. thunderbolt), the Vajrayāna.

The terms Vajrayāna and Mantrayāna describe a heterogeneous collection of esoteric practices that represent the most ritually evolved expression of Indian Mahāyāna Buddhism. Tantra was at its peak in India from the eighth to the eleventh centuries CE, but its origins can be traced back much earlier, depending on how scholars wish to define the term. Vajrayāna Buddhism relies on the cultivation of pure awareness and the purification of every aspect of perception, in the transformation of senses and mind into conduits of enlightening expression. This is accomplished through training in an elaborate system of interrelated ritual activities, visualizations, and recitations grouped together in what sometimes is called deity-yoga. In deity-yoga the practitioner visualizes himself or herself to be already fully enlightened in the body and with the speech and mind of a particular Buddha or chosen deity (*yidam*) drawn from the Vajrayāna pantheon. Vajrayāna is also called the vehicle of the fruit or result (Phalayāna), for it presupposes the inherent Buddha-nature of the practitioner working to a state of realization from inside out – exemplified in the union of 'acting like a Buddha' and 'being one'.

Tantric training is also said to impart a wide range of supernatural abilities, or *siddhis*, such as clairvoyance and clairaudience, increased lifespan, power and wealth, and so forth. Tibetan religious literature delights in the magical feats of great adepts or *mahāsiddhas* who displayed great mastery over their minds and the world of forms as a result of Tantric schooling.

The most celebrated of all *mahāsiddhas* in Tibet is Milarepa (1052–1135), the cotton-clad recluse from Mila whose *Hundred Thousand Songs*, a collection of vivid spiritual poetry (Skt. *dohas*), continue to inspire Buddhist ascetics the world over.

In these narrative songs of spiritual realization, we read of magical contests against the Bön priest Naro Bhun Chon, reflecting an actual historical confrontation between the Buddhist factions competing with the indigenous caste of Tibetan priests known as Bön. The didactic and symbolic potency of these songs celebrate the re-emergence of Buddhism, destined from the eleventh century to become again the dominant religion of Tibet.

[Naro Bhun Chon]
In our Bon religion the Immutable One is the Swastika-Body – the Lord Ye Shin Dsu Pud, and other heavenly beings. The fierce blood-drinking Deity with gaping mouth has nine heads, eighteen arms, and many miraculous powers. His sister is the World-Conquering Mother. I, the Bon novice, am her disciple. Look at me! See how I demonstrate my miraculous power!

[Milarepa]
To you, the wrong-view-holder Bonist, I now give answer with this song:
The famous Di Se Mountain blanketed with snow symbolizes the pure, white Buddhist doctrine. The streams flowing into the famous Blue Lake of Ma Päm symbolizes one's deliverance to the Realm of the Absolute.
I, the famous Milarepa, the old man who sleeps naked, am he who now transcends the dualistic realm!
The little songs springing from my mouth are but the natural outflow of my heart; they tell of, and describe the Sūtras of the Buddha.
The staff held in my hand symbolizes the crossing of the ocean of Saṃsāra. I have mastered both the minds and forms; unaided by worldly deities I can perform all miracles... This place belongs to Buddhists, to the followers of Milarepa.
If you, Bon priests and heretics, will now practice the Dharma, you, too, will soon be able to benefit all; if not, you should depart and go elsewhere, because my powers of magic are greater far than yours. Watch closely now and see what I can do!

(Chang 1977)

The story of how Mahāyāna reached Tibet and how it came to be established in opposition to native religious cults constitutes a fascinating and essential chapter of Tibet's adaptation to Buddhism. Before telling this story we must bear in mind that the relationship between Buddhist traditions prevalent in the south, such as Sri Lanka and Southeast Asia, and Mahāyāna schools active in north India is complex and need not be reduced to geography (south vs. north) or mere chronology (early vs. late). Contemporary scholars have shown these designations to be as problematic as they are informative. We know for example, that by the tenth century, monks from different citizenries and Buddhist persuasions lived together, debated and practised their own diverse traditions in large Indian Buddhist universities like Nālandā in the Northeast. This being said, the division between other forms of Buddhism and Mahāyāna does reflect different phases in doctrinal interpretation. If philosophically inclined, we could become enmeshed in long discussions concerning a number of subjects which have been of interest within many Buddhist traditions:

1   The ontological qualities of the enlightened-state (innate vs. acquired enlightenment)
2   The singularity or plurality of Buddhas and Bodhisattvas at any given time in any given system
3   The possibility and expediency of the highest goal of the Buddhist path (partial vs. complete Buddhahood; realization in one life-time or in several)
4   The use of ritual practices as effective or not as a means of mental cultivation.

The list of such issues is potentially very long.

Mainstream, Mahāyāna and Vajrayāna Buddhist orientations did not grow in stark isolation from each other, nor did they, in their ritual and doctrinal developments, ever give rise to religious schisms like the ones we encounter during the Reformation in Christian Europe. By contrast, Buddhism as it is understood in Tibet reflects the continuity and union of the three *yānas*. Vajrayāna Buddhism is seen as an extension of the skilful means of Mahāyāna, with the *Vinaya* (monastic rules) of the mainstream schools governing monastic practice. Tibetan Buddhist monks ordain by the *Vinaya* of the *Mūlasārvastivāda*, a school close to Theravāda, and a number of Pāli scriptures from the Southern schools can be found in Tibetan translation.

These texts occupy nowadays but a small section of the Tibetan Buddhist canon containing in all some five thousand *sūtra* and *tantra* texts distributed in the Kanjur (words of the Buddha) and the Tenjur (commentaries) consolidated in the fourteenth century by the librarian-scholar Buton (1290–1364).

THE GREAT DEBATE AT SAMYE: GRADUAL OR SPONTANEOUS ENLIGHTENMENT?

The first king of the Tibetan Dynasty, Nyatri Tsenpo (c. second century), is said to have descended to earth from a lineage of sky-kings, physically connected by a rope to Heaven. In his court Bön priests served as religious advisers and specialists over fertility rituals and funeral rites. The earliest mention of Buddhism dates to the reign of the twenty-eighth king of the dynasty, Lhato Thori Nyentsen, who seems to have been acquainted with Buddhist *sūtras* and religious objects through contact with Central Asian missionaries. However, it was not until the reign of the Tibetan emperor, Songtsen Gampo (c. seventh century CE), that the first Buddhist temples were built and Buddhist scriptures began to be translated from Sanskrit and Chinese into Tibetan. In the eighth century, during the reign of Trisong Detsen (742–97), the first Buddhist monastery Samye was built in the shape of a giant *maṇḍala* modelled after the Indian temple of Odantapuri in Bihar. At the same time, Buddhism was officially declared the state-religion of the vast Tibetan empire extending across Central Asia and reaching Ch'ang-an, the capital of Tang China (modern day Xi'an).

After its foundation in 775 CE, Samye became a renowned seat of learning attracting many Buddhist masters and disciples from China, India and Central Asia. Here many languages were taught, Buddhist scriptures were translated into Tibetan from Chinese, Indian and Central Asian languages, and the Tibetans were gaining enough confidence in these new doctrines to compose their own Buddhist treatises. Samye fostered the monastic codes of the *Mūlasarvāstivādin* school and promoted a refreshing synthesis of two prominent and competing Indian philosophical schools, the Yogācāra, who posited a doctrine that phenomena were mind-only, and Madhyamaka, who posited the middle-way approach. It is not surprising that the monastic ethos and philosophical views of these two schools prevailed in Tibet and inform, to this day, the practice and scholastic foundation of all Tibetan Buddhist schools.

This holds true of the school of the Nyingma (holders of Ancient *Tantras*) which is the only Buddhist meditative tradition in Tibet to trace unequivocally its origins back to the imperial times when their semi-legendary founder, the Tantric master Padmasamhava from Uddiyāna, was invited by king Trisong Detsen to subdue the indigenous 'demonic parties' that were opposing the construction of Samye monastery. Such was the gratitude of the king that he became a disciple of the great master and gave him his queen Yeshe Tsogyal as a student and consort. Yeshe Tsogyal's secret life as a *yoginī* and the songs of her spiritual realization are among the finest indigenous lyrical and instructional portrayals of a woman's enlightenment played out on native Tibetan soil.

There are a few stories of strife and reconciliation associated with the history of the grand monastery of Samye. Although it is not altogether clear, different support groups in the imperial court may have been responsible for the growing antagonism between the Chinese and Indian Buddhist factions leading to the famous Samye debate. This confrontation may have lasted for as long as three years, after which, according to Tibetan historical sources, King Trisong Detsen pledged for the superiority of the gradual approach to enlightenment promoted by the Indian scholar Kamalaśīla, to the disadvantage of Mo-ho-yen's party from China. They had advocated a type of Chan (see Chapter 9), a non-gradual and effortless path to enlightenment. Although the king's decision did not mean the elimination of Chan views, it does mark a declining influence of Chinese Buddhism in Tibet, confirmed in the sheer numbers of religious texts surviving today in Tibetan. These are mainly of Indian origin, with only a meagre section bearing witness to the wealth of Chinese doctrines available in Central Asia at the time.

Chan lineages, however, were not altogether lost in Tibet. Many of the doctrines survive in the highest Buddhist teachings of the Nyingma School, known as the Great Perfection or *Dzogchen*. In *Dzogchen*, not unlike Mo-ho-yen's enlightenment through non-activity, a view of the inherent perfection in all phenomena and effortlessness are essential for attaining supreme liberation. In the *Lamp of the Eye of Meditation*, a unique work dated from that period, the views of Kamalaśila and Mo-ho-yen were juxtaposed, to the advantage of Dzogchen:

(The Great Perfection) is the mother who produces all Buddhas. It is the antidote of all activity that involves effort. Whichever path one follows and whatever method one adopts, without realisation of the Great Perfection, one cannot attain Enlightenment.

Karmay (1972: 113)

Dzogchen lineages of the Nyingma are traced to Padmasambhava and other early masters active in Samye. These lineages continued to flourish and became systematized in the fourteenth century by Longchenpa (1308–64), the great *Dzogchen* exponent and scholar of the Nyingma School.

Neither the imperial glory of Samye nor the political might of the empire lasted beyond the tenth century. This effectively ended the first large-scale transplantation of Buddhism in Tibet and saw the decline of a generous imperial patronage of Buddhist monasticism. The emergence of new Buddhist schools, with their own sets of the latest *Tantras* imported from India in the eleventh century, was the cause of tension with the older Nyingma on issues related to scriptural authenticity, canonical legitimacy and patronage. Spiritual leaders of the Old School continued to promulgate the eighteen great *Tantras*, like the *Guhyagarbha Tantra*, *Vairocana's Net of Magical Display*, and so forth, while producing extraordinary new Buddhist teachings

Figure 8.2 **Tibetan religious trumpet, Bimahali Museum, Sarahan, Kinnaur**

of their own. These were said to have been previously buried as Treasures (Tib. *gter-ma*) in earth, water, and space or in the minds of select disciples of Padmasambhava. The concealment of Vajrayāna teachings as treasures came along with a prophetic injunction requiring their rediscovery by realized treasure-discoverers at an appropriate time in the future when they would be of most benefit to mankind. Visionary Buddhist teachings continue to be produced in this way and to contribute to a large array of ritual and meditative Buddhist literature that is, in its mode of propagation, uniquely Tibetan.

THE NEW TANTRIC SCHOOLS: SAKYA, KAGYU AND GELUG

The religious, cultural and political history of Tibet is bound up with the formation and development of its Buddhist schools, which are commonly divided into the old and new orders. The new, typically divided into Gelug, Kagyu, Sakya and the Kadampa, trace the Vajrayāna lineages of their teachings to the new translation of the *Tantras* dating from the second major dissemination of Buddhism in Tibet. Although the divisions between schools are meant to represent accurately a major internal diversity, there are no essential differences in doctrine between all the various orders. Their main differences consist in their traditional attachments to different lines of realized teachers, sacred texts and particular Buddhist divinities.

The revival of Buddhism commenced in the late tenth century in Western Tibet when the monk-king Lha Lama Yeshe Ö dispatched twenty-one intelligent young Tibetans to Kashmir, which was then a thriving centre of Buddhist scholarship. From those who survived the arduous journey over the Himalayas, one figure stands out prominently: the great translator, Rinchen Zangpo (958–1055), who spread the Buddha's doctrine through translation, teaching and establishing monasteries in Kinnaur and Western Tibet. During his time, Jangchub Ö, the nephew and successor of Yeshe Ö, wishing to receive the latest esoteric teachings from India to revitalize the monastic culture, invited the reputed Bengali scholar and monk Dipamkara Atīśa (982–1054) from the Buddhist University of Vikramaśīla. The arrival of the *paṇḍita* in Tibet in 1042 heralded what was to become a Buddhist renaissance − a burst of artistic, intellectual and spiritual activity that followed this second major translation phase of Indian Buddhist literature into Tibetan.

Atīśa is fondly remembered for translating and synthesizing many Buddhist *sūtra* and Tantric scriptures. Urged by his disciple, the monk-king Jangchub

Ö, he produced *A Lamp on the Path to Enlightenment*, a concise treatise for aspiring Bodhisattvas. This work is well known in Tibet as it set the pattern for many Lam-rim styled teachings (graded paths to enlightenment) that comprise a unique genre of Tibetan Buddhist literature. Atīśa's attempt at a synthesis between the *sūtras* and *Tantras* came to be a defining characteristic of Tibetan Buddhist theory and practice. Among Atīśa's many gifted Tibetan disciples, it was Dromtön who later consolidated his teachings and founded the Kadampa School. The teachings of the early Kadampa masters from Central Tibet were sober and down-to-earth, focusing on the practical aspects of Buddhist training and not on philosophical musings and scholastic refinement. Their stress on step-by-step training gave rise to a fixed set of contemplations for mind training that recur in almost all Tibetan Buddhist teachings: the preciousness of human birth and recognition of favourable conditions to practice the *dharma*, the impermanence of life, the karmic consequences of actions and the suffering and dissatisfaction of *saṃsāra*.

New developments occurred in Southern Tibet when the householder, Marpa the Translator (1012–99), began studying Sanskrit with one of the most famous and productive translators of the eleventh century, Drogmi Lotsawa (992–1072). Inspired by his teacher, he departed for Nepal and India to find the source of the Buddhist teachings. With the *mahāsiddha* Naropa he trained in the *Hevajra Tantra* and the *Six Yogas*, and from Maitripa he received the precepts of *Mahāmudrā*, the highest teachings of the Kagyu and Gelug schools. When he finally settled back in Tibet he became the founder of what is commonly known as the Kagyu school (order of oral transmissions). He had many disciples, the most famous being the yogi Milarepa, who came to exemplify the trials and accomplishments of ascetics in Tibet.

It was not until the time of Milarepa's 'heart-disciple', the illustrious scholar and physician Gampopa (1079–1153), that the order established a solid monastic foundation. His teaching lineage continued with the line of the Karmapas, the highest religious representatives of all Kagyu orders. The first Karmapa, Düsum Khyenpa (1110–93), was a charismatic teacher, as all of his line have been, right up to the present-day seventeenth Karmapa, Ogyen Drodul Tinley Dorje (born in 1985), currently residing in India. Integral to the principal teachings of all Kagyu lineages is Naropa's *Six Yogas*: the generation of psychic heat; attainment of the illusory body; dream yoga; recognition of the radiant mind of clear light; mind-transference at the moment of death; and forceful projection into another body. The quintessential instructions of the school, however, are preserved in the tradition of the Great Seal (Skt. *Mahāmudrā*); a direct method of introducing one into the radiant 'nature of mind' (Buddha-nature), inherent in all beings and beyond cognition.

This extract from 'A Song on the View of Voidness' demonstrates Kagyu teaching within a precise poetic form. Tibetan poetry of this kind is often chanted on meditation courses, and is intended to arouse careful attention in the reciter:

When the secret of appearance is revealed,
Everything arises in a tone of voidness,
Undefined by the marks of identity,
Like a sky that is nothing but image...

When the secret of meditation is revealed,
However much one meditates, it's but a state –
Undistracted, and in natural restfulness,
Free of exertion and constraint.

Karma Trinly (1456–1539), Kagyu monk
Jinpa and Elsner (2000: 147–9)

For the Kagyu and Sakya schools the synthesis of the scholarly with the yogic ideals exemplified in one person, the 'scholar-siddha', sustained an exciting and prolific ritual and philosophical monastic life. Whereas for the Kagyu orders, monastic leadership was passed down through teacher–disciple or incarnation lineages, for the Sakya school, succession of leadership through the family line, such as through nephews, became the norm. The Sakya, historically bound up with the Khon clan, had its roots in the Tibetan Empire. Although the monastery of Sakya (grey-earth) was founded in 1073 by Khon Konchog Gyalpo (1034–1102), we cannot properly speak of the Sakya order prior to the early twelfth century. The Sakya religious system developed from the doctrinal reforms of Sachen Kunga Nyingpo (1092–1158), the son of Konchog Gyalpo. He was spiritually inclined from a very young age. In his liberation-narrative (Tib. *nam-thar*), a popular genre of Tibetan Buddhist literature, we read that when he was just eleven years old, and six months into meditation retreat, he was blessed by a vision of Manjuśri, the Bodhisattva of Wisdom, and with these words came thereafter to understand all Buddhist teachings:

> If you are attached to this life you are not a religious person.
> If you are attached to the cycle of existence you do not have renunciation.
> If you are attached to your own goals you do not have the enlightened motivation.
> If grasping occurs you do not have the view.
>
> Lopez (1997: 189)

The Sakya School produced many distinguished Buddhist scholars, like Sakya Pandita (1182–1251), who also served as religious preceptor to the Mongol sovereign Godan Khan. Sakya scholarship greatly contributed to the development of scholastic subjects, like Madhyamaka philosophy, epistemology and logic, and is well represented in the nineteenth-century non-sectarian movement known as Ri-me. The meditation system of the school is an amalgamation of Tantric traditions that include the Vajrayāna cycles of Mahākāla, Vajrakilaya and Guhyasamaja; transmissions by Padmasamhava to Khon Nagendrarakṣita and the Lam-drë (lit. path and result). The latter,

Sakya teachings also produced poetic expression, based, as these passages indicate, on close experiential observation:

On how to engage in a Meditative Path

For deep meditation, you need firm resolve,
Rooted in the bone of your heart,
Renunciation, the core of mountain solitude.
Give up the concerns of everyday life...
In meditation, be free of all apprehension,
In radiant experience, be free of all grasping,
Find a haven, though the ground is lost.
Tread beyond every word, every thought.

Drakpa Gyaltsen (1147–1216), son of one of founders of Sakya schools

Jinpa and Elsner (2000: 127–8)

based on the *Hevajra Tantra* and related esoteric scriptures, derives from the teachings of the Indian *mahāsiddha*, Virupa. Its meditation instructions form the core curriculum in Sakya monasteries.

Unlike the Sakya and Kagyu schools that held Indian masters at the source of their lineages, the last major Tibetan school, the Gelug (the order of the virtuous) was founded by the renowned scholar-yogi and monastic reformer Tsongkapa (1357–1419). This order is also known as the 'New Kadampa' based upon its self-perception as the revival of the original Kadampa tradition inspired by the teachings of Atīśa. Naturally, the school held in high esteem the *Lam-rim* teachings (stages of the path) and incorporated into their curriculum new highest yoga *Tantras* imported from India corresponding to the *Guhyasamāja*, *Cakrasaṃvara*, *Yamāntaka* and *Kālacakra* deities.

Through the work of many gifted Gelug masters and the establishment of three prosperous monasteries in Lhasa – Ganden (1409), Drepung (1416) and Sera (1419) – the Gelug school became, by the seventeenth century, the most politically assertive order of Buddhism in Tibet. From the seventeenth century onwards, during the reign of the fifth Dalai Lama until the Chinese takeover of Tibet in 1949, the Dalai Lamas, through successive incarnations, held for the most part religious and political authority over Tibet. Tenzin Gyatso, the current and fourteenth Dalai Lama (born 1935) and leader of the Gelug school, continues to promulgate Buddhism around the world through public teachings, lectures and books, while his exemplary efforts for the promotion of non-violence and humanitarian values has earned him international esteem and recognition. For the faithful, he is a manifest expression of Avalokiteśvara's compassionate vow to return to the world for as long as sentient beings remain.

In addition to the Nyingma, Gelug, Kagyu and Sakya monastic orders there have been a number of peripatetic lineages formed around charismatic teachers, greatly enriching the religious life in Tibet. Most prominent are the itinerant traditions of the *Zhije* system (pacification) and the teachings of *Chöd* (cutting through the ego), credited respectively to the unconventional Indian *siddha*, Padampa Sangye, and the controversial female *yogi*, the Tibetan Magic Lobdron. These traditions are shared by different schools, as is a variety of teachings and genres of texts. Pure-Land related Buddhist practices (see Chapter 9), ranging from aspiration prayers for birth in Sukhāvatī to Vajrayāna techniques for attaining to Pure-Lands, are shared by all four Tibetan Buddhist schools, reflecting a strong devotional side to Tibetan Buddhism.

More daring examples of 'enlightened eccentricity' are found in stories of Buddhist adepts like Drukpa Kunley ('Brug-pa Kun-legs), a sixteenth-century adept seen as a madman, by some counts, or master of 'crazy wisdom' by others. His antinomian behaviour, startling anecdotes and blatant mockery of conventional deceit and stifling monastic institutions won him the admiration, love and respect of many Tibetans. He is well remembered for introducing joy, humour and bewilderment to Buddhist narratives of liberation:

> Drukpa Kunley, the Master of Truth, himself said,
> 'If you think I have revealed any secrets, I apologize;
> If you think this is a medley of nonsense, enjoy it!'
> Such sentiments, here, I fully endorse.
>
> Dowman (1984: 35)

A brief overview of dominant trends in Tibetan Buddhism would not be complete without reference to the emergence of other minor orders like the Jonang and Bodong, which added fuel to sectarian tensions between monastic schools. This was especially true with the foundation of the Jonang school, which claimed one of the sharpest religious thinkers of fourteenth-century Tibet and one of the most controversial Buddhist scholars the tradition has ever known. Versed in a wide range of Buddhist subjects, Dolpopa Sherab Gyaltsën (1292–1362), the 'Buddha of Dol-po', is best known for his controversial and stunning contributions to the philosophical interpretation of emptiness. Architect of the Zhen-tong (Tib. *gzhan-stong*; other emptiness) view he sought to reconcile the Yogācāra-linked notion of an enlightened essence, or Buddha-nature, present in every living being with the Madhyamaka position on the lack of an enduring substance. In what may be characterized as a Yogācāra–Madhyamaka philosophical synthesis, Dolpopa boldly reformulated 'Buddha-nature' as being *zhen-tong*, that is, 'empty of other relative phenomena' but not empty in 'itself'.

Sectarian tensions leading to the persecution of the Jonang views during the reign of the fifth Dalai Lama, eventually inspired the formation of an ecumenical movement in Eastern Tibet known as Ri-me (Tib. *ri-med*; without boundaries), dedicated to the appreciation, preservation and synthesis of all Tibetan Buddhist traditions. Jamgon Kongtrul (1813–99) is credited with a number of literary works that contributed to this nineteenth-century cultural renaissance. His earliest manifesto of non-sectarian views is found in an encyclopaedic treatise, *Encompassing all Knowledge* (*Shes bya kun khyab*), a masterful work that competes in erudition with some other ninety volumes of writings, classified in four extant treasuries.

VAJRAYĀNA ANATOMIES OF ENLIGHTENMENT

There are literally thousands of Vajrayāna texts and commentaries, which fill the libraries of Tibetan Buddhist monasteries. The subject-matter of these works varies widely and is perplexing to the uninitiated, as it may encompass complex deity and *maṇḍala* visualizations, alongside intricate descriptions of an internal subtle-body anatomy. Drawing on the more creative recesses of the human mind, Vajrayāna techniques aim at transforming relative reality by harnessing an underlying power of the mind. This can be utilized either for attaining the ultimate goal of 'Tantric enlightenment' or towards the ritual manipulation of the ephemeral, as seen in many practical manuals of this genre.

There are different classification schemes for a wealth of esoteric scriptures. The Nyingma employ a nine-vehicle system, with the *Tantras* occupying the lower vehicles of *Kriyāyoga*, *Upayoga*, and *Yoga*, or the higher or inner *Tantras*, designated as the *Mahāyoga*, *Anuyoga* and *Atiyoga* classes. The highest of them, *Atiyoga*, encompasses the teachings of *Dzogchen*, further divided into those meditation instructions belonging to the Mind-class (*Sem-de*), Space-class (*Long-de*) and the class of Pith Instructions (*Menang-de*). The new schools employ the divisions of *Kriyāyoga*, *Caryāyoga*, *Yoga*, and *Anuttarayoga* to classify their large collections of Vajrayāna scriptures. Most of the ritual practices of these schools involve training in the *Anuttarayoga*, or *Highest Yoga Tantras* which are further divided, according to content and view, into Mother, Father and Non-Dual *Tantras*.

Although there are differences in theory and practice between large Vajrayāna cycles, like the *Guhyasamāja* and the *Kālacakra* for example, they all contain esoteric instructions on how to perform *yoga*, literally a union, with the main Buddhist deity of the cycle. The term often used for this core Vajrayāna practice is 'deity-yoga'. These are considered advanced meditation techniques and there are preliminary practices, the *Ngöndro*, to be completed before one enters properly the path of deity-yoga. The aim of the *Ngöndro* is to stabilize the practitioner's body, speech and mind by completing a set of each one hundred-thousand prostrations, Vajrasattva mantras, *maṇḍala* offerings, and guru yoga. These may take a minimum of one year of committed practice, after which the mind of the practitioner is prepared to hear and train in the most esoteric teachings of the *Highest Yoga Tantras*.

Going for refuge to the Three Jewels (Buddha, *Dharma*, *Saṅgha*) is common to all Buddhist traditions, but for a Vajrayāna trainee the place of refuge is also understood as the *Three Roots* of Tantric practice. These are:

1 invoking the guidance and blessings of the Lama (teacher) who is equal in all respects to the Buddha
2 supplicating the *Yidam* (deity) whose meditation is supreme of the *Dharmas* and
3 looking for direction and support in the community of the *Kandro ḍākinīs* (sky-goers).

The first root, the Lama (Skt. *Guru*), is of paramount importance to the practice of the Vajarayāna. Without granting an oral transmission of the Tantric scriptures, empowerment/initiation into work with the Vajrayāna deities and oral instructions on how to perform the appropriate *sādhana* (liturgical text for Tantric meditation), one should not commence, nor could one succeed in Tantric training.

As far as the effectiveness of Tantric meditations is concerned, no distinction is made in terms of gender, although women are considered physically better predisposed for success in the practice. Unlike *sūtra*-type meditations, which do not require the permission of a Lama, no Tantric meditation can be practised without the permission of a qualified Vajra teacher. There are many religious texts which discuss in detail the ideal attributes that teachers and disciples must have and how they should check for these in each other.

Indispensable to most Tantric meditations is the correct physical position, known as the seven-point posture of Vairocana. Some techniques may require the practitioner to emulate the form of the deity (Buddha) one is invoking, which may include visualizing or enacting a specific hand gesture, or *mudrā*, a physical register of an enlightened aspect or attribute. Physical gestures and postures are also ritually enacted in offering ceremonies and during Vajrayāna recitations. The use of mantras (mystic formulae) may be seen as ritual appropriations of the deity's speech. Each Buddha of the Vajrayāna pantheon has its own unique mantra. Oral recitation of the mantra of the appropriate chosen deity (*yidam*) is common during the Development stage (Tib. *bskyed rim*). This is the first section of deity-yoga practice, where one is

Figure 8.3 **Counting mantras with a rosary in Lhasa; rosaries usually have 108 beads**

instructed to contemplate: all beings in the form of female or male Buddhas (*yidam*) and the world as their Buddha-fields (pure-lands), all sounds as transmissions of enlightened voice and all thoughts as reflections of the wisdom-minds of deities.

During the second stage of deity-yoga, known as the Perfection stage (Tib. *rdzogs* rim), training is reserved for recognizing the nature of mind as the union of bliss, clarity and freedom from conceptual elaborations. This stage of deity-yoga often involves studying the physiognomy of the subtle-body, the *vajra-body* comprised of conduits, nodes, movement and vital essences, or drops. The physical posture prescribed in Tibetan meditations corresponds to theories of subtle-body anatomy. According to these, located inside the physical body is a subtle-body. This possesses three main channels (left, central, right), five main energy nodes intersecting with the central channel (cakras); wind (Tib. *rlung*) moving through the main channels and 72,000 smaller conduits as well as white and red vital drops (Skt. *bindu*), located at different parts of the body.

According to Vajrayāna theory most sentient beings possess a subtle-body with more or less the same constituents. The difference between an ordinary being and a realized master is that for the first, impure karmic winds circulate in his subtle-body reflecting impure mental states, while for a liberated being, wisdom-energy flows without restriction and the blocked nodes are released of their primordial bondage. Here wisdom-energy may be understood as the outcome of the transmutation of the five poisons of ignorance, anger, pride, passion and envy into the corresponding wisdoms of five Buddha families. These are:

1   Buddha Vairocana's wisdom of spaciousness
2   Akṣobya's mirror-like clarity and precision
3   Ratnasambhava's generosity
4   Amitābha's discriminating awareness
5   Amoghasiddhi's all-accomplishing action without struggle.

Vajrayāna meditative theory and practice is complex and requires many years of study and training. Tibetan Buddhist scholars from all schools have written many important commentaries and treatises on the subject and the Tibetan *Treasure* literature abounds with new and reformulated Tantric lineage-based meditations. A well-known Vajrayāna text of the *Treasure* genre is the *Tibetan Book of the Dead* (*Bardo Thodol*); said to have been written in the eighth century and hidden thereafter to be rediscovered some four hundred years later by treasure-discoverer Karma Lingpa. It has been translated into many Western languages and given rise to many scholarly discussions and cross-cultural interpretations, praised in particular by Carl Jung for its unique psychological insights.

The subject of death had been an important meditation topic for early Buddhists (see Chapter 4) and there is no shortage of theoretical discussions and ritual manuals dealing with it in Tibet. The ritual performance of *phowa*, a Vajrayāna mind-transference technique to be performed at death, is an important ceremony led by specialized Lamas on behalf of the departing. One of the best known of the *Six Yogas* of Naropa, *phowa* is practised by monks and lay practitioners of all Buddhist schools in Tibet. The Nyingma school claims an even earlier lineage traceable to its founder Padmasambhava. Buddhist narratives and examples of the impermanence of life are not confined to the monastic curriculum. They are witnessed in Tibetan sky-burial grounds as the corpse is dismembered and fed to the vultures, and can be read in less gruesome accounts of Tibetan lay people with near-death experiences becoming Buddhist preachers, the Delog or the ones who 'passed over and returned' (Tib. *'das log*).

THE 'STANDING BLADE OF GRASS': A TIBETAN PRACTICE

Across Buddhist countries, the performance of after-death rituals is of paramount importance. The main purpose of such rites is not just to dispose of the corpse, but to secure for the deceased auspicious rebirths or liberation from the cycle of *saṃsāra*. The technique of transferring one's consciousness at the time of death (*phowa*) is well known. It is performed by Buddhist masters for the deceased, as well as by lay practitioners instructed by a teacher on the subtle visualizations and instructions of the *phowa sādhana*. According to the Vajrayāna tradition, one must first receive the oral transmission (*lung*), empowerment (*dbang*) and instructions (*khrid*) from a qualified master. The process and instructions for subtle-body visualizations are given orally. Their success is said to be dependent upon the blessings of the teacher and so they are usually not recorded.

The technique of mind-transference, or 'enlightenment without meditation', can be applied with the objective of taking birth in a Buddha-field of one's choice. To the best of our knowledge, it was recorded for the first time in the fourteenth-century Tibetan text, *The Standing Blade of Grass* (*'Pho ba 'Jag tshugs ma*). Said to have been entrusted to non-human beings (*Nāgas*) by its author, Padmasambhava, it was destined to be rediscovered, centuries later, by the treasure-revealer, Nyida Sangye:

> The extraordinary phowa lineage of the 'Standing Blade of
> Grass' is very precious for it goes back to the eighth century
> and Padmasambhava in Tibet. According to the history, when
> Padmasambhava was residing at the Chimpu caves near Samye
> monastery, one of the Tibetan king's ministers, called Nyima,
> experienced an unexpected tragedy. While moving between houses
> he accidentally caused a fire that burned his house to ashes, killing
> both of his parents, thirteen people and all his livestock. The minister
> remained inconsolable. The Tibetan King, desiring to see an end
> to his suffering, went to Chimpu to beseech the help of Master
> Padmasambhava. Out of compassion for his plea, Padmasambhava
> travelled through magical means to Sukhāvatī to request the aid
> of Buddha Amitābha. Amitābha granted to Padmasambhava the

teachings of mind-transference, instructing him to pass them to minister Nyima as a single-lineage (one master to one disciple). Not long after receiving Amitābha's instructions, minister Nyima renounced all worldly activities and dedicated himself to their practice. After death, his physical body dissolved into light and he attained the rainbow body, displaying that he had successfully accomplished the transfer to Amitābha's pure-land.

The 'Standing Blade of Grass', named after the kusa-grass traditionally used to test the aperture at the fontanel, stands at the core of a major festival, the Great Drikung Phowa, traditionally held in Central Tibet once in twelve years. The lineage of this text and its practices is kept alive by the Drikung Kagyu order in India. It is transmitted and taught annually to Tibetans and Westerners in Bodh Gayā (Bihar) by foremost *phowa* master, K.C. Ayang Rinpoche (1942–).

Technical accounts of the dying process can be found in the *Highest Yoga Tantras*, where descriptions abound on how to transform the processes of 'dying' and 'what lies beyond' into Buddhahood. This is accomplished through a series of *yogas* that are modelled on the processes of death, the intermediate state and rebirth. Through practice, the *yogi* eventually attains control over them and is no longer subjected in the usual way to dying. Tantric descriptions of these techniques are based on subtle-body theory of the winds said to serve as bases of consciousness during life and dissolving in sequential stages during death. In an eighteenth-century Gelug treatise of the *Guhyasamāja* cycle, we read that in the eighth dissolution of consciousness, the last phase of the dying process:

T]he white and red indestructible drops dissolve [respectively] into the white and red indestructible drops [at the heart], and all the winds inside the central channel dissolve into the very subtle life-bearing wind. Through this, the very subtle wind and mind that have existed in the ordinary state from the beginning [in a non-manifest state] are made manifest, whereby such an appearance dawns... This is called the 'clear light of death' and 'the all-empty'... It is actual death.

(Lati Rinbochay 1985: 45)

Figure 8.4 **Tibetan prayer wheels**

Just as Buddhist teachings in Tibet may be classified according to the *sūtras* and the *Tantras*, the latter requiring, as we have seen, a distinct course of training, meditations can be divided into two types. Both of these require extensive familiarization with a large body of theory and practice. In short, there are meditations that employ a cognitive or physical object (deity, *mudrā*, mantra, breath, etc.) and there are those without an object. Non-dual meditations, which do not employ a reference point (meditator, meditation and object), belong to the highest teachings of the Tibetan Buddhist tradition. For the new schools these meditative traditions are styled under the heading of *Mahāmudrā* and for the Nyingma under *Dzogchen*. These teachings may appear less complicated than some of the Vajrayāna practices we have examined so far, but in fact presuppose an unmistakeable recognition of the 'nature of mind' as pointed out by a qualified Buddhist master to his disciple. As to the essence of *Mahāmudrā* practice, Kyemé Zhang Rinpoche offers the following condensed points of instruction:

> Do not withdraw your consciousness, but let it go free.
> Do not crave anything, but rest in openness.
> Do not focus on an object, but rest in openness.
> Do not engage in many tasks, but rest in being present.

Without trying to direct the mind,
Let it be without ground, like the intervening space.
Without thinking of the past, future, or present,
Let your consciousness be fresh.

Chagmé (2000: 146)

There are many similarities between the philosophy of *Dzogchen* and *Mahāmudrā*, especially in their emphasis on the pointing-out instructions by a qualified master and the yoga of non-meditation. In terms of the result, or the fruition of practice, however, *Dzogchen* is alone in claiming as its highest achievement the attainment of the rainbow body. This is a form of manifest enlightenment, explained as the dissolution of the physical body at death into light.

THE WESTERN REDISCOVERY OF TIBETAN BUDDHISM

One of the most striking features of Tibetan Buddhism is the system of monastic and spiritual succession based upon reincarnation. According to Buddhist doctrine, each being's mind-stream, as if flows from life to life, finds itself in innumerable embodiments, at times as a god, demi-god, animal, human, hungry ghost, or as a being suffering in hell. The wheel of compulsive incarnations and their accompanied sufferings are distinguishing features of *saṃsāra* and liberation from them has been the *summum bonum* of Buddhist practice. With the advent of Mahāyāna, however, the conception of what it means to be a Buddhist shifted from aiming at one's personal liberation – a goal viewed to contain a tint of self-interest – to aiming at completing an impossible task: the liberation of all beings. This missionary task entailed for Bodhisattvas to keep incarnating repeatedly and willingly endure the anguish of this world to reach enlightenment together with all existing forms of sentience. The implication of this doctrine had a profound effect on the religious and political landscape of Tibet and became a unique feature of Buddhism in Tibetan society.

The first recorded incident of a self-pronounced incarnation is said to have occurred in the monastic compounds of the Kagyu School in the early parts of the eleventh century. Düsum Khyenpa (1110–93), the first Karmapa, is said to have disclosed to his foremost disciple Drogon Rechen, before he died, details of the place where his next incarnation could be found. Furthermore, he declared that in the future there will be many Karmapas and even that there were other incarnations of him in existence. His prophesy

TĀRĀ

Originally an Indian deity, the goddess Tārā is said to have entered Tibet during imperial times and her worship has continued ever since. As an object of popular veneration she is the only other deity in Tibetan Buddhism to match the Bodhisattva of compassion, Avalokiteśvara. There are numerous meditations, ritual practices and visualizations associated with her and, on a more pragmatic level, she is celebrated for being swift in answering prayers due to her immeasurable compassion in assisting all in need. As the personification of the wisdom of all Buddhas and Bodhisattvas she has many iconographic representations. She is most commonly worshipped through the Praises to the Twenty-one Tārās. Her manifold aspects include:

* White Pacifying Tārā, offering protection from adversity, and attack from physical and immaterial beings
* Bhagavati Vajra Tārā, who protects against harm from the earth, including earthquakes and avalanches, as well as inner sickness and evil influence caused by pride
* Red Tārā who protects against harm from water
* Tārā who protects against harm from fire
* Tārā who protects against harm from wind in the outside world, hurricane, and storms caused by evil spirits
* Yellow Tārā of Enrichment, who increases all kinds of prosperity and wealth in the world.

Other manifestations are associated with intelligence, eloquence and so forth. Her mantra is *oṃ tāre tuttāre, tuttāre ture svahā!*

was fulfilled and spiritual-succession through a system of incarnations was established in the Kagyu school. Soon after, other Tibetan Buddhist schools adopted the system, giving rise to many returning-bodhisattvas occupying high seats in monastic institutions and enriching Buddhism by perpetuating their own spiritual lineages.

In the wake of the Tibetan diaspora after the Chinese invasion in 1950s, Tibet and its unique Buddhist heritage became known in the West. This was due in part to the charismatic leadership of the fourteenth Dalai Lama and learned representatives of other Buddhist schools. Most of the religious leaders of the four Tibetan Buddhist schools reside in exile in India where they have established monasteries, a dim glow compared with the thriving Buddhist monasticism in Tibet prior to the Chinese take-over. The future of many Tibetan Buddhist lineages remains uncertain. The support shown by some Western and Eastern countries for their plight as refugees and for the preservation of Tibet's endangered cultural heritage has raised many poignant ethical questions and stirred international discussions on how to combine democratic principles, human rights and commercial interests in dealings between powerful nations and minority cultures.

The encounter of Tibetan Buddhism with the West has been fruitful and enriching, as indicated by the increasing numbers of Westerners adhering to Tibetan Buddhism and new dharma centres opening in Europe, Australia and America. When examining the symbiotic relationship between the two, critics have rightly pointed to the dangers of Orientalism, or 'exoticization of the other' at the detriment of seeing, let alone understanding Tibetan Buddhists as a people whose rich history and culture is not reducible to the spiritual accomplishments of a few. We should bear in mind that clerical Buddhism, for all its inspiring scholastic and meditative traditions, is not exactly represented in lay Buddhism. Here, illiteracy or the lack of time to read and study the scriptures has yielded more popular varieties of Tibetan worship, such as: spinning mani-wheels, reciting mantras, making offerings, circumambulating *stūpas* and holy objects, going for pilgrimage to sacred places and so forth.

The engagement of Tibetan Buddhism with the cultural fabric of the West is most striking in a young generation of Tulkus, or reincarnating Tibetan Lamas being reborn in the West. It begs the question, whether some of these recognized incarnations of past Tibetan teachers – who have been raised in the West and are without traditional monastic education – may be considered authentic representatives of the Tibetan Buddhist tradition. Detached from the lay and state support that Buddhism once enjoyed in Tibet, the future of Tibetan monasticism in exile is precarious and it remains to be seen when distinct meditative lineages and orders of Tibetan Buddhism will develop within a Western context.

THE BÖN

Any exposition of Tibet's meditation traditions is incomplete without reference to the Bön. The Bön is Tibet's oldest spiritual tradition and predates the advent of Buddhism. Unlike Tibetan Buddhist schools that trace the origins of their traditions to India, Bön monastic and lay lineages hold Tönpa Shenrab to be the enlightened founder of their religion. He is said to have been born in the mysterious land of Olmo Lung Ring, identified as Tazig (Persia), in the West. Because of its spiritual sanctity it was also said to be transcendent and eternal, accessible only through an arrow-path, a great tunnel created by Shenrab shooting an arrow on his way to Tibet. For some scholars, Olmo Lung Ring is to be found in western Tibet, around Mountain Kailash, the holiest site of present-day Bön and once under the jurisdiction of the great kingdom of Zhang Zhung.

With the official adoption of Buddhism in Tibet, court Bön was discouraged, faced persecution and eventually went underground. Experts are still trying to piece together information about the royal priestly class of the early period. The Bön that emerged with the foundation of monasteries from the eleventh century onwards shares so much with the Buddhists, in terms of monastic structures, meditative practices and types of scriptures, that they are almost indistinguishable from each other. This is not to say that they are the same, a claim that neither party would be willing to make. Where these two similar, but rival, traditions clearly differ is in their remembrance of history and telling of their sacred origins. Whether the Bön can be rightly called a heterodox form of Buddhism depends on whether we accept the traditional claim that religious systems are based on lineages – and not on texts. Despite the fact that both schools share the same soteriological and ethical goal, enlightenment or release from *saṃsāra*, the Bön continued to suffer persecution up until the seventeenth-century, if not for their non-Buddhist origins, at least for their resistance to the fifth Dalai Lama's envisioned pan-Tibetan sovereignty.

The doctrines taught by Tönpa Shenrab and a rich tradition of commentaries can be found in the Bön canon, containing nowadays some 300 volumes of ritual and meditation texts including works on arts and crafts, logic, medicine, astrology, divination, cosmogony, poetry and so forth. This enormous collection of knowledge is classified either as the *Four Bön Portals and the Treasury as the Fifth* or the *Nine Vehicles of Bön*. Resembling numerically the Nyingma system of classification, the *Nine Vehicles of Bön* contain:

1   The *Vehicle of Prediction*, dealing with divination, astrology, ritual and medical prognostication
2   The *Vehicle of the Visual World*, explaining how to placate gods and demons of this world

3 The *Vehicle of Illusion*, which gives details of the rites for dispersing adverse forces through the use of *Tantras*

4 The *Vehicle of Existence*, which explains funeral and death rituals for the salvation of beings in the state between lives, the *bar-do*

5 The *Vehicle of a Lay Follower*, providing instructions for practising the ten virtues and the ten perfections

6 The *Vehicle of a Monk*, where rules and regulations for monastic asceticism are laid out

7 The *Vehicle of Primordial Sound*, which explains the transformation of the practitioner in a *maṇḍala* of Tantric enlightenment

8 The *Vehicle of Primordial Shen*, which explains the need for a suitable master, a suitable partner, and a suitable site, among other things

9 The *Vehicle of the Unsurpassable Doctrine*, which is dedicated to the doctrines and practices of the Great Perfection, *Dzogchen*.

The Bön schools of Tibet suffered more or less the same fate as the Buddhists in the aftermath of Chinese aggression and had to re-establish themselves in India and Nepal. They also propagate their teachings in Europe and the US, where several Bön centres exist. Old rivalries have been put aside, and they have received open support from the fourteenth Dalai Lama, who has stressed the importance of preserving the Bön tradition, as representing the indigenous source of Tibetan culture, in addition to acknowledging the major role it has had in shaping Tibetan Buddhism's unique identity.

TIMELINES

c.5th century Reign of Latotori Nyentsen, twenty-eighth king of the Dynasty; first recorded introduction of Buddhist scriptures and religious objects to Tibet.

c.622–49 Reign of King Srongtsen Gampo and expansion of the Tibetan empire; official introduction of Buddhism to Tibet and construction of the first Buddhist temples in Lhasa, Jokhang and Ramoche.

754–97 Reign of King Trisong Detsen and inauguration of Buddhism as the state-religion; foundation of first Tibetan Buddhist monastery, Samye, and ordination of the first seven Buddhist monks. Persecution of the Bön.

763 Tibetan empire extends to the capital of China, Ch'ang-an.

792	Sino-Indian Buddhist debate in Samye over spontaneous vs. gradual enlightenment.
c.800	Reign of King Trisong Tsen; prohibition of translating Tantric teachings and revision of all Buddhist texts in Tibetan translation.
c.838–42	Reign of King Langdarma; persecution of Buddhist monastic establishments resulting in the decline of Buddhism in Central Tibet and the fragmentation of the Tibetan empire.
970	King of Western Tibet, Lama Yeshe Ö, patron of Buddhism during the second dissemination of dharma to Tibet.
1012–96	Life and works of Marpa; first Tibetan lineage teacher of the Kagyu school.
1040–1123	Life and works of *mahāsiddha* Milarepa.
1042	Arrival of Atisha to Tibet, well-known Indian master from Bengal.
1056	Foundation of Reting monastery by Dromton, Atisha's main disciple; origins of the Kadampa school.
1073	Foundation of Sakya monastery by Könchok Gyalpo.
1182–1251	Life and works of Sakya Pandita, major scholar of the Sakya school.
1290–1364	Life and works of Buton, compiler of the Tibetan Buddhist canon.
1357–1419	Life and works of Tsongkapa; founder of the Gelupka school.
1617–82	Life and works of the fifth Dalai Lama; consolidation of the Tibetan empire.
1912	The thirteenthth Dalai Lama declares the independence of Tibet from China.
1935	Birth of the fourteenth Dalai Lama, current spiritual leader of Tibet.
1950	Chinese People's Liberation Army invades Tibet.
1959	The fourteenth Dalai Lama seeks political asylum in India; formation of the Tibetan Government in exile.
1989	The Nobel Peace Prize is awarded to the fourteenth Dalai Lama for his campaign against violence and support of peaceful resolutions to the contested status of Tibet.
2000	The seventeenth Karmapa, Ogyen Thinley Dorje, flees Chinese occupied Tibet and seeks asylum in India.

FURTHER READING

Batchelor, S. (1979) *The Guide to the Bodhisattva's Way of Life. Translation from Tibetan*, Dharamsala: Library of Tibetan Works and Archives.

Chagmé, K., Wallace, B.A. trans. (2000) *Naked Awareness: Practical Instructions on the Union of Mahamudra and Dzogchen*, Ithaca: Snow Lion.

Chang, C. trans. (1977) *The Hundred Thousand Songs of Milarepa*, London: Shambala.

Dalai Lama XIV, Jinpa, T. trans. (1995) *The World of Tibetan Buddhism: An Overview of Its Philosophy and Practice*, Ithaca: Snow Lion.

Dowman, K. (1984) *Sky Dancer: The Secret Life and Songs of the Lady Yeshe Tsogyel*, Boston: Routledge & Kegan Paul.

Eimer, H. and Germano, D. (2002) *The Many Canons of Tibetan Buddhism*, Leiden: Brill.

Hopkins, J. (1983) *Meditation on Emptiness*. London: Wisdom.

Jinpa, T., and Elsner, J. trans., 14th Dalai Lama foreword (2000) *Songs of Spiritual Experience: Tibetan Buddhist Poems of Insight and Awakening*, Boston/London: Shambala.

Karmay, S. (1972) *The Treasury of Good Sayings: A Tibetan History of Bon*, Oxford: OUP.

Lati Rinbochay and Hopkins, J. commentary and trans., 14th Dalai Lama foreword, Napper, E. ed. (1985) *Death, Intermediate State, and Rebirth in Tibetan Buddhism*, Ithaca: Snow Lion.

Lhalungpa, L. (1977) *The Life of Milarepa: a New Translation from Tibetan*, New York: Dutton.

Lopez, D. (1997) *Religions of Tibet in Practice*, Princeton: Princeton University Press.

Lopez, D. (1999) *Prisoners of Shangri-la: Tibetan Buddhism and the West*, Chicago: Chicago University Press.

Mackenzie, V. (1995) *Reborn in the West: the Reincarnation Masters*, London: Bloomsbury.

Powers, J. (1995) *Introduction to Tibetan Buddhism*, Ithaca: Snow Lion.

Roerich, G. (1976) *The Blue Annals*, Delhi: Motilal Banarsidass.

Samuel, G. (1993) *Civilized Shamans: Buddhism in Tibetan Societies*, Washington DC: Smithsonian Institution Press.

Shaw, M. (1994) *Passionate Enlightenment: Women in Tantric Buddhism*, Princeton: Princeton University Press.

Snellgrove, D. (1987) *Indo-Tibetan Buddhism: Indian Buddhists and their Tibetan Successors*, London: Serindia.

Sogyal Rinpoche (1992) *The Tibetan Book of Living and Dying*, London: Rider.

Thubten Yeshe, Lama. (2001) *Introduction to Tantra: the Transformation of Desire*, Boston: Wisdom.

Tsultrim A. (1984) *Women of Wisdom*, Boston: Routledge & Kegan Paul.

Tulku Thondup Rinpoche (1997) *Hidden Teachings of Tibet: An Explanation of the Terma Tradition of Tibet*, Boston: Wisdom.

Tulku Urgyen Rinpoche, et al. (2007) *Skillful Grace: Tara Practice for our Times, Kathmandu*: Rangjung Yeshe Publications.

WEBSITES

Tibetan and Himalayan Digital Library: http://www.thdl.org

Tibetan Buddhist Resource Centre: http://www.tbrc.org

Berzin Archives: http://www.berzinarchives.com/index.html

Tibetan Studies WWW Virtual Library: http://www.ciolek.com/WWWVL-TibetanStudies.html

Himalayan Art Resources: http://www.himalayānart.org

Meditation in China
Nine

If one's body is pervasive as space,
Abiding at rest, immovable, filling all directions,
One's actions will be beyond compare,
Unknowable to gods and men.

Avataṃsaka Sūtra (Thomas Cleary trans.)

BUDDHISM ENTERS CHINA

What has become known as the third great tradition of Buddhism developed in and around China in the first few hundred years of the first millennium. The earliest records we have for Buddhism in this region date from the first century CE. Traditionally, it was thought to reach the area first through the 'Silk Road', the arterial network of highways, roads and tracks that connect eastern parts of Asia to Central Asia, India and Europe. Early evidence, however, from Southeast Chinese shore regions, suggests that Buddhism may have come first via sea-faring mercantile routes. The Buddhists, unlike practitioners in other early Indian traditions, did not regard sea travel as polluting; several Jātaka stories describe the Bodhisattva as a sailor in earlier lives. The land route to India did, nonetheless, come to provide the main thoroughfare for influences to travel, cross-fertilize and develop, offering a means for the Chinese to learn from Indian texts and practitioners; art and early stories also betray the influence of Buddhist iconography.

From the outset, meditation seems to have been the most attractive feature of this new tradition. In 148 CE a Buddhist Parthian prince, An Shigao, arrived at the then Dao Han capital, introducing meditative techniques and initiating the first translations of Buddhist texts from Sanskrit through informal writing bureaux: a version of the breathing mindfulness sūtra from this time is the earliest Buddhist meditation text extant. This process continued with the more explicitly Mahāyāna focus of Lokakṣema, who imported texts relating, in particular, to the recollection of the Buddha and to the Pure-Land presided over by Buddha Amitābha: the Pratyutpanna-Sūtra was probably translated in 179 CE. A systematic attempt at translating Indian texts was undertaken by the famous pilgrim Faxian (338–422), who travelled to India to learn the full monastic rules (Vinaya), and described the Buddhist traditions he saw there. A Central Asian monk, Kumarajīva (344–413), was also responsible for the translation of many of the first scriptures to arrive in Chinese terrain. Later another monk, Xuanzang (596–664), instigated another wave of translation, introducing much of the by now more self-consciously discrete Mahāyāna *sūtrapiṭaka*, after an epic journey described in *Journey to the West*. He was subsequently mythologized in a sixteenth-century novel and features in many modern comic books, accompanied by a mythical stone 'monkey king' who comes to use supernatural power to support the pilgrim on his heroic journey. Although there was some Southern Buddhism influence in China, particularly in the northern areas, the predominant textual imports were largely those that had arisen in mainland India, though differentiation between various schools of Buddhism was in these centuries far more fluid than is now generally supposed. In India, until then, monastic rules had tended to be constant where doctrinal difference had not and, in the early centuries of Buddhist practice, were often retained from school to school where doctrinal and philosophical issues, and hence spiritual practice, may have been the cause of debate and divergences.

YOGALEHRBUCH

As Buddhism spread from India through Central Asia on the Silk Road, many variations on traditional meditative practices seem to have been developed, where Buddhist stories, practices and traditions travelled to China on the one hand and to Iran and Turkey on the other. A number of texts involving visualization are associated with the area around Kashmir and further out of India into Central Asia. These extracts are taken from fragments of a fifth-century meditation text, the *Yogalehrbuch*, as it is now called, found by the Buddhist caves at Kizil, Xinjiang province, in China, which gives some indication of the kind of material emerging during this period, often difficult to assign to any particular school. The whole text is structured around the forty meditation subjects described by Buddhaghosa. Even though sections are missing one can see it recounts, however, a very different type of practice from that described by Buddhaghosa within these categories, including elements of visualization that have come to be associated more with other forms of Buddhism. At this stage in history, there is considerable fluidity between the ideas and practices of the

Buddhist traditions. The style is more freely associative and less formal than subsequent practices associated with, for instance, the Tibetan schools. This extract describes the basic breathing mindfulness at the point of calming or concentrating the mind (11) to seeing cessation (16) (see Chapter 2).

Then the body of the practitioner of yoga appears shining like the moon's disc. An inner sea arises, and a second one outside. When the practitioner of yoga breathes in, the *citta* held fast to the inbreath plunges in the form of a young boy into the inner sea; when he breathes out, the *citta* held fast to the outbreath does the same within the outer sea – while concentrating the *citta*.

Finally he sees the young boy sunk in the inner sea, given over to the happiness of concentration. Thousands of torches fall into the inner sea; they burn brightly and hiss, and likewise in the outer sea. The young boy held fast to the inbreath sinks in the inner sea and the one linked to the outbreath does so in the outer one. Finally, the practitioner of yoga sees the boy as if surrounded by crystal shrine-halls. He has many hundreds of followers and is covered with pearls. Then the Lord, associated with mindfulness, arises, and ties a pale silk cloth around the practitioner's head.

Strings of pearls go out all around from his head; through the silk cloth and strings of pearls ... in a similar way appear countless world systems, filled with crystal shrine-halls, and inside these Lord Buddhas with many hundreds of followers. Similarly ... they envelop their followers and abide, while experiencing freedom (i.e. freeing the *citta*).

Then the inbreaths and outbreaths become covered with diamonds. The world crumbles into dust – at the vision of impermanence.

Then thirdly ... the inbreaths and outbreaths set the whole world on fire – at the vision of letting go.

Like a mass of foam it afflicts the whole world seething with these very flames – at the vision of dispassion.

> ... the body of the practitioner of yoga ... he sees the mass of foam crumbling and coming to peace, as if sprinkled with cool water – at the vision of cessation.
>
> At the time of emerging there arises a palace covered with pearls and the body of the yoga practitioner therein (is similarly covered) with pearls. The Lord ties a silken cloth around his head and says: 'Mindfulness of breathing should be practised in this way. If it is practised in this way, it is very complete.' Devas fill the whole sky and release a rain of flowers and jewels.
>
> This is the practice of breathing mindfulness for the present time.
>
> Extract from A. Lindop and L.S. Cousins (1998), unpublished trans. of Dieter Schlingoff (1964) *Ein Buddhistisches Yogalehrbuch*, Berlin.

The Buddhist emphasis on meditation and a spiritual life beyond the pragmatic, the secular and the familial, however, seemed strange to the Chinese. Since unification under the first emperor in 221 BCE, the Chinese governing classes had been primarily interested in the practical difficulties of defending and establishing comprehensive administrative, financial and legal systems to deal with vast populations of very diverse local interests. For the peasant classes, life was governed by harsh conditions and the long hours associated with farming: rice in the south and wheat in the north. The caprices of nature, in the form of flooding, irregular rainfall and crop failure, which could, at a stroke, threaten the livelihood of thousands of people, provided a constant threat to the wellbeing and survival of individual communities. Confucianism, with its careful emphasis on societal relationship and a highly nuanced arrangement of hierarchy, extended an appeal through all social classes by providing a way of accommodating conditions peculiar to areas of densely populated, close-knit communities, often separated by large masses of uninhabitable, barren land. Some basics of Buddhist organization were also culturally unfamiliar: almsgiving to a celibate monastic order, separated from their relatives, who did not pay taxes and brought no obvious material benefit to society, was not considered natural or desirable. Indians of all traditions perceived holy men as bringing merit to others by supporting their holy life but Chinese customs, however, demanded changes in this regard. From the outset, monks started to work more within lay communities and to participate in the social life regarded so highly by Chinese society; texts on filial piety were favoured. Attempts at assimilating Buddhism into a Confucian society started early. Sun Zhuo (c.300–80), for instance, a layman who wrote extensively on Buddhism and Confucianism, noted that Buddhism tended to focus on the inner while Confucianism focused on the outer. The good Chinese lay person could, he argued, espouse both philosophies within the area of activity where it was most appropriate. Despite continued Confucian opposition, such accommodation allowed Buddhist influence to grow over the early centuries of the first millennium, with its methods shaping and being themselves shaped by, in particular, another element of Chinese thought, Daoist religious and spiritual practice.

Although Laozi had lived centuries before, Daoism was emerging as a self-conscious tradition, with its own texts, around the same time as Buddhism entered China. Daoist respect for the powerful forces of the natural universe, skilled action in accordance with these, a sense of the power of the ineffable 'Way' and the limits of language in expressing that, had already started to percolate through all areas of Chinese life. Buddhist meditation became popular in the South, where Daoist techniques already involved close exploration of the breath and circulation of the subtle energies associated with the life force (qi). The practice of alchemy, and the search for the elixir vitae, whether literal or metaphoric, formed the basis of Daoist methods. The vocabulary of much of the first wave of Buddhist writing on meditation reflects this preoccupation in its choice of imagery and terminology, with, for instance, reference to internal 'cinnabar fields' sited in the head, the chest and just below the navel and a 'palace' at the heart. Buddhist meditative methods were soon assimilated into Daoist doctrinal understanding too, revitalizing it and perhaps contributing to its great success around the same time as Buddhism. The dynamic between Daoism and Buddhism in China is a long and complex dance, ranging from absorption of one another's key ideas, to wariness. In the long run, both seem to inject something new into the other, and the two are not always distinguishable. On a logistical level Daoism also embraced monasticism, and set up its own temples after the arrival of Buddhism: Laozi was considered as an emanation of the same principle of compassion as the Buddha. Until the twentieth century Chinese thought and custom was never far from Daoist: so throughout its history in China Buddhist doctrine has inevitably been shaped by the Daoist attitude to practice, language and the limits of verbal formulation.

From the fifth century, with the arrival of Kumarajīva in Chang in 401, one of the problems of absorbing Buddhist ideas into Chinese culture was perceived as a hermeneutical one, associated in part with these two indigenous traditions. The pragmatic Chinese wanted health, wealth, happiness and, in particular, a long life. Buddhists clearly did too, but Chinese as a language just did not have terms for the many subtle meditative states and philosophical Indian ideas that would introduce the Buddhist way of bringing these about. China was also developing its own richly various intellectual philosophies, which posed different questions and searched for different kinds of verbal formulation to express its doctrines. Any attempt at integration inevitably required some creative exploration and adjustment. Unlike the Tibetans, who systematized the translation of Indian texts with a uniform word-for-word terminology, Chinese interpreters and translators, working in special bureaux, developed their own different use of Indian terms. Sometimes 'misinterpreting' key notions into Chinese or, in a perhaps more likely scenario, consciously adapting them or recreating them to render them assimilable within a Chinese intellectual and linguistic framework, they produced new and creative ways of capturing the flavour of a text, an approach suggested by Kumarajīva. The verities of Chinese life were those that could be seen in the world. At death beings joined their ancestors: the idea of a different life after this body had gone was not familiar, nor, more subtly, was the notion of a discrete 'self' (ātman) or a 'suchness' of things that might need transcending. These core ideas, central to the formulation of Buddhism in an Indian setting, needed scrutiny, amplification and a new terminology. How is it possible to introduce the idea of saṃsāra, the endless wandering of existence, and its end, nirvāṇa, in a culture without a sense of continued rebirth? Was enlightenment a gradual process or an instantaneous one? What kind of language could express the ineffability of enlightenment? Could language indeed be effective at all to express the transient manifestations of any single moment? Such questions, although hinted at in Indian forms of Buddhism, initiated a fascinating and productive period of meditative and intellectual exploration, during which Chinese Buddhism emerged with its unique identity. In part as a consequence of this creative process, various philosophical schools emerged and flourished in China in the fifth and sixth centuries CE, with implications that affected day-to-day practice on a very basic level. During this period San-Lun (Three-treatise school), emerged as a Chinese form of the Madhyamaka; Faxiang that of Yogācāra.

Neither of these survived intact themselves, but were the precursors to four major schools of Chinese Buddhism: Tiantai, Huayan, Chan and Jingtu. All of these schools, influenced deeply by, and indeed influencing themselves, Chinese social values, philosophical assumptions and meditative interests, emerged over several centuries with identities quite distinct both from each other and from other forms of Buddhism. While many of its roots lie in teachings derived from itinerant teachers, texts and practices imported from India and Central Asia, Chinese meditative practice, growing in such a different environment to that of India, emerged as a quite distinct and highly varied phenomenon of its own.

TIANTAI

From the outset, Buddhism seems to have been introduced in China through individual wandering monks teaching meditation and theory, with key texts providing an underlying doctrinal basis for the adoption of specific techniques and practices. These waves of distinct teachings from differing schools of Buddhism must have proved a little confusing, or at any rate in need of some classification, as well as some assimilation into the pre-existing traditions associated with Daoism and Confucianism. In part a reflection of this need for systematization and in part, perhaps, a peculiarly Confucian way of accommodating diversity through hierarchical differentiation, the scriptures themselves came to be ordered according to a chronological sequence based upon what they thought were the stages of teaching within the Buddha's lifetime. Founded by a great creative synthesizer, Zhiyi (538–97), the Tiantai school developed a meditation method based on the Mahāyāna idea of emptiness. In the first stage, the meditator realizes, through calm, the emptiness in all things and all names, but does not have the wisdom to see the Buddha nature. In the second, through more developed wisdom, he sees the 'seeming' and the creation of all things, but now lacks the calm necessary to realize the Buddha nature. In the third stage he sees both emptiness and the seeming of things, and calm and wisdom come into balance. Zhiyi also systematized the various levels of Buddhist scriptures, following some earlier Indian guidelines, into a hierarchy according to their levels of truth. The Tiantai system of Panjiao classified Buddhist literature according to what they believed to be the historical periods of the Buddha's life, each offering a new form of Buddhist understanding. This kind of classification became one of the hallmarks of Chinese Buddhism.

HOW TIANTAI VIEWED THE BUDDHA'S LIFE

Panjiao: five stages of the Buddha's teaching

1 Huayan, attributed by them to the three weeks after the enlightenment.
2 A modification of this doctrine, adapted for the average person, said to be taught over the next twelve years.
3 Concepts such as the Bodhisattva, and elaborations of earlier teachings, supposedly taught in a third period.
4 Complex metaphysical ideas, formulated in the *Prajñāpāramitā* literature, taught in a fourth period, included the notion of non-duality, and that divisions were illusory and disappeared with insight. The *śūnyatā* doctrine of emptiness, which became so influential in China, was also believed to have characterized this period.
5 The *Lotus-Sūtra*, thought to have been taught in the final eight years of Buddha's life, was regarded as the summit of his teaching. It was termed the *Ekayāna* (one vehicle), a development from the idea of three *yānas* (see Chapters 7 and 8). It was supposed to offer the means to provide salvation from the wheel of suffering and rebirth for the entire human race.

While the Tiantai movement acknowledged that elements of all five teachings could be found at different stages, this hierarchical arrangement also governed an attitude towards text itself that was subsequently of great importance in China and Japan. The notion that any single *sūtra* represented the summation of the Buddha's teaching has continued to exercise an influence down to the present day, particularly in Japan. Tiantai influenced subsequent schools of Buddhism by providing a way of reconciling Chinese pragmatism with a sense of the numinous, and by describing the interpenetration of the spiritual with the material. So Tiantai did not devalue the visible world: rather it demonstrated that each activity, each being and each entity is imbued with significance. Zhantan (711–82), a later Tiantai leader, argued that even inanimate objects such as mountains and rivers possessed Buddha nature.

SACRED CALLIGRAPHY

This sort of thinking, alongside a sense of the primacy of a single text, has accompanied the idea that renderings of the teaching in physical form, through such means as ola leaf inscription, brush stroke calligraphy and, later, woodblock printing may itself not only serve to preserve Buddhism but can also be a means of bringing meditative calm and even insight into being. If there really is an interpenetration of the physical and the spiritual, then a perfectly executed text should bear the imprint of the mind of the practitioner upon its appearance. The Chinese loved writing: unified by a single script since the time of the first emperor, they found it natural to record *dharma* on paper, invented there in the second century CE. Emperors commissioned the copying of texts as a meritorious act and teachers encouraged their students to perform these tasks as an act of devotion. From the fourth century CE thousands of texts were lovingly reproduced, on mountain sides, caves, large *sūtra* pillars at crossroads, silk and paper, as the art of calligraphy emerged as a meditative discipline in itself. Art also reflected this interest: the depiction of Buddhas and Bodhisattvas became regarded as an auspicious activity, as did the translation of Buddhist principles into the act of painting itself. The robustness, spaciousness and flourish of Chinese art seems sometimes like an enactment of Chinese Buddhist principles in practice.

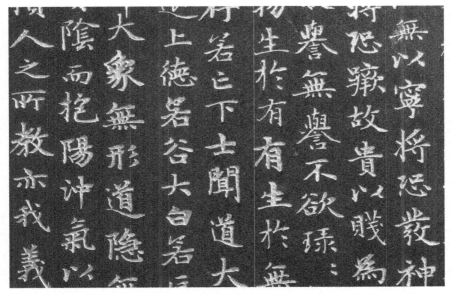

Figure 9.1 **Chinese gold calligraphy on a black background**

ZHIYI AND THE FOUR KINDS OF *SAMĀDHI*

Zhiyi studied under the meditation teacher Hui-ssu and is said to have attained enlightenment on Mount Ta-su. He left to teach and write on meditation in 568, before decamping in 576 to Mount Tiantai, where he founded his own school. Tiantai was characterized by a strict monastic discipline that placed great emphasis on community, co-operation, repentance practice and meditation. Zhiyi maintained that there were two kinds of meditative practice: one to be pursued in seclusion, in forests and mountains, the other to be pursued as part of daily life, as part of a community. The last part of his career was his most prolific, and in a series of manuals he sought to provide comprehensive advice for meditators in all Buddhist traditions. The system of four kinds of *samādhi* delineated here is of this kind, though it is tailored primarily to those in the Tiantai system of repentance practices and concentration methods. On his death bed, when asked by his disciples who should be their teacher, Zhiyi reminded them of the Buddha's dying words: that they should be a refuge to themselves, and that they should take the monastic rule and the teaching, in this case embodied in the four kinds of *samādhi*, as their spiritual guides.

1 Cultivating concentration through constant sitting. This arduous practice is to be performed in a bare secluded room, for ninety days, either alone or in a small group. With brief periods of respite for walking, eating, relieving himself, the meditator sits and does not sleep or lie down, or lean against a wall. He contemplates the *dharmadhātu*, the *dharma* body (*dharmakāya*) of the Buddha, or the attributes and visualization of a particular Buddha. If the meditator is inexperienced or tired, he entrusts his fate to a Buddha of his own choosing, chanting and offering up his shame to him. Eventually he perceives all Buddhas face to face, and ascends to become an advanced Bodhisattva. Details of this practice are no longer extant.

2 Cultivating *samādhi* through constant walking. This is associated with a practice called *pratyupanna-samādhi*, introduced from India, whereby the meditator finds himself standing with all Buddhas. The meditator makes extensive offerings, washes, puts on new robes and goes to a chamber for meditation. Whenever he enters this room he purifies himself. For a period of ninety days the meditator circumambulates a shrine to the Buddha Amitābha, ceasing only to eat and relieve himself. He is cared for by an attendant. The practice is a visualization of the thirty-two marks of

the Buddha in oneself, practised while walking backwards and forwards. This culminates in an investigation of the process of discernment in the mind itself, so that the meditator enters into the Pure-Land and stands face to face with all Buddhas, of all the directions, but also has direct experience of emptiness: 'As many stars as a person with clear sight can see on a clear night – that is how many Buddhas he sees!'

3   Cultivating *samādhi* through part walking and part sitting. This is also conducted under conditions of ritual purity in a secluded hall. The meditator makes a shrine with thrones for twenty-four patron deities, a mirror to dispel evil and a five-coloured cloth canopy above. Numerous banners, paintings, flowers, rare incense and fragrant broths are placed around to create a miniature Pure-Land. Up to ten people may be involved, who make offerings, circumambulate, prostrate themselves and sit, in turn. Walking and chanting is constantly mixed with sitting. A protective *dhāraṇī* is recited. The practitioner can take the ritual at any level: it works for the beginner as a first stage, or, for the experienced, as way of freeing the mind from defilement so that the *dharmadhātu*, the radiant mind beyond duality, is perceived. Through engagement with this constantly repeated ritual, the practitioner gradually sees the nature of the mind itself. Alternatively the practitioner can practise the Lotus *samādhi*, whereby recitation of the *Lotus-sūtra* is interspersed with chanting and repentance. These practices involve confessing errors, pleas to the Buddha to remain in the world, rejoicing in the merit of other beings, dedicating all merit to all sentient beings and making the Bodhisattva vow. No set time limits are given for walking, sitting or chanting and the practices are adjusted according to ability. The mind eventually becomes settled and enters *samādhi* in all activities.

4   Cultivating *samādhi* through neither walking nor sitting. This practice includes any practice not included in the other categories, but emphasis is placed on the repentance practice (Ching Kuan Yin practice).

ZHIYI ON CHANTING

Zhiyi describes the awakening power of the *dhāraṇī*, in the final stages of its use as a meditation:

> When [the practitioner] discerns the sound of the voice while he is reciting the spell, he finds that the sound cannot be apprehended. It is without substance, like an echo in an empty valley ... the merits of the wisdom

and *samādhi* that he has acquired are completely inexpressible. Once you have experienced awakening like this, you will know for yourself that your obstructions have been eliminated, and you will not [need to] wait for further discrimination [regarding this fact].

Stevenson (1986: 65)

As this short summary indicates, with the emergence of Tiantai, Chinese Buddhism had started to move in its own way. It absorbed many key ideas from Indian Buddhism, with the idea of emptiness and by the employment of some techniques also found in Southern Buddhism. With its use of walking practices, thirty-two marks visualization and the use of repetitive ritual as a means of allowing the mind to observe its own formations, as well as its new doctrinal understanding of meditative practice, it had begun to assert its own distinct nature, practices and interests.

HUAYAN

Another school, considered by some, if not all, as the most intellectually highly sophisticated of all Buddhist traditions, developed an epistemological teaching on the basis of the *Gaṇḍavyūha-Sūtra*, the *Avataṃsaka-Sutra* (*Hwayan Ching*), *The Flower Ornament Scripture*, and a translation of an Indian text known as *Satyasiddhi-Sastra*, by Harivarman (c.250–350 CE). The earliest text, written when boundaries between schools were less well defined, has been termed, perhaps rather as a distinction made after the event, Theravādin. It exhibits features, however, that seem to be associated with many other Buddhist traditions. The subsequent translations and new versions of the text incorporate notions, many of which were present in other schools, but which find creative fusion in the development of Huayan thought:

1 Emptiness: the concept of the emptiness (*śūnyatā*) of all things, that comes to be associated with the Mahāyāna.

2 The *Tathāgatagarbha*: the idea that there is an embryonic Buddha latent in all beings. Although this had featured in some schools of Buddhism since a third-century *sūtra* on the subject was composed in India, it was more comprehensively developed in China, where it became a key factor in arousing faith and motivation amongst practitioners of all levels of attainment.

3 The interpenetration of all phenomena: the notion of the *dharma* realm (*dharmadhātu*) of the radiant mind.

4   The idea that principle or the noumenal (C. li) and the phenomenal (C. shi) cannot be separated from one another. If everything reflects everything else, then any phenomenon embodies principle.
5   The realization of 'suchness', the inherent, concept-transcending nature of things.
6   The teaching of totality, whereby everything in the universe contains and reflects everything else.

The most famous exposition of Huayan philosophy was delivered to the Empress Wu in 699 CE, by Fazang. Brilliant though she was, she found Fazang's discourses difficult to understand. So, employing an image used in his 'Treatise on the Golden Lion', he constructed a hall of mirrors. On the ceiling, around the walls, on the floor and even in the four corners large mirrors were placed. Inviting the Empress to watch, he placed a torch and a Buddha image in the centre of the room, so that the whole hall was filled with infinite inter-reflections. Basing his work on the theory of emptiness, Fazang said that when one *dharma* arises, all others do too, and that each reflects and interpenetrates the others. 'Right here we see an example of one in all and all in one – the mystery of realms embracing realm ad infinitum is revealed ... These infinite reflections of different realms now simultaneously arise without the slightest effort; they just naturally do so in a perfectly harmonious way.' He then took out a small crystal ball and placed it in the centre too, to demonstrate the vast in the tiny, and the tiny in the vast, before explaining that the same principle operated through all times as well, and that the past, present and future are all reflected within one another.

After 845, with the persecution of Buddhism in China, the school did not fare well. Its teaching, however, continued in the Kegon school in Japan.

THE FLOWER ORNAMENT SCRIPTURE

The *Avataṃsaka-Sūtra* is held in high esteem by the Northern but, in particular, the Eastern schools of Buddhism. The date of its composition and its author are unknown, but it is thought to have been composed by several hands in India during the first and second centuries CE: at this and subsequent times many texts are attributed to Buddhas or enlightened beings communicating through revelation or vision. It is thought to have been translated into Chinese by Buddhabhadra around

420 CE, and by Kumarajīva. It was particularly popular in the Tang period (618–907). The Chinese versions, of which there are about thirty in the first centuries CE, become heterogeneous compendiums of Buddhist texts and practices, all unified by a wonderful extravagance of expression that generates vast eulogies and declamations in poetry and prose. Exuberantly discursive dialogues include lists of apparently limitless perfections and attributes, hyperbolic evocations of vast areas of space and time, and countless Buddhas, Buddha-fields, Bodhisattvas, and world-systems interpenetrating one another. The sense of intellectual search that characterized much of Huayan, however, permeates the discourses and the message of the text is enacted in its style. The listener or reader participates in the doctrine of mutual interpenetration through a kind of technicolour multi-dimensionality, where each part of the text does seem to mirror and reflect the others. No small extract can do justice to writing which seems designed to be recited in grand sweeps of several pages. This one is taken from a translation of one of the Chinese versions:

Chief in Goodness

If one's body is pervasive as space,
Abiding at rest, immovable, filling all directions,
One's actions will be beyond compare,
Unknowable to gods and men.
Enlightening beings practice acts of great compassion,
Vowing to liberate all successfully;
Those who see, hear, listen, accept and make offerings,
They cause all to attain peace and happiness.
Those great beings have magnificent spiritual powers;
Their eye of reality is always complete, without any lack;
The wonderful practices of virtuous ways and other such paths
Are supreme jewels they cause to appear.
Just like clusters of diamonds in the ocean,
By their mystic powers they produce many jewels;
Without decrease or increase, and inexhaustible;
Such is the mass of the enlightening beings' virtues...

> They enter concentration on one atom
> And accomplish concentration on all atoms,
> And yet that particle doesn't increase:
> In one are manifest inconceivable lands...
> What in one atom is manifest
> Is also manifest in all atoms;
> This is the mystic power of concentration and liberation
> Of these sages of great renown.
>
> Cleary (1993: 338–9)

CHAN AND PURE-LAND (JINGTU)

Who is reciting the Buddha's name?

Two other major schools emerged in China, whose teachings were to prove particularly effective in popularizing Chinese Buddhism. Indeed their methods to a certain extent transcended the notion of a school and have been found in many other Buddhist traditions to which they are only loosely aligned. Oddly resistant to all kinds of persecution, both these traditions and their offshoots in other Far Eastern countries have survived well into the twenty-first century, adapting and adopting different forms. These were Chan and the Pure-Land.

Chan

The word Chan, which gives the word Zen, is derived from the word jhāna/ dhyāna in Indian Buddhist literature, which denotes in Southern Buddhism a deep meditative state, where concentration (samādhi) is brought about through samatha/śamatha meditation. The school developed around the intuitive, visionary insights of Kāśyapa, a disciple of the historical Buddha, who was said to have received an inspirational transmission of his teachings, through his smile and gift of a flower at Vulture's Peak in India. A primarily teacher/pupil based tradition, it places very little emphasis on scriptures and doctrines. Transmission of the teaching is based on silence as much as speech, and the hallmark of this school has been the elliptic saying, gongan, and methods such as a clap or even a light blow with a stick at a particular point in the meditator's development. Bodhidharma, a sixth-century monk, is supposed to have introduced the tradition into China, linking it to contacts with Daoism. The leadership has sometimes been contested – one group, the Northern, argued for Shenxiu (606–706), who taught a gradual path to enlightenment and the other, the Southern, for Huineng (638–713), who taught the suddenness of the awakening experience (wu), stressing emptiness. Bazhang Huaihai (720–814) introduced rules geared to the Chinese lifestyle. Two schools emerged as a result of the cross-fertilization with Dao: Linji and Caodong. Chan's popularity increased during the Sung Dynasty (960–1269).

Bodhidharma was an itinerant monk from either Central Asia or India who introduced radical new Buddhist teachings to China. One biographer said that he was the twenty-sixth patriarch in a line of transmission going back to the Buddha. His teaching, marked by an emphasis on silence and the intuitive apprehension of truth, shaped the perception of how Buddhist meditation was undertaken and taught throughout China, Korea and Japan. Some credit him with inventing gongfu/kung fu, an unlikely attribution, which indicates, however, the popular association of Chinese monasticism with acrobatic and martial skill.

- A special transmission outside the scriptures
- No reliance on words or letters
- Direct pointing to the heart of humanity
- Seeing into one's own nature.

According to one account, Bodhidharma, after nine years in China, wished to go home and gathered his disciples around him to test their understanding. Dofuku said: 'For me, truth is beyond affirmation or negation, for this is the way it moves.' In reply Bodhidharma said: 'You have my skin.' A nun, Soji, said: 'To me, it is like Ānanda's sight of the Buddha-land – seen once and for ever.' Bodhidharma replied: 'You have my flesh.' Doiku said: 'The four elements of light, air, water and earth are empty and the five skandhas are No-things. In my opinion No-thing is reality.' Bodhidharma commented: 'You have my bones.' At last, another disciple, Eka, bowed before his teacher – and remained silent. Bodhidharma said: 'You have my marrow'.

Despite the apparently rebellious nature of some of its teachings, the Chan tradition represents a profound synthesis of Daoist, Confucian and Indian Buddhist traditions. Throughout all areas of Eastern Buddhism, the practice of Chan meditation pays particular attention to the area beneath the navel, called the Tantian. This term, derived from Daoist terminology, denotes the 'cinnabar field', one of the areas associated with alchemical practice. The maturation of the process of awakening is described as 'the long nurturing of the holy fetus', a reference to the idea of the alchemical process as the sustaining of a fetus of immortality, nurtured within the physical body through the containment of sexual energy, diet and meditation. To this day some practitioners within the many Chan schools that have arisen throughout Eastern Buddhism place particular attention on keeping the breath and the centre of gravity low within the body, to ensure the practice remains steady and grounded in a strong physical base.

GONGAN (J. KŌAN)

From the earliest days of Buddhism, meditators have recorded different hindrances and distractions besetting their minds. To those who have tried calming the mind with various practices, sleepiness is, from the earliest texts, often noted as a besetting problem, as is a lack of zest for investigation and search. This was perhaps the case for monks in the early days of the Chan tradition. Legends say that during the early part of the Tang period (618–907), when Chan was flourishing in China, some monks were enlivened in their practice by a number of electrifying teachers, who liked to ask absurd and sometimes violently inspired questions for them to think about. This disturbed their sense of peace to arouse a more challenging sense of doubt within the practice. This was not the corroding kind of doubt that demotivates or deadens, but an unsettling of views, for an often particularly advanced meditator, that required them to experience what came to be known in later centuries, in Japan, as the 'Great Doubt'. The stimulus of these questions and, sometimes, answers, varied from simply asking, 'Who is dragging this corpse around?' to the more disturbing answer to the question, 'What is a Buddha?' to which the reply was 'A dried shitstick!', a *gongan* that emerged in Japan in the twelfth century. In time this often repeated question, answer or oblique remark required the meditator to dissolve usual boundaries of self and object, and the relationship between knower and known.

From the 800s, despite the persecutions of 845, anthologies started to be collected of phrases, stories and anecdotes about great teachers, the product of a long process of development in the Chan movement during the later Tang period in China. They were called in Chinese *gongan* and in Japanese *kōan*, and feature prominently in all the subsequent Eastern forms of this school. They put an end to private understanding (*gong*) and were supposed to accord with what the Buddhas and patriarchs would say (*an*).

The intention of these was to cut through the entanglement of concepts and language to produce awakening. These 'public cases' – the term derives from a metaphor of a magistrate passing public judgement on a legal case – were insisted upon by some teachers as an extreme antidote to the threat of quietism of those who had become passive and escapist. Acting a bit like a kind of sharp seasoning to the meditation, such questions could not be called quite *samatha* or *vipassanā*. Rather, as in so many new formulations of Buddhist meditative principle, they seem to act sometimes as a catalyst for the fusion of the two, resulting in a sometimes sudden, momentary experience of awakening. From the earliest days of Indian Buddhism elders, both men and women, produced poems on attaining enlightenment, some of which seem remarkably like Chan formulations. There is a unique freshness about Chan meditative techniques and *gongans* however: the practitioner's argument would be that when enlightenment occurs the world seems arrestingly beautiful and different, a way of seeing particularly promoted within this Buddhist tradition.

The creativity of such expressions, though not at first intended as literary, was indicative of the vitality of Chan in China; such writings have contributed to the great popularity of the school in the West. Indeed it has long been a truism of Chan practice that this school of Buddhism has produced a far greater literature than any other in China. The circumstances of the events that lead to awakening provide a fund of constantly retold anecdotes and stories.

A CHAN STORY

Dahui decided to spend nine years with his teacher, and if that did not work he would give up. So he threw himself into intense struggle and was told to work on the *gong'an*, 'The East Mountain walks over the water'. He made forty-nine attempts to answer it, but was rebutted each time. On the thirteenth day of the fifth month in the year 1125, he experienced a breakthrough at last. He recalled the event in this way. His teacher ascended the seat for *dharma* and said, 'Once a monk asked Yun-men this question, "Where do all the Buddhas come from?" Yun-men answered. "The East Mountain walks over the water". But, the teacher said, I would have given a different answer to the question, "Where do all the Buddhas come from?":

"As the fragrant breeze comes from the south, a slight coolness naturally stirs in the palace pavilion."

When Dahui heard this, all of a sudden there was no more before and after. Time stopped, he ceased to feel any disturbance in the mind and remained in a state of complete calm. The first answer still implied a dichotomy between movement and rest. His teacher had stressed the unity of the two.

Abbreviated version of story in 'Ta-Hui Tsung-Kao and Kung-an Ch'an',
Yu (1979) '(*Dahui Zonggao* and *Gong-an Chan*)'

HUANG PO (?–849): A CHAN TEACHER

One of the most influential Chan teachers was Huang Po. Trained first in the Linji (J. *Rinzai*) tradition, he was called 'a tiger' by his own teacher, yet seems to have earned the love of the great crowds that came to listen to him. He argued that awakening was momentary, comparing it to the point at which water boils and changes state. The practitioner should not reject any phenomena: he sees their illusory nature, transcends duality but, at awakening, also perceives the fullness of the world as it is.

Many people are afraid to empty their minds lest they may plunge into the Void. They do not know that their own Mind is the void. The ignorant [seekers] eschew phenomena but not thought; the wise [seekers] eschew thought but not phenomena.
Blofeld (1994)

Walking is Chan, sitting is Chan
During speech, silence, action, and stillness, the essence is at peace
Yung Chia (665–713)
Buswell (1981: 192)

FAITH IN THE MIND: THE XINXINMING

This extended poem has been one of the most influential pieces of Chan writing. Previously wrongly attributed to the patriarch, Sengcan, it seems to have been written sometime during the Tang dynasty (618–917), and has assumed the status of a sacred text for Chan practitioners. Drawing on notions of emptiness that can be traced back to Nāgārjuna, it combines a Daoist understanding of living the 'Way' with notions of non-duality and transcendence:

Objects are objects because of the mind;
The mind is the mind because of objects
Understand the relationship between these two
And what is real: one emptiness

(paraphrase)

THE OX-HERDING PICTURES

Chan also seems to have been associated with other particularly popular and productive artistic expressions. One of the simplest and most effective ways of communicating Chan theory has been in Chinese, Korean and Japanese painting and poetry, with the Chan/Seon/Zen story of the ten stages of taming an ox. Depending on his audience, the Buddha often employed similes relating to well-trained creatures such as elephants, horses and other standard work animals of Indian domestic life. Ox-herding is also an ancient simile for meditation, dating from the earliest canonical texts. An early example of its use in China as a metaphor for practice can be found in a story from the Tang Dynasty (618–906). A monk was working in the monastery kitchen when his teacher came in and asked what he was doing. He replied, 'Nothing much, just herding the ox (the mind).' The teacher asked, 'How are you herding it?' The monk replied, 'Every time the ox wanders off to eat grass when he should be working, I rein him in and put him back to work.'

During the Sung Dynasty (960–1279) the stages of Chan practice were depicted, usually within temples and often accompanied by poems, comparing each stage of training the ox to one in the process of training the mind in the Chan method. Oxen had always formed an integral part of Chinese peasant life and the focus on this image is perhaps indicative of the cross-class appeal which Buddhism was starting to exert. The most famous of these were by K'uo-an Shih'yuan, a twelfth-century Chan master of the Linji school. The pictures demonstrate ten levels of Chan practice, culminating in the recognition of the Buddha nature. The ten vary, but the subject has continued historically to be a popular expression of Buddhist principle.

K'uo-an

1   In the first picture the ox-herd is shown, searching for the lost ox.
2   The ox-herd finds its tracks, giving hope that it has not been lost forever.

3 He catches sight of the ox.

4 He has caught the ox, but with the help of the bridle, the Chan training. This is like the strict discipline needed by a child in its early days.

5 The ox follows the ox-herd home voluntarily, without a bridle, but not in a careless way.

6 There is tranquillity and joy that reunion with the source of existence brings. The ox-herd rides joyfully playing his flute, in perfect harmony with his natural surroundings.

7 Having reached the point of no-return, the ox-herd realizes his identity with the ox, for he sees that it is his true self: his selfless nature. The illusion of selfish ego and individualism is finished, so allowing ego-lessness to shine forth unimpeded. Further pictures are different perspectives on the same experience.

8 A circle is drawn on the ground, symbolizing the all-encompassing emptiness that makes the ground of all things. The reality of the self and the ox are forgotten.

9 Flowers bloom and birds sing in the air. The fullness or emptiness, the 'suchness' of things as they are, is displayed. It is an affirmation after the negation or rejection of the world. When self and things, described in Yogācāra as temporary constructs, are forgotten or left behind, the true nature of things is revealed.

10 In the tenth picture the ox-herd enters the bustle of the market place, doing ordinary daily activities. The fully enlightened being does not retreat from the world, but comes back, sharing his experience and leading ordinary people to the way of the Buddha.

The last three pictures describe the life of a Buddha after his enlightenment.

This series has become one of the classical demonstrations of Chan practice.

Martial arts are also of interest in this regard. Space does not permit closer consideration of this subject, but the adoption of martial disciplines (gongfu) in the Shaolin temple in the seventh century, was perhaps a comparable development to, say, the gongan, in this case a response to pressing external events: military attacks from outside. While it is still unclear to what extent the monastic orders practised the arts, acrobatic and physical prowess are attributed to monks by early texts. Perhaps such disciplines also addressed a meditative need. Indian monastics, whose life often involved travel by foot, arduous almsrounds and conditions of 'sleeping rough', had no need for demanding physical exercise. Chinese monks, however, had very different circumstances and seem to have developing stimulating bodily, as well as intellectual, correctives for potential imbalances in the contemplative life.

ZEN AND THE WEST

At this point a few words should be said about the popularity of Chan (Zen) in the West. From its inception the traditions associated with Chan have, from distaste for excessive scriptural study, tended to describe themselves and been perceived as somewhat removed from other Buddhist traditions. A love of practical and immediate revelation, combined with its own tradition of free religious expression and a new espousal of moral relativism have been contributory factors in drawing many Americans to Chan in the twentieth century, popularized in waves such as the Beat movement in the 1950s. It should be remembered, however, that Chan emerged within an environment, as we have seen, steeped in subtle textual study, gradual meditative work and monastic discipline. Developed in part as a response to this, its apparent iconoclasm, which includes stories of teachers burning sacred texts, requires some appreciation and practice of forms for those forms to be transcended: their aim is non-attachment, not rejection. The deep learning and respect for discipline amongst those fully trained in Chan practice can sometimes surprise Westerners. We know from textual evidence that from the tenth century, and in all likelihood before, Chan monasteries often adhered to an austerely beautiful daily routine that included sitting meditation, chanting and prostrations. Indeed in modern monasteries a humbling sense of devotion is evident, despite, or perhaps as a necessary accompaniment to, the immediacy of a sometimes forceful 'anti-text' Chan approach. The tradition is only really appreciated by some sense of the conditions in which it has operated historically.

JINGTU (PURE-LAND)

What proved to be the most popular form of Buddhism in East Asia, Pure-Land, centred on devotion to the figure of Buddha Amitābha. Founded by Tanluan (476–542), it exercised a particular appeal to the laity for a number of reasons, most obviously for its promise of rebirth in Amitābha's Pure-Land or Western Paradise, where enlightenment was assured, accessible to anyone who called in good faith upon the name of the Buddha. This practice, known as *Nianfo*, a translation of *Buddhānusmṛti*, Buddha-recollection, was popular as a complement to the pre-existing folk belief of the continued presence of ancestors. Rebirth in a Pure-Land is like a very long-term heavenly sojourn, though those present in these heavenly paradises are said to be committed to helping less fortunate beings in the realm of the humans.

Although there are 290 Chinese translated scriptures in the Chinese canon that also discuss Amitābha and his realms, the core texts are the smaller and larger *Sukhāvatī-vyūha-Sūtras* (*The Magnificent Display of the Happy Land*) and the *Amityāyur-buddhānusmṛti-Sūtra*. All of these texts display affinities with the descriptions of the cities of Universal Monarchs and the great heaven realms described in early Buddhism. The latter is certainly designed as a graduated visualization exercise. These arouse an imaginary world in which the practitioner can sense an almost immanent presence of a realm with a blissful freedom from physical pain, worry about events of the world of more obvious suffering, impermanence and illness. The Pure-Land is removed spatially, and said to be trillions of miles away, as other Buddhist heavens are removed. Indeed although such a hypothesis might be rejected by some Pure-Land traditions, including, for instance, the Japanese Jōdo Shinshū 'True Pure-Land' School, the school's roots seem to lie within the context of the practices which gave rise to many other Buddhist meditative traditions. The text delights in visual detail, and includes jewelled trees, nets and balustrades, lengthy timescales − the favourite Indian concomitants of the 'realms' of blissful states of mind − in an evocation of a paradise removed from life's usual pains, distractions and cares. These features align it to other embodiments of how the world is sometimes 'glimpsed' or 'remembered' differently when there is a skilful mind (*kusala citta*): the human realm of the *Mahāsudassana-Sutta*, or the heavens described in Pāli and Sanskrit Buddhist texts. The description of the Pure-Lands evokes the deep calm of the *jhānas*, an ever possible yet usually obscured potential. For ordinary people the bridge to this is faith; the obscurations make them seem 'far away'. Incidentally, those that teach meditation based on the use of visualization and such texts usually stress the importance of letting go of any visual images when a practice is finished. They were usually recited in contexts where there would be some preliminary setting aside of worldly activities, such as in a temple. Throughout *sūtras* of this kind there is also the reminder that for many humans, much of the time, the world just is not quite like that. Transience, pain and loss are recurring and stark features of daily, timebound existence. The effect of the *sūtras* seems to rest upon this curious interplay and, perhaps, mindfulness lies in finding the middle way within this contradiction.

In China, from the outset, with the teachings of Shandao (613–81), one of its earliest teachers, some association between the idea of the Pure-Land and inner state was stated. When one uttered the syllables of the mantra, he said, one was in the Pure-Land. In many popular schools of practice this connection does not seem to have been promoted, though some intimation of such a correspondence is sometimes implied. The idea that 'The Pure-Land is the mind itself', and hence capable of realization within a present human rebirth, is stated by some practitioners, including, later, in Japan, Hōnen and Shinran and, in Korea, Jinul. One feature of the Pure-Land heavens is that they are more explicitly *dharma* based than those of other traditions, justifying the lengthy existence in them that they extol for those who work for their enlightenment under the auspices of the Buddha Amitābha. There are many Buddhas and Bodhisattvas, who do not feature in the Pāli versions of such realms. Birds sing the *dharma* continuously, while the trees murmur it when moved by the breeze. This aural element seems to be the one which was supposed to be introduced into daily practice. A chant is a good way of keeping something working in the background of the mind in daily life where a visual practice is unsuitable.

THE PURE-LAND

6 ... Shariputra, (when) in that Buddha land a gentle breeze happens
to blow, the precious trees in rows and the begemmed nets
emit a delicate enrapturing tune, and it is just as if a hundred
thousand musical instruments played at the same time. Everybody
who hears that music naturally conceives the thought to invoke
the Buddha, to invoke the Dharma, and to invoke the Sangha.
Shariputra, that Buddha land is arrayed with such good qualities
and adornments.

7 Shariputra, what do you think in your mind, for what reason
that Buddha is called Amita(-abha)? Shariputra, the light of that
Buddha is boundless and shining without impediments all over

the countries of the ten quarters. Therefore he is called Amita(-abha). Again, Shariputra, the life of that Buddha and of his people is endless and boundless in Asamkhya-kalpas, so he is named Amita(-ayus). Shariputra, since Buddha Amitayus attained Buddhahood, (it has passed) now ten Kalpas. Again, Shariputra, that Buddha has numerous Shravakas or disciples, who are all Arhats and whose number cannot be known by (ordinary) calculation. (The number of) Bodhisattvas (cannot be known) also. Shariputra, that Buddha-land is arrayed with such good qualities and adornments.

8   Again, Shariputra, the beings born in the land Sukhavati are all Avinivartaniya. Among them is a multitude of beings bound to one birth only; and their number, being extremely large, cannot be expressed by (ordinary) calculation. Only can it be mentioned in boundless Asamkhya-kalpas. Shariputra, the sentient beings who hear (this account) ought to put up their prayer that they may be born into that country; for they will be able to be in the same place together with those noble personages. Shariputra, by means of small good works [lit. roots] or virtues no one can be born in that country.

9   Shariputra, if there be a good man or a good woman, who, on hearing of Buddha Amitayus, keeps his name (in mind) with thoughts undisturbed for one day, two days, three days, four days, five days, six days, or seven days, that person, when about to die, (will see) Amitayus Buddha accompanied by his holy host appear before him; and immediately after his death, he with his mind undisturbed can be born into the Sukhavati land of Buddha Amitayus. Shariputra, as I witness this benefit, I say these words; every being who listens to this preaching ought to offer up prayer with the desire to be born into that country.

From The Smaller Sukhāvatīvyūha-Sūtra, Utsuki (1924)

Shariputra = Sāriputta P /Śāriputra Sk; Shravaka = *śrāvaka*, disciple (see Chapter 7). The names of many of the beings of these realms are linked to light and radiance.

The straightforwardly practical appeal made this school of Buddhism so contagious in a Chinese context: daily life for the Chinese peasant was ruthlessly tough, with little time for textual study or secluded meditation practice. From the earliest days of Buddhism the recollection of the Buddha had been recommended to those busy in the lay life. By a gradual metamorphosis, this meditation seems to have changed into a constant possibility, with the internal murmuring of the mantra that evokes the Buddha associated with the Pure-Land, Amitābha. Adapted in this way, it could be employed alongside other activities such as farming and manual work, thus ensuring that activity thought to be salvific was not perceived the sole province of the monastic orders or an intellectual lay elite. Anyone could chant the name, at any time, and still participate in the path to liberation. Allowed to become a constant background presence, the mantra is felt to become part of the unconscious mind, conditioning responses and behaviour so that at the moment of death the being will experience the requisite moments of real faith. These are described in different contexts as varying from ten successive moments to seven successive days. Thereupon he will be instantly reborn in the heaven, becoming, it is implied, a benign, guarding presence able to help relatives and friends on their way to enlightenment.

Amongst the great Pure-Land teachers were Daochuo (562–645) and his student Shandao, who made more than ten thousand copies of the *Sukhāvativyūha-Sūtra*. The former advocated the use of beans to mark the number of times one said Amitābha's names, a variation on the use of rosaries which were and are linked to mantric meditations in Northern and Central Asian forms of Buddhism. This was perhaps helpful advice for impoverished peasants, unable to afford rosaries. Five elements were codified by Shandao:

1 Uttering the name
2 Chanting the Pure-Land *sūtras*
3 Meditating on the Amitābha Buddha
4 Worshipping images of the Buddha
5 Singing praises of the Buddha.

Pure-Land Buddhism exercised an immediate and popular appeal, although it did come into conflict with other schools of Buddhism as it grew in popularity.

This school of Buddhism has always proved resistant to persecution and lack of prestige. Daochuo emphasized the idea that the world in general was in a degenerate age (*mappō*) and needed such simple devotional exercises, and perhaps as a consequence of this it has not been seen by some as an entire salvific path. But its emphasis on the Bodhisattva vow, a heaven that offered solace for the present and the promise that the practitioner would be in close proximity to his or her descendents after death, perhaps allowed a more ancient Chinese reverence for the protective power of ancestors and familial loyalty to find a wholehearted Buddhist outlet. Personal accounts attest that this practice continued in China well into the twentieth century, despite communist persecution, and continues now. In *Ten Thousand Miles without a Cloud* (2004), filmmaker Sun Shuyun gives an eloquent evocation of her earliest memories of a gracious and tiny peasant grandmother, with whom she shared a bed 'head-to-toe', her face next to the woman's continuously painful and stinking bound feet. Despite the terrible grief of the loss of seven of her nine children in infancy the old lady remained dignified and strong, through recitation of the forbidden Pure-Land mantra. She maintained this by secretly passing beans through her hands into a bowl as she chanted – the method recommended by Daochuo centuries before – on waking and entering sleep.

With the development of Pure-Land Buddhism one sees yet another way in which the Buddhist meditative system was transformed and invested with entirely new elements in China.

CONCLUSION

As can be seen by this brief introduction, Buddhist meditation practice in China did not emerge in isolation. Influenced by Indian and Central Asian translations and teachers on one side, its meditative tradition shares many features with that of its other neighbours, Korea and Japan, who also contributed to the form of Buddhism we now call Eastern Buddhism. This is evident both in the schools that developed in those countries, but also in the effect the practices of all these countries have had on one another. The Tang dynasty represented a high point of Buddhism in China. After 845 CE, however, a wave of anti-Buddhist persecution began as powerful land-owning monasteries were perceived as a threat to the state. In one year, temples were destroyed, monasteries disbanded and monks and nuns made to return to lay life. Buddhism, though producing many great teachers, and, in the twelfth century receiving some renewed vitality from Tibetan sources, never regained its pre-eminence in China. After the 1911 revolution Buddhism lost hold in China completely: monasteries were desecrated, monks tortured and imprisoned. In recent years there has been some thawing of attitudes. According to recent surveys, three hundred million Chinese now admit to being Buddhist, often, by a curious irony of fate, influenced by 'back-packing' trips and coach tours to Tibet. There are probably more Buddhists; the numbers of meditators amongst these are not known.

Taiwan

In the last few centuries one of the principal upholders of Chinese Buddhist practice has been Taiwan, which received its first Buddhist influences during the mid-1600s under the Ming dynasty. Although primarily Chinese in orientation, Taiwanese Buddhism was greatly influenced by the Japanese, when under their control from 1895 to 1945, and more recently by Tibetan Buddhism. Buddhism has undergone a great surge of popularity there in the late twentieth century, with an estimated five million people now practising Buddhists. The orders of nuns still retain the ancient ordination line from China, and are highly regarded in society as a whole. Taiwan is regarded as a repository of Chinese Buddhism by the Chinese, and in recent years has started to see its own forms of Buddhist practice. Malaysia and Singapore have strong Chinese Buddhist communities, with Pure-Land Buddhism being particularly popular.

TIMELINES

221 BCE	Unification of China under first Emperor
c.65	First written reference to Buddhism in China
c.150	An Shigao arrives at Han capital
344–413	Kumarajīva, great translator of Buddhist texts into Chinese
399–414	Faxian travels to Central Asia and India
476–542	Tanluan, popularizer of Pure-Land Buddhism
520	Daoists and Buddhists engage in first of several public debates
520 or 526	Bodhidharma arrives in China
538–97	Zhiyi, founder of Tiantai Buddhism
549–623	Jizang, exponent of Madhyamaka form of Buddhism
562–645	Daochuo, Jingtu teacher
596–664	Xuanzang, Buddhist pilgrim to India
613–81	Shandao, Jingtu teacher

638–713	Huineng, founder of Southern school of Chan
641	Marriage of Chinese princess to king of Tibet: first movement of Chinese Buddhism to that country
643–712	Fazang, founder of the Huayan school
807–69	Liangjie, founder of the Caodong school of Chan
845	State persecution of Buddhism marks the beginning of the decline of Buddhism in China
867	Death of Yixuan, founder of the Linji school
972	The printing of Buddhist canon begins
c.1150	Zonggao, a Chan meditation teacher, formalizes *gongan* system
1949	Large numbers of Buddhist monks flee China for Taiwan
1965	Cultural revolution under Mao Zedong and widespread destruction of Buddhist sites

FURTHER READING

Blofeld, J. trans., H'siu P. preface (1994) *The Zen Teaching of Huang Po: On the Transmission of Mind*, New York: Grove Press.

Bucknell, R. and Kang, C. (1997) *The Meditative Way*, London: Curzon.

Buswell, R.E. (1981) *Tracing Back the Radiance: Chinul's Korean Way of Zen*, Kuroda Institute, Honolulu: University of Hawaii Press.

Chang, G.C.C. (1972) *The Buddhist Teaching of Totality: the Philosophy of Hwa Yen Buddhism*, London: George Allen & Unwin.

Clarke, R.B. trans. (2003) 'The Hsin Hsin Ming by Seng T'san' (Xinxinming) http://home.att.net/~paul.dowling/archive/zen/hsin.htm

Cleary, T. trans. (1993) *The Flower Ornament Scripture: a Translation of the Avataṃsaka Sutra*, Boston/London: Shambala.

Collins, S. (1998) *Nirvana and other Buddhist Felicities: Utopias of the Pali Imaginaire*, Cambridge: CUP.

Cousins, L.S. and Lindop A. (1998) unpublished trans. of Dieter Schlingoff (1964) *Ein Buddhistisches Yogalehrbuch*, Berlin.

Gomes, L.O. (1996) *The Land of Bliss: The Paradise of the Buddha of the Marvellous Light*, Honolulu: University of Hawaii Press.

Gomes, L.O. (2004) 'Pure-Land', Robert Buswell Jnr. (ed.), *Encyclopedia of Buddhism*, 2 vols., New York: Macmillan, 2, 703–6.

Hawkins, B.K. (2004) *Introduction to Asian Religions*, New York: Pearson Longman.

Heine, S. and Wright, D.S. (eds) (2000) *The Kōan: Texts and Contexts in Zen Buddhism*. Oxford/New York: OUP.

Kit, W.K. (1998) *The Complete Book of Zen*, Shaftesbury, UK: Element.

Luk, C. (2002) *Ordinary Enlightenment: a Translation of the Vimalakirti Nirdesa Sutra*, Boston: Shambala.

Reps, P. (1957) *Zen Flesh, Zen Bones*, Harmondsworth, Middx: Penguin.

Shahar, M. (2000) 'Epigraphy, Buddhist Historiography, and Fighting Monks: The Case of The Shaolin Monastery', *Asia Major Third Series* 13 (2) 15–36.

Shuyun, S. (2004) *Ten Thousand Miles Without a Cloud*, New York/London: Harper Perennial.

Sponberg, A. (1986) 'Meditation in Fa-hsiang Buddhism', in Gregory, P.N. ed., *Traditions of Meditation in Chinese Buddhism*, Kuroda Institute: Studies in East Asian Buddhism, 4, Honolulu: University of Hawaii Press, 15–41.

Stevens, J. (1995) *Sacred Calligraphy of the East*, Boston: Shambala.

Stevenson, D.B. (1986) 'The Four Kinds of Samadhi in Early T'ien-t'ai Buddhism', in Gregory, P.N. ed., *Traditions of Meditation in Chinese Buddhism*, Kuroda Institute: Studies in East Asian Buddhism, 4, Honolulu: University of Hawaii Press, 45–97.

Williams, P. (1989) *Mahāyāna Buddhism: the Doctrinal Foundations*, New York/London: Routledge.

Yu, C.–F. (1979) 'Ta-Hui Tsung-Kao and Kung-an Ch'an', *Journal of Chinese Philosophy*, 5, 211–35.

Yu, L.K. (Luk, C.) (1964) *The Secrets of Chinese Meditation*, Maine: Samuel Weiser.

Yun, H., Graham, T. trans. (1999) *Only a Great Rain: a Guide to Chinese Buddhist Meditation*, New York: Wisdom.

WEBSITES

Chan

'Teachings of Sudden Illumination' (2007)
http://www.selfdiscoveryportal.com/ChanMasters.htm
'Western Chan Fellowship' (2005)
http://www.westernchanfellowship.org/selected-articles.html
'Life in a Chan monastery' (2005)
http://www.westernchanfellowship.org/life-in-chan-monastery.html
'Ten ox-herding pictures' (1996) *Chan newsletter* No.119, November
http://www.chan1.org/ddp/channews/11-1996.html
'The Ten Ox-herding pictures of Zen : Series 2' (2008) Zen Buddhist Order of Hsu Yun
http://www.hsuyun.org/Dharma/zbohy/VisualArts/OxHerdingPictures/oxherding2.html
Yu, C.-F. (1979) 'Ta-hui Tsung-kao and Kung-an Ch'an', *Journal of Chinese Philosophy*, 6, 211–35:
http://ccbs.ntu.edu.tw/FULLTEXT/JR-JOCP/jc22069.htm
Xinxinming: 'Hsin Hsin Ming' (2003):
http://rightviewonline.org/BOOKSHELF/Faith%20in%20Mind,%20Review.pdf

Pure-Land

Utsuki, N. (1924) *The Smaller Sukhāvatīvyuhā Sūtra* or *The Sutra on the Buddha Amitayus Translated from the Chinese Version of Kumarajiva*, Educational Department of the West, Hongwanji, Kyoto, Japan. Also on:
http://web.mit.edu/stclair/www/smaller.html
Pure-Land chants:
http://www.buddhanet.net/audio-kmspks_chant.htm
Buddhist poets:
http://www.poetseers.org/spiritual_and_devotional_poets/buddhist/huang/
http://www.poetry-chaikhana.com/Y/YungChiaChue/index.htm

Meditation in Korea and Vietnam
Ten

KOREA

By tranquillity a mountain raises up, and to this movement a valley responds

The austerely rugged beauty of the Korean peninsula, with its Chinese neighbours by land on one side and the Japanese by sea on the other, has fostered a form of Buddhism that has developed its own identity, while sharing many features with the Buddhist schools of its neighbours. It was, and to a certain extent still retains, elements of a Shamanist society, which came under the control of expansively imperialist China in 100 CE. A Chinese style academy for sons of the aristocracy was established in 372 in Taehak and from that time a Confucian ethos continued to influence the ruling classes and their system of government. The first evidence of Buddhist practice occurs around the middle of the third century CE, which gradually spread, along with Confucianism, throughout the whole country. Buddhism was officially instated as the state religion in some northern areas by King Sosurim (r. 371–84) in 372, in the south-western state of Baekje in 384, and the south-eastern state of Silla, over a century later, in 527. A process of conversion, absorption and meditative exploration followed. At first, like Confucianism, the appeal of Buddhism lay primarily with the court, by whom it was adopted, however, with the intention of popular dissemination. In the sixth and seventh century, waves of monks, sent to study and practise in China, introduced key texts from the main Chinese schools for this purpose: one, Seungrang (450–530?), studied with the famous Kumarajīva. King Seong (r. 523–54) sent monks to Japan in 538, 545 and 552, with the intention of transmitting the teachings, a project carried on by his successors. Uisang (625–702) made a great pilgrimage to China and introduced Huayan (Hwa-eom (K)) to Korea, adapting the idea of the Buddha nature for Korean practitioners. By the Goryeo period (935–1392), Buddhism had been adopted amongst the populace as a whole: in 1036 Buddhist monks succeeded in getting the death penalty abolished. In the twelfth and thirteenth century the entire Chinese canon was printed; this edition, of 81,258 wooden blocks, is still in existence.

Attempts at syncretism and the development of a Korean form of Buddhism that reconciled differences between the tenets of Chinese schools seem to have been a feature from early times. This took place at local levels, where Shamanist mountain shrines often came to be associated with Buddhist temples, and at the level of practice and doctrine, as key figures attempted to reconcile apparently opposing doctrines in new formulations of the Buddhist path. Such an approach was inspired by the work of Wonhyo (617–86). A colourful and innovative thinker, after studying the *Lotus-Sūtra* and the *Mahāparinirvāṇa-Sūtra* he set off for China to learn texts with his companion, Uisang. The story goes, however, that he mistakenly drank from a skull when staying overnight in a cave that had once been a grave and was now open and desecrated by robbers. He became enlightened on the following morning: when he realized what he had drunk from a skull, his disgust was so powerful that it inspired an insight into 'non-self' that freed him from all attachments to the body. This event occurred in Korea itself: significantly, he never went to China, but returned to his native Silla, where he remained as a teacher. This decision seems crucial in establishing a particularly Korean distillation of doctrine and practice: Wonhyo formulated a synthesis of the approaches of the various schools through the Eastern idea of 'One mind'.

WONHYO'S NINE KINDS OF ABIDING MIND

1   Remaining introspective
2   Equanimous abiding
3   Peaceful abiding
4   Intimate abiding
5   Pacification
6   Tranquillity
7   Absolute tranquillity
8   Abiding solely in one principle
9   Equanimous retention

Wonhyo classified *śamatha* according to these nine stages. At the final stage, the mind remains and settles into the *samādhi* of true suchness. This is the unitary characteristic of the *dharmadhātu*, and produces innumerable *samādhis*, starting with the single practice *samādhi* (*ekakarasamādhi*), that is characterized by equanimity and non-duality. Insight into dharmas inevitably involves insight into impermanence, suffering, wandering (*saṃsāra*) and impurity. He describes four types of insight (*vipaśyanā*):

*   Insight into *dharmas*
*   Insight into the great compassion
*   Insight into vows
*   Insight into energetic effort

Wonhyo said that the practices of *śamatha* and *vipaśyanā* need to be completed together. They are like the two wings of a bird: if there is only one, the bird will not be able to soar in the sky. Or it is like two wheels of a cart: if both are not present, the cart will not be able to move and carry anything. The path of awakening (*bodhi*) requires both, working together.

Wonhyo's approach was itself challenged, however, by the introduction of 'Seon' (Chan) schools in the ninth century, which promulgated realization through intuitive, direct contact and a 'sudden' approach to enlightenment. Uicheon (1055–1101) again attempted balance, seeking to stress the importance of both the schools based on the study of *sūtras* and practices based upon them and the more iconoclastic Seon approach. 'Success' or 'lack of success' are perhaps not appropriate terms to apply to such work on establishing a form of Buddhism natural to the Koreans: the process seems to have been ongoing and creative, over centuries of experimentation and changes in emphasis.

A different kind of integration was initiated by the great Seon monk, Jinul (1158–1210). At a time when Korean spiritual practice was becoming somewhat institutionalized and possibly corrupt, he espoused the Huayan idea of the Buddha nature and the importance of texts and gradual work on self-development in the search for this. He also acknowledged the importance of initial illuminatory insight, which revealed the 'empty' nature of reality. He posited that a moment of illumination may be a necessary precursor to the Bodhisattva path, but that this path was long and needed study and meditative discipline, until a moment of final realization, where both approaches could come to fruition together. Drawing on methods suggested by earlier teachers, he compared this combination of sudden awakening and gradual cultivation through a number of similes. It is like the appearance of the sun at dawn: when it first appears it shines on the ice that has formed on water, but it takes time before the ice is completely thawed. Or it is like the birth of an infant (sudden awakening) who is endowed with the potential of an adult but has to bring these qualities to fruition (gradual cultivation). His work on integrating practices, textual work and his experiential observation of contact with a number of different schools and practitioners led him to a synthesis of Seon (Chan) with the Huayan method, explained in a series of texts and manuals on the subject of meditation and theory. He organized a Buddhist congregation named Jeonghye (meaning 'the cultivation of wisdom and concentration in unison') at a mountain monastery called Gilsang-sa (now Songgwang-sa); his work is felt to represent the high point of Korean Buddhist creativity.

JINUL'S SCHEME FOR MEDITATION PRACTICE AND SUITABILITY FOR DIFFERENT PEOPLE

9   **The cultivation of wisdom (*prajñā*) and concentration (*samādhi*) in unison** This method – which gave its name to his congregation – may be practised as a way of spiritual development, but also suggests an equilibrium enjoined for all stages of meditative practice and all methods.

10   **Faith and understanding according to the complete and sudden school** This is the process of tracing back the radiance of the mind, a practice suggested in the very earliest texts (A I 10; see Chapter 3), yet emphasized by the Chinese schools. All beings trace their origin back to the purity of the *dharmadhātu*. The meditator searches and finds this through continued practice. This kind of meditation is considered suitable for the average person.

11   **Hwadu (lit. head of speech)** This depends upon a typically Chan 'short cut' approach to meditation, of observing the *hwadu*, a method associated with the Chinese *gongan*. Jinul regarded it as useful primarily for those of considerable meditative experience. 'Dead' words (*sagu* (K); *siju* (C)) only appeal to logic, reason and usual meaning: this is the usual kind of intellectual investigation. But 'live words' (*hwalgu* (K); *Huoju* (C)) free the mind by offering nothing that the deluded mind can grasp. The *hwadu*, the central point of a *gongan*, needs some linguistic explanation but is closer to an authentic description of the unconditioned than most speech. At a later stage that insight needs to be transcended: a non-verbal

shock, such as a slap, a clap, a shout, or even plain silence may be needed to loosen all attachment.

12 **No-thought** This is the stage of no-mind (musim), the suspension of conventional thought, that Jinul described as being important for all meditations, whether those included in the recollection of the Buddha, or the direct, Seon methods. It provides a path where any kind of language or conceptualizing is transcended. In *Straight Talk on the True Mind* he says it is only possible for the advanced practitioner.

13 **The recollection of the name of the Buddha** This technique, practised throughout the Pure-Land schools, goes, Jinul says, through ten stages, culminating in its use as no-mind. After long practice in the Bodhisattva path, the practitioner is ready, at the tenth and final stage, for the recollection of the Buddha in 'suchness', where he or she understands the one true *dharmadhātu*. This can even be pursued by the lay practitioner while conducting usual daily activities: while the practice starts in a simple way, with the hope of fulfilled aspirations and a heavenly rebirth, and may remain so for most people, it requires the participant to see, after various stages of refinement, the Pure-Land as the purified mind itself.

All of these methods, cultivated correctly, will, Jinul says, lead to awakening: an important acknowledgement of the validity of the variety of techniques and approaches that have come to characterize Eastern Buddhism.

Jinul's *Linji gongan* method of Seon practice has tended to prevail in Korea: while there have been and are differences between groups and sects, historically these have tended to arise perhaps more from geographical and property-owning interests rather than doctrine or methodology.

Buddhism suffered a series of setbacks as it endured persecution under the Confucian Joseon dynasty (1392–1910). It was associated with women and the uneducated: monks were even banned from Seoul, and classed with vagabonds as amongst the lowest strata of society. Monks retreated to the mountainous regions, still regarded as the heartland of Korean

Chinul: Do you hear the sounds of that crow cawing and that magpie calling?

Student: Yes.

Chinul: Trace them back and listen to your hearing nature. Do you hear any sounds?

Student: At that place, sounds and discrimination do not obtain.

Chinul: Marvelous! marvelous! This is Avalokiteśvara's method for entering the *noumenon* [*li*]. Let me ask you again. You said that sounds and discriminations do not obtain at that place. But since they do not obtain, isn't the hearing-nature just empty space at such a time?

Student: Originally it is not empty. It is always bright and never obscured.

Chinul: What is the essence which is not empty?

Student: As it has no former shape, words cannot describe it.

Chinul: This is the life force of all the Buddhas and patriarchs – have no further doubts about that.

Note: Chinul = Jinul

Buswell (1981: 104–5)

Seon Buddhism. In the 1890s, at a time, oddly enough, of a resurgence of Korean nationalism, Buddhist practices and doctrines started to become again incorporated into the mainstream of cultural life, though the Japanese occupation from 1910 to 1945 created some tension between local Buddhist customs and the incoming Japanese orders, some of which permitted the marriage of monks. After the Second World War, Korean forms were re-established. The re-acceptance of Buddhism, however, alongside global trends, has meant that from the late twentieth century the practice of Seon meditation has undergone a surge of popularity in South Korea. There is a large monastic order whose members specialize in either texts or meditation after a certain training period. The Korean orders of nuns have become increasingly prestigious: their temples also retain a direct ordination line, through China, dating from the earliest bhikkhunī orders. Nuns of some other Buddhist countries, where the full ordination lineage has been lost, are sometimes reticent, perhaps coming from poor and uneducated classes. While this may or may not have any bearing on their meditative achievement,

Figure 10.1 **Buddhas carved into stone on a hillside in Korea**

it does mean that they have sometimes had less access to teachers, time for practice and a chance to learn languages and doctrine in a formal way. In the twentieth century Korean nuns, however, have become highly regarded, well-educated and, in a culture where the monastic orders have access to land and funds, live in prosperous temples: some have become internationally renowned as scholars and eloquent teachers of meditation. They have been involved with the ordination of women in Northern Buddhism and attempts to reintroduce the nuns' lineage in Southern Buddhism.

A STORY

A famous modern Seon master in Korea was Man'gong (1872–1946), who became a monk when he was fourteen years old and then studied Zen under the famous Zen master Kyongho. Kyongho gave him the following kōan:

The ten thousand *dharmas* return to the One
Where does the One return?'

Man'gong meditated on this day and night for many years. At last, when he was staying in a temple near Sosan, he sat facing the wall meditating on this. For several days he forgot to eat or sleep. Then one night, he opened his eyes and the wall had disappeared. There was only a single bright circle of light like moonlight. Early that morning, he heard a monk chanting while ringing the temple bells:

The triple world, all Buddhas, everything is created by only One Mind.

Man'gong was abruptly enlightened. Clapping his hands he laughed and sang the following song of awakening:

The true nature of empty mountains is beyond the millions of years of
past and future,
White cloud, cool wind come and go by themselves endlessly,
Why did Bodhidharma come to China?
The rooster cries before dawn and then the sun rises over the
horizon.'

Adapted from: *Korea Journal*, May 1, 1972
Tedesco (1992: 32–3)

With the notable exception of the devotional chanting of the names of Bodhisattvas and Buddhas – which, Jinul argues, can be refined through stages of subtlety and meaning – meditative practice in Korea has tended, until recently, to be regarded as the province of the monastic orders. In the last decades of the twentieth century, with a surge of interest in new translations of Buddhist texts, the intelligentsia gravitated towards Seon practice. The 2005 census recorded 10,726,000 Buddhists, 22.8 per cent of the South Korean population. Christianity has become increasingly popular in Korea. The situation regarding Buddhism in communist North Korea is unknown, but Buddhism is thought to have been suppressed.

The mountain

Mountains are the more beautiful
After the sun has gone down
And it is
Twilight. Day closes, darkness
Settles. Boy:
Watch out for tigers, now.
Let's not
Wander about in the field.

Yun Seon do (1587–1671)

Throughout Eastern Buddhism and, in particular in Korea, the mountain is used as a place for quiet meditation, a site for establishing monasteries and as an image of the union between opposing elements: according to Daoist principle it is said to be the place where the female, earth principle (*yin*) meets the male sky (*yang*). In Korea, Shamanist sites on mountains soon became associated with Buddhist temples. The mountainous region is the home of many Seon monasteries, whose monks represent a reasonably unbroken line of meditative practice going back for several hundred years: despite some persecution, practices long since lost in China, for instance, have been retained. The following is the oldest explanation of Seon for the royal family, given during the ninth century in the reign of King Hungdok by a Seon master on his return from China:

Whatever practicing you may do, there is no practice at all.
However enlightened you may be, there is no enlightenment at all.
By tranquillity a mountain raises up, and to this movement a valley responds (by appearing).
Hence the benefit of non-action is like winning without a fight.

Koh (1991: 99)

Figure 10.2 **Korean *stūpa* set on the side of a mountain**

The daily routine in a Seon monastery is austere and disciplined, as this personal account by a practitioner attests:

A Buddhist Monk's Life

Quite often the meditation monk will spend some months or years in a kangwon before starting the tough regimen of sitting meditation. The Son master gives the new monk a hwadu or koan – a meditation technique using a paradoxical topic to develop the monk's power of intuition, e.g. What is the sound of one hand clapping? Much of the monk's day is taken up with meditation and with meeting the master to discuss the koan. It may take several years for the monk to give a response that satisfies the master, who then gives his disciple another of the 1800 standard koans.

There are various intensities of meditation. During kyol-je (retreat sessions), monks meditate for a minimum of eight hours, divided into four two-hour units (50 minutes sitting and 10 minutes walking). Each session begins with three slaps of the bamboo rod or chukbi and ends with one slap. The monks face the wall seated in full lotus position. During meditation, if a monk should begin to nod or slouch, he receives a warning, usually in the form of a stroke of a bamboo stick to improve his concentration. The job of monitor rotates every hour.

The monks meditate and sleep on the same mat, all together in a big room. Meals are taken in silence and, of course, there is strict silence during the meditation sessions; but the rule of silence is not so strict between the sessions. However, individual monks take a vow of silence for long periods (100 days, 1 year, 1000 days, 3 years, etc) and hang a 'Don't disturb' badge on the front of their robes.

This is usually combined with extended meditation and perhaps, living in a hermitage and eating cold food. Once or twice a year, many monasteries have an intensive one-week sitting – up to twenty hours of meditation each day.

Dwan (1991: 17–18)

TIMELINES

109 CE	Korea annexed to Han empire
313	Chinese lose control of Korea
372	Buddhism adopted as official religion in northern areas at same time as establishment of Confucian academy
384	Buddhism adopted as official religion in Baekje
527	Buddhism adopted as official religion in Silla
538–52	King Seong sends Buddhist texts and statues to Japan
617–86	Wonhyo, who first attempted to unify divergent sects in Korea
625–702	Uisang, founder of Korean Hwayan Buddhism
c.650	First Seon monastery established in Silla by Korean, Beobrang, a pupil of Daoxin (580–651), fourth patriarch of the Chinese Chan lineage
c.700	The establishment of five orthodox schools of Buddhism in Silla
751	Buddhist scroll dating from this period, found in Kyongju, the oldest printed material in the world
c.770	Establishment of Cheontae (Tiantai) school

c.900	The emergence of the Nine Mountains (Gusan) school of Seon
918	The Goryeo dynasty begins. Buddhism supported but strictly controlled
1011	First complete woodblock edition of Buddhist texts
1055–1101	Uicheon and further attempts to unify Korean Buddhism
1158–1210	Jinul
1251	New edition of Buddhist scriptures
1392–1909	Suppression of Buddhism under Joseon dynasty
1910–45	Korea Japanese colony
Mid-1950s	Split between North and South Korea

VIETNAM

One writer, Wong Kiew Kit, refers to the 'the quiet grandeur of Vietnamese Zen': it is a country famous for some of its kings who abdicated to become monks. Another beautiful, yet ravaged terrain, Vietnam differs from other Southeast Asian countries in that while Buddhism arrived in the first centuries CE from India it was superseded by Chinese elements; the Chinese rather than the Indic world-view has been more influential. With the arrival of the Zen monk Vinitaruci from mainland China in about 580 CE, a form of Buddhism was introduced that interacted with other forms of Tantra and Pure-Land as well. Because of this Buddhism in Vietnam is characterized by elements that align it more closely with Eastern Buddhism, though it is mixed with some derived from other Southeast Asian countries.

Under the Ly dynasty in 1010 Buddhism continued to flourish, notably amongst the royalty as well as the general populace; kings were usually of the Thao Duong sect of Thien (Chan/Zen) Buddhism. From the eleventh to the fourteenth century, Buddhism developed rapidly, was adapted as the state religion, and permeated all aspects of social and private life. From the tenth and eleventh century the Vietnamese are said to have loved *dhāranis*, particularly 'The Heart of Great Compassion' (*Mahā-karuṇa-hṛdaya-dhāraṇī*). One monk, Ma Ha, recited the Buddhist scripture Dai Bi Tam, a *Tantra*, continuously over a three-year period. The wealth of *saṅgha* also gradually grew, as rice-growing land was donated to monasteries, although there was some loss of reputation for Buddhist monasticism as Confucianism established itself. The emperor Tran Thai Tong attempted a synthesis between Zen, Pure-Land and Daoism/Confucianism. In 1299 one of his successors, Tran Nhan Tong, became a monk, founding the Truc Lam sect of Thien, a syncretic movement that is still popular. Truc Lam's Zen Monastery, in southern Vietnam's highland Da Lat City, has for many decades been operating under the auspices of the Venerable Thich Thanh Tu, a renowned teacher in meditation.

In this period of a real establishment of Buddhist practice, the form that emerged was strongly influenced by Confucianism, but, with the Daoist practices to which Buddhist techniques were often associated, offered a more spacious, spiritual dimension that was seen to complement Confucian social considerations. As with the arrival of Buddhism in other countries, local animist practices contributed a ritual element that seems to have nurtured and sustained Buddhism in the country. After a period of decline that lasted until the nineteenth century, Buddhism saw a resurgence of influence from the early part of the twentieth century. Over 90 per cent of Vietnamese people are Buddhist, practising a tradition still also steeped in local animist customs. The influence of Pure-Land, Zen and Vajrayāna is strong. Amongst modern Vietnamese, Pure-Land seems to exercise the greatest appeal, while Zen meditation is preferred amongst the monastic orders. Many of the monastic orders of Vietnam, however, by adhering to a strictly Southern *vinaya* are distinct from other Eastern forms of Buddhism. Theravāda Buddhist forms are found in many practices. In this regard, they perhaps follow a model that is more closely allied to the situation in the early centuries in India, when a *vinaya* was still shared by monks of all traditions, where their doctrinal understanding and practices might differ.

Vietnam was and still is a profoundly Buddhist country, despite the troubles of the past fifty years. Indeed some have argued that the lack of the influence of the West and consumerism in recent years has, oddly enough, helped to retain the great dignity of the country's Buddhist heritage. In the south, where there is a strong Khmer population, there is a sizeable minority of Theravāda Buddhists. Monks and nuns from all traditions tend to be well educated and there are thriving meditation centres, open to the laity too.

SOME VIETNAMESE GONGANS

Tue Trun Thuong Si (1229–99)

A Buddhist layman, general and soldier, he took up Thien (Chan) later in life and was renowned for his calm and silence:

Walking or sitting is meditating
In flaming fire appears a lotus

Tran Thai Tong (1218–77)

Born of a fisherman family from Nam Ha, he was the first king of the Tran dynasty. He took the throne at the age of eight, and vowed to consecrate himself to Buddhism. He reigned for 32 years, building monasteries, supporting Buddhism and practising meditation, before handing the kingdom to his son. He claimed that the aim of the Thien practitioner is like the return to a native land:

> The day has ended, but one is ten thousand miles from the native land.
>
> (*Tu Son*)

> On the long way, one does not walk but one arrives at home
>
> (*Niem Tung Ke*).

Thich Nhat Hanh (1926–)

This Zen monk has found world recognition as an eloquent spokesman for peace and reconciliation. He is a Buddhist scholar, practitioner and founder of the Plum Village community in France. His many writings include *gongans*, translations of twelfth-century poems and expressions of his doctrine of 'interbeing'. This adaptation of the idea of interpenetration gives a modern interpretation of theory for meditation and social relationships.

FURTHER READING: KOREA

Buswell, R.E. (1981) *Tracing Back the Radiance: Chinul's Korean Way of Zen*, Kuroda Institute, Honolulu: University of Hawaii Press.

Buswell, R.E. (1983) *The Korean Approach to Zen: the collected works of Chinul*, Honolulu: University of Hawaii Press.

Buswell, R.E. (1986) 'Chinul's Systematization of Chinese Meditative Techniques in Korean Son Buddhism', in Gregory, P.N. ed., *Traditions of Meditation in Chinese Buddhism*, Kuroda Institute: Studies in East Asian Buddhism, 4, Honolulu: University of Hawaii Press, 199–242.

Chanda, E.R. (Sept 1980) 'The Korean Mountain Spirit', *Korea Journal*, 11–16.

Dwan, S. (Summer 1991) 'A Buddhist Monk's Life', *Inculturation*, 8–21.

Jae-ryong, S. (1999) *Korean Buddhism: Tradition and Transformation*, Seoul: Jimoondang.

Koh, I.-J. (1991) 'Introduction of Ch'an (K. Son) in the Later Silla', in Lancaster, L.R. and Yu, C.S. (eds) *Assimilation of Buddhism in Korea: Religious Maturity and Innovation in the Silla Dynasty*, Berkeley: Asian Humanities Press.

Lee, P.H. compiler and trans. (1974) *Poems from Korea*, Honolulu: University of Hawaii Press.

Shindai, S. ed. (1977) 'Wonhyo's calmness and insight', *Bukkyo no jissen genri* (Buddhist soteriological principles), Tokyo: Sankibo Busshorin, 429–45.

Tedesco, F. (1992) *Collected Articles on Contemporary Korean Buddhism*, Seoul: privately published.

Websites

(2007) 'Buddhism in Korea': http://www.buddhanet.net/e-learning/buddhistworld/korea-txt.htm

(2007) On the *hwadu*: http://www.koreanbuddhism.net/hwadu/

(2005) Golden Wind Zen Group 'Man'gong': http://www.goldenwindzen.org/mangong.htm

Audio link to Korean chanting: http://www.koreanbuddhism.net/library/music/list.asp

FURTHER READING: VIETNAM

Hanh, Thich Nhat (2006) *Present Moment, Wonderful Moment, Mindfulness Verses for Daily Living*, Fitchburg, MA: Parallax.

Kit, W.K. (1998) *The Complete Book of Zen*, Shaftesbury, UK: Element.

Thien-An, T., Smith, C. ed., (1975) *Buddhism and Zen in Vietnam*, Rutland, VT: Charles Tuttle.

Websites

'Prominent Figures of Vietnamese Buddhism', Ven. Thich Thien Chau http://www.quangduc.com/English/vnbuddhism/010prominent.html

Meditation in Japan
Eleven

No more water in the pail!
No more moon in the water!
Emptiness in my hand.

The history of Buddhist meditation in Japan is linked to the development of various strands of Eastern Buddhism, whose diversity is reflected in the many different forms of Buddhist schools that have existed there. A number of factors, however, have meant that Japanese Buddhism, and hence its meditative practices, has developed features quite distinct from those of Korea and China, with emphases that those countries do not share. Some of these may be summarized briefly as follows: the custom of some monastic orders embarking on marriage and inheriting familial roles as custodians of particular temples; an emphasis on a single text as being the repository of the teaching and the development of a number of formal and independent disciplines, in part extensions of and in part developments away from meditative training. A curious and apparent contradiction of Japanese Buddhism is also its precise and even sharp differentiation between various schools, with, at the level of domestic and monastic practice, greater fluidity of movement in Buddhist identities than in some other countries. Family groupings, still associated with local connections, often have their own 'mix' of texts as sacred objects, often from highly disparate traditions.

The history of the tradition in Japan is helpful in explaining some of these features. The earliest accounts of Japanese religion come from Chinese travelogues that predate Buddhism, which note a stratified society made up of individual communities (uji) coming from a divine ancestor (kami no uji), who presided over the wellbeing of his descendents. This system gradually transformed itself into the practice of Shintō (Shindao: way of the gods), at that time an unformed collection of folk-beliefs from around the Japanese archipelago. By the sixth and seventh centuries CE these traditions were largely being absorbed by and adapted to the practices of Buddhism. This is thought to have reached Japan from Korea in 538 CE, with a monk who arrived with texts and a gilded Buddha figure, anxious to promote a friendly alliance between the two states. In 539 a piece of wood is said to have been washed up, to the accompaniment of Buddhist chants; two more images of the Buddha were made from that. Buddhism started to take root, primarily because one clan, the Soga, wished to make closer links with China.

Buddhism's appeal in Japan was at first primarily diplomatic, with the ruling classes anxious to form links with their powerfully expansive and proselytizing neighbours, China and Korea. But within fifty years of Buddhism reaching Japan the regent, Prince Shōtuku (573–622), a ruler often compared to Aśoka, declared Buddhism to be the state religion. Close ties between the *saṅgha* and secular power were established from the outset. Buddhist monks tended to teach the higher ranks rather than the general populace, perhaps on the grounds that this was the most effective means of exporting their tradition. Buddhism had, however, still to establish a relationship with the powerful *kami no uji* of individual clans, whose influence was threatened by imported beliefs and customs that could undermine their primacy.

In the Nara period (710–84) the devout emperor Shōmu (701–56) ordered extensive temple construction, including a temple enshrining a 16-metre tall image representing Vairocana, the central Dharma body, who had been described in Huayan philosophy as the Buddha who penetrates all directions. The figure was a significant symbol of a process which had been going on some time, and was effective in communicating Buddhism to the Japanese court. Six schools of Chinese Buddhism were introduced, the most influential being the Kegon, a version of the Chinese Huayan school. As the *Avataṃsaka* tradition suggests, Kegon saw ultimate truth as an interpenetrating phenomenal reality, without impediment. This doctrine seemed not only unthreatening but encouraging, in that it allowed imperial power to be perceived as permeating that of the state. This heralded the way for the acceptance of Buddhism in Japan. Shintō had always regarded the emperor as a living god, an idea that could persist under Buddhist auspices. Buddhism was, however, also so linked to Daoism and Confucianism, both of which accompanied its arrival, that its presence in Japanese intellectual training and meditative practice always seemed syncretic.

At this point it is interesting to consider which elements of Buddhism and its practice prove attractive on its arrival in a new setting. We probably tend to assume now that the most persuasive features of Buddhism are the intellectual, in its adventurous exploration of the parameters of philosophical discourse, or the specifically meditative, in its varied range of technique and forms of practice. Historically this has sometimes certainly been the case, as in China, where meditative and philosophical texts brought by monks do seem to be the first to be translated and discussed. In Tibet the idea of being a scholar and a meditating monk was appealing. In Japan a number of other features seem to have been more important. Buddhism ensured Japan's participation on an equal footing with other powerful nations and prescribed an ethical rule of conduct that could be applied universally to the ruling classes. This code could be applied both within the country and in the nation's relationships with other states. Other factors came into play too. The figure of the Buddha seems to have been a focus from the start, and was appreciated by a culture that seems to have intuitively responded to visual objects rather than, at first, ideas. An image of the Buddha heralded the introduction of Buddhism to Japan, wooden images made from driftwood marked some sort of acceptance of the tradition, and the construction of the great image of Vairocana proclaimed Japanese espousal of Buddhism. The physical appearance of the Buddha, rather than written or spoken text, seems to have elicited the deepest feeling of the Japanese converts. Another attractive feature was the intricacy and sophistication of its magical ceremonies, said to avert all kinds of misfortune and illness. One of the central preoccupations of Japanese life had always been the use of ritual and ceremony as an outlet for emotional and physical expression. Visual and ritual aspects of Buddhism shaped much Japanese meditative and doctrinal development and were in turn influenced by them. A sense of the moment, so important to the Japanese, came, over centuries, to encompass the idea that by emulating and acting as a Buddha, awakening was realized. It was a crucial development, which arose from earlier Tiantai teachings of the inherent Buddha nature. As we see, it seems to influence much Japanese meditative practice, even amongst schools who do not formally adopt such doctrines.

Over the next few centuries, a process of gradual absorption allowed Buddhism to be included in and to transform Shintō practice, so that by the early modern period a number of peculiarly Japanese forms of Buddhist practice emerged. This is in part evident in the development of some esoteric schools, which demanded a complex interplay of mantra and visualization, particularly popular in the court and the higher social classes. An appreciation of expressive action can also be seen, however, in the emergence over several centuries of specific arts, such as archery, calligraphy, Nō theatre, flower arranging and gardening. All of these seem to gratify a love of drama, a poised sense of dignity and a testing through physical action. They offered, through a single or repeated ritual, ways of bringing into being, through external embodiment, a transformed inner state. Such forms of spiritual training, some of which emerged first in China, are popular in Japan to this day, not necessarily in an overtly Buddhist context but as offshoots that express its basic principles. They are considered beautiful or enlivening in themselves, by allowing mindfulness, the transcending of hindrances and appropriate and well-timed bodily movement or movements to come to bear on a specific 'way' (dō).

In the gradual development of these forms, and in daily religious practice, Japanese Buddhism absorbed many Shintō, Daoist and Confucian elements. Shintō itself, deeply embedded before the arrival of Buddhism, featured less obviously in Japanese life after its arrival; most of its priesthood became Buddhist. Rural areas, however, in particular retained strong Shintō influences, in a synthesis with Buddhism known as Ryobu, 'dual aspect'. Local deities and kamis were considered Buddhas and Bodhisattvas, benignly disposed towards their local populations and family groupings. Indeed it was argued by the Japanese historian Kuroda (1926–93) that the fluidity of movement between, in particular, Shintō and Buddhist practices by the early modern period suggests that the two traditions in practice permeated one another. The distinction between them seems artificial until well into the nineteenth century, when self-consciousness promoted some external differentiation: their still symbiotic relationship is shown by the fact that in the twentieth century many houses had both Buddhist and Shintō shrines.

However the influences worked, the two seemed to have found some way of welcoming one another. In the early centuries of its arrival in Japan, other aspects of Buddhist practice, such as meditation, also started to be disseminated and there was a widespread and unmodified import of Chinese texts. In 794 CE the capital moved to Heian, modern day Kyōto, and Buddhism was ready to blossom in Japan.

TENDAI (CHINESE TIANTAI)

This Chinese school, with Mount Hiei near Kyōto as a head monastery, was introduced to Japan by the Japanese monk, Saichō (767–822), who established a twelve-year training regime of meditation and academic study around 805 CE. In China, Tiantai came to be closely associated with Pure-Land. In Japan it also become more directly linked to esoteric Buddhism, adopting the teachings of the Lotus-Sūtra (Hokekyō) and absorbing Shinto elements. Saichō built a meditation hall in 812 and introduced the Pure-Land chant, gradually incorporating other elements of this practice. After his death another monk, Ennin (793–864), introduced Tantric rituals, with *maṇḍalas* and visualizations of deities as well as Zen meditation. This kind of ritual and ceremony was perceived as a colourful way of arousing and sustaining the practitioner's full attention, so effecting a process of deepening concentration. For these, as in the Tantric practices of other Buddhist countries, the practitioner needed first to pay homage and establish awareness of four directions for protection. Mindfulness is maintained by being aware of the whole field of the meditation, both outside and within. The visualization and *maṇḍala* (*mandara* J.) is then internalized in the mind's eye and seen in the practitioner too. After the mind has been fully engaged, and is able to unify the outer visualization with an inner one, the practitioner asks the various deities, Buddhas and Bodhisattvas that have been invoked, to depart. He or she lets all images dissolve, and allows the mind go to a bright emptiness. At the end of the practice, the practitioner is required to make a clean break with the ritual and re-enter wholeheartedly activities in the world.

Tendai had lost some of its influence by the early modern period, but some of its arguments, for instance that there was an original Buddhahood (*Hongaku*) and that this state was attainable by the common man, did persist, influencing subsequent Japanese meditative developments in other schools which might not have formally espoused this doctrine. Tracing its roots back, in particular, to the Yogācāra traditions of India, it also fostered most of the other major meditative traditions in Japan, through founder monks first trained in this school. Although it has an intellectual bias, it is also associated with a strong traditional meditative tradition that seems to have fostered an expansive, sometimes assertive creativity. Adapting the *Avataṃska* idea of the penetration of principle in the phenomenal world as an expression of *dharma*, for instance, poetry and the arts were actively encouraged.

The Japanese monk Kūkai (774–835) introduced the Mantrayāna Shingon school from China in 816, establishing a central temple on Mount Kōya, fifty miles from the capital. A man of immense prestige within the court, he also made a notable impact on the arts, and helped to establish modern written Japanese. Kōya was at one time home to 1000 temples and, for a period, Shingon outshone Tendai, superseding it at the court. Shingon rested upon two foundations. One was the preaching of the *dharma*. The other was the practice of the 'three mysteries' of mind, body and speech. For the mind, complex visualizations were made of *mandaras* with colours representing the six elements; for the body, the practice of *mudrā*, employing gestures and postures that enacted the balance of the elements in the body. For speech, *mantra* (*shingon* or *myō* J.) embodied the six elements through different sounds. The practitioner finds union with the *Dharmakāya*, the 'body' of the enlightened mind, with the intent 'to achieve Buddhahood in this very body' (*sokushin jōbutsu*). The luminous nature of the awakened mind can then be brought into being in the world. The complex symbology and relation of the microcosm, the body, with the macrocosm, the universe, were seen as a means of expressing this, so exerting great influence on poetry, in the *waka* and *renga* poets, art and ritual.

Both Tendai and Shingon were popular in court circles. The esoteric practices of these schools, involving the *mandara*, the visualization of deities and emanations and carefully graded ritual, further translated much Shintō and local practice through a visual vocabulary of Buddhas and Bodhisattvas. By the end of Heian period (794–1185), both schools went into slight decline. They have, however, survived into the twenty-first century, and much of the thought, rituals and meditations with which they were associated were subsumed into other forms of Buddhist practice.

PURE-LAND (JŌDO)

The Heian period was also characterized by bitter struggle and poverty amongst the peasantry. Buddhism was at that time a primarily aristocratic tradition and although Kūkai had shown great kindness to poorer elements of society, Buddhist monks had to fight against considerable social pressure to communicate their tradition as they would wish. The Pure-Land school, which had in part been developed in response to peasant needs, was naturally suited also to Japanese land-workers. The monk Kūya (903–72) found converts from all social classes when he travelled in Japan disseminating Pure-Land teaching and meditation through the short chant encapsulating the teaching. Little is known about Kūya, except that he was a lay practitioner from an early age, travelled throughout Japan and then took full ordainment in 948, when initiated in Tendai precepts. His commitment was always, however, to the commoner. He retained his old name, eschewed government posts, and travelled widely. During this time he studied texts, made up songs about the Pure Land, and made statues of the Buddha, regarding the physical form of the image of the Buddha as a teaching mechanism to arouse intuitive wisdom in the often illiterate peasant. His life story, of works for public benefit, suggests he would not have regarded this as a second-best alternative. Rather, he may have felt, in the manner of some modern Buddhist practitioners, that constant, daily bodily exercise may make the land-worker more awake to the 'text' of a representation of the Buddha. Someone who uses the body for physical work all day may be more sensitive than one who does not to the tranquillity of an arm and hand resting on the Buddha's lap, or the relationship between even, relaxed shoulders and an upright back. It is worth remembering that from the earliest times social status and education were not perceived as either a hindrance or a help in meditation.

The teachings of Hōnen (1133–1212), and his disciple Shinran (1173–1262), the principal early proponents of Pure-Land Buddhism, ensured that it became the largest single Buddhist school in Japan. The idea of *mappō*, that the *dharma* was in decline, had been a feature of Eastern Buddhism for centuries. Reintroduced by this school, it instigated a wave of interest in the simple devotional element that it suggested as the only effective means to liberation in a time when other forms of spiritual practice were difficult. Hōnen was born during the ascending fortunes of the warrior Samurai class, and became a Tendai monk early on in life. After spending years studying, it is said, the entire Buddhist canon and reciting the Amida chant (*nembutsu*), he decided in 1175 to commit himself to the *nembutsu* and founded the Jōdo (Pure-Land) sect, dedicated in particular to the poor and oppressed. His focus on this simple formula led him to reject all other Buddhist schools, a tendency towards exclusivity that from this period characterizes many Japanese Buddhist traditions.

As in China, the Pure-Land traditions have exercised a widespread popular appeal and today account for more practitioners in Japan than any other Buddhist path. Deeply devotional and, in its Japanese manifestations, often remarkably akin to monotheistic worship, Japanese Pure-Land represents a kind of practice which is perhaps most highly differentiated from the forms found in other traditions elsewhere. In what seems now a particularly Japanese accommodation of Buddhism, which allowed the custodianship of specific texts and rituals to become associated within a familial, Shintō context, the school encouraged marriage amongst the priestly orders. This was justified on the grounds that celibacy was likely to lead to pride and the entanglement of the ego: mastership of the temple lines in this school became patrilineal, a practice that continues to this day. The inheritors of these traditions, initiated by Shinran, are known as the *Jōdo-shin-shū*, or 'True Pure-Land School'.

NICHIREN

One of the most powerful figures in shaping Japanese Buddhism is Nichiren (1222–82), a fisherman's son, who, at the age of fifteen, took Tendai vows at a local temple. Detecting a quietism and complacency in the practices conducted there he initiated a new school, in 1253, based on the *Lotus-Sūtra*. He encouraged his followers to seek for the fulfilment of all aspects of liberation, worldly and spiritual, by employing the chant *Namu-myōhō-renge-kyō* (*Homage to the Lotus of Fine Dharma*), a distillation of the qualities of the *Lotus-Sūtra*. An iconoclastic preacher, he was banished from the mainland twice. After the first time he returned, and after the second miraculously escaped a death sentence, dying naturally in exile. His attempts to introduce a new element in Japanese Buddhism were successful, however; he also sought to institute social and political changes at a national level, and integrated these within his own religious system. There are now millions of followers of Nichiren Shoshū and its offshoot Sōka Gakkai (founded in 1930), which now has no formal connection with Nichiren groups. There are deep differences between these movements but all use chanting, usually a single formula, for solitary and group practice. The use of chanting as a means of attaining worldly aims as well as spiritual ones has brought them some criticism. Associated Nichiren movements have, however, been very successful globally. The followers of Sōka Gakkai around the world, now into the third and fourth generation, have different perspectives from earlier generations. There is less political emphasis. With regard to the charge of worldliness, longstanding practitioners point out that while some, though not all, use chant with a wish for worldly success, the motivation with which people undertake chanting changes in time. The chant's promise of success in achieving goals is an example of 'skill in means', encouraging, eventually, deeper spiritual practice.

The efficacy of chanting in Japanese schools is supposed to lie in origins described, in the manner of much Japanese meditative practice, in ancient Yogācāra terms. This sort of language was adopted by the Hossō (Faxiang C.) sect, which came to Japan in 660, and continued to influence many Japanese schools of meditation. The Buddha nature is latent, overlaid or hidden in human beings by a 'storehouse' (*ālayavijñāna*) of tendencies, from which the seeds (*bīja*) of all phenomena emerge. By frequent chanting, the practitioner gradually contacts deeper levels of the Buddha nature so that it can be allowed to percolate through these tendencies, in time gradually transforming them. Action in the world is then more likely to arise from contact with the intuitive knowledge that resides in the suchness (*tathatā*) of the Buddha nature, not from selfish wishes.

LOTUS-SŪTRA

The great text the *Sūtra of the Lotus Blossom of the Fine Dharma Saddharmapuṇḍarīka-Sūtra* (Sk), *Miao-fa Lien-hua Ching* (C), *Myōhō-Renge-Kyō* (J) is one of the earliest Buddhist scriptures, dating from the second century CE in an extant Sanskrit version. While the Chinese were quick to translate the texts of India into their own language, the Japanese preferred to keep them intact as they received them from China, regarding their inscribed or chanted forms as sacred material objects, that should not be changed in any detail. The text rests upon two principal ideas: that the Buddha is not confined by time and space, and so is always present to help suffering beings. All Buddhist paths lead to the awakening attained at Buddhahood.

The text employs an urgent and dynamic parable. A man has a house, in which children are playing. The house starts to go up in flames. How can he persuade the children to leave? He encourages them by telling them they will find various kinds of carriages when they leave, so that they escape the house of their own accord. One type is drawn by goat, symbolizing the *śrāvakayāna*, one by deer, the *pratyekabuddhayāna* and one by ox, the *bodhisattvayāna*. When they ask for their carriages, he gives each a large, beautifully adorned carriage to keep for themselves. It is of the great white ox (*Buddhayāna*). This is usually interpreted as giving pre-eminence to the third part, an emphasis the text certainly implies. It has been argued, however, that the parable is also subtle: the vehicles the children find after leaving the house are, for all three groups, both much better than they had imagined and equally splendid, for each of the categories of children. It seems that at the moment of awakening all three paths are transcended.

In a series of visualization exercises, presumably to be undertaken while listening to the recitation, the *sūtra* describes a vast *stūpa* which emerges from the ground and describes it containing the body of a Buddha named Prabhutaratna, who in a previous age taught the Lotus-Sūtra. The splendid Buddha emerges and gives half his seat to the Buddha. The sūtra says that the 'death' of the historical Buddha was an example of skilful means, to frighten people into taking the medicine they need. In this, the highest teaching, they find that the Buddha is always there to help them, if they will just utter his name.

In Nichiren schools it is said that just chanting the name of the Lotus-Sūtra elicits the quality of awakening in the practitioner, whose faith will then understand at the level of intuition its innermost teachings.

ZEN

The Chan/Zen schools arrived in Japan several centuries after other forms of Buddhist practice had set down roots. In the troubled Kamakura period (1192–1333), Japan came under the rule of the military Shōguns and Samurai, and there was a shift in power from the capital to the provinces. This movement allowed Buddhism to become more widely disseminated under the influence of the Samurai, who helped Zen in particular to spread

Figure 11.1 **Kinkakuji, a Rinzai Zen temple formerly known as Rokuonji, originally built in 1397**

more generally to the general populace. Its directness and a warrior-like emphasis on action and a few, apt and even enigmatic words captured the populist and even pugilistic mood of the times.

Eisai Zenji (1141–1215) started the Rinzai Zen school on his return from a trip to China in 1191. Like other schools it acknowledged that on the spiritual path there would be moments of awakening (wu (C) / satori (J)). The school also maintained that such sudden illuminations require gradual prior development and should not be clutched for their talismanic value, as was felt to be the case in some Zen schools. Insights are to be allowed to mature and tested through experience, so that they are integrated and not forgotten. In Japanese Rinzai, interactions between teacher and disciple take place in frequent private interviews known as *sanzen* consultation, held to be important for the testing of experience and for dispelling illusions that, for instance, some awakening is of a higher order than it is. The Rinzai school places particular emphasis on concentration, and, as Peter Harvey notes (1990: 270), seems more aligned to the *samatha* schools of Indian Buddhism. Modern forms teach a careful appreciation of the movement of the breath, which leads gently to a state of *samādhi*. The breathing is of a very long and relaxed kind, which draws attention down to the 'tanden' (*tantian*) below the navel, and allows the practitioner

Figure 11.2 **Detail of Kinkakuji temple**

to find a barely perceptible breath, which brings great peace. From here the practitioner comes to rest in the radiance of the mind. *Gongans/kōans* are used to test the intuition of the meditator, until he attains *jhāna/dhyāna* and can then apply investigative insight to that: the specially chosen phrase or sentence acts both as a means of producing concentration and as a catalyst for insight on the basis of that.

The Sōtō Zen school was started by Dōgen (1200–53), who had travelled in China in search of teaching. Dōgen attained enlightenment on being given the phrase, 'Cast off body and mind' by his teacher: by relinquishing identification, the practitioner becomes aware of the constant teaching in the universe around, and awakening becomes possible. Upon his return from China in 1227, Dōgen wrote a manual, *Shōbōgenzō*, with instructions for *Zazen*, 'sitting and opening the hand of thought', a form of meditation he describes as not leading to *jhāna/dhyāna* itself, but to awareness in the midst of process. In time he established his own school, loosely aligned to the Chinese Caodong. Disappointed with much Chan teaching in China, Dōgen did not promulgate sudden revelatory experiences, on the grounds that if they occurred they were part of an ongoing development. Earlier Tendai teaching had suggested awakening was already present: the practitioner just needed to discover it in any given moment. The Buddha nature is there to be realized. One of the school's notable developments was the practice of 'just sitting' (*shikantaza*). While meaning 'sitting', *Shikantaza* has also been described as the practice of doing each activity in life for the sake of that activity, regardless of whether one is sitting, lying, walking, or standing, or working. It attempts to arouse in practitioners an awareness beyond any particular method or goals. In practice it does employ many traditional meditation practices, such as watching the breath, for preliminary concentration (*samādhi*), in order to achieve this. In spirit, however, it seems kin to the basic mindfulness and *vipassanā* techniques of other schools, though the method is to try to avoid labels or excessive classification – or just to notice these when they arise in the mind too. One can see in *Zazen* and *shikintaza* an example of an integration of a new formulation of the teaching, meditation practice and a Japanese emphasis on physical external expression working hand in hand. If the Buddha is already present, then the job of the practitioner is simply to let him or herself manifest this; if the activity is 'just sitting', as the Buddha did, then that is what the practitioner does. The school is the most popular Zen school to this day.

THE SOUND OF ONE HAND CLAPPING

In the seventeenth century, Japanese kōans started to be schematized, and collections were compiled with 'correct' answers. The most famous, apparently composed during this period, is 'What is the sound of one hand clapping?' attributed to Hakuin Ekaku (1686–1768). This has continued to be popular for centuries. At Kennin Temple, in Gion, Kyōto, a thirteenth-century Zen monastery, there was a teacher in the nineteenth century called Mokurai, or Silent Thunder. One story told about him describes a boy of twelve called Toyo, who saw older disciples visit the master for *sanzen* each morning. Despite the teacher's refusal, Toyo wished to visit too. He struck the gong, bowed three times and went to listen in silence. Mokurai gave his teaching:

'You can hear the sound of two hands when they clap together. Now show me the sound of one hand.'
Toyo bowed, went to his room and heard some geishas.
When the teacher asked him the sound of one hand, Toyo played the geisha music.
The teacher was dissatisfied and told him to try again.
Toyo moved to a quiet place and heard some dripping water.
When he next visited his teacher, Toyo imitated dripping water.
'That is the sound of dripping water. What about the sound of one hand? Try again!' said Mokurai.
Toyo meditated and heard the sound of the wind.
But that was rejected too. As was the cry of the owl and the buzz of locusts.
For almost a year he meditated and wondered about the sound of one hand.
At last he entered true meditation. All sounds were transcended.
'I could collect no more,' he explained, 'so I reached the soundless sound.'
It was at this point, it is said, that the boy had understood the sound of one hand.

POSTURE

Perhaps because the realization of Buddhahood in the moment is considered so important, Zen schools pay particular attention to posture. Bodily carriage is the expression of and guide to mental state: to assume and sustain the posture with care is a way of bringing into being awakening. The half-lotus posture is favoured, or kneeling, either on the haunches, a husk-cushion or a specially made stool. As in other traditions, the back should be straight. There should be no tilt backwards or forwards. Slumping is an indication of loss of awareness and self-possession. The left hand is placed gently over the right, the opposite way around from the Indian *samādhi* posture, though the thumbs are also supposed to just touch one another so that the hands rest in a tranquil oval shape. The hands should be held as if bearing a precious object. In some the thumbs are held raised slightly, close to the navel, rather than resting on the palms. Whereas in Southern Buddhist schools meditation is usually conducted with the eyes shut, the eyes are sometimes half-open, in order to ensure that there is no distraction but that the meditator is awake too. For 'just sitting', practitioners sit in lines facing a wall. Sometimes one practitioner walks around and hits practitioners with a stick: this is to wake anyone slumping, to relieve tension points where the back and shoulders have become too rigid or tense, and sometimes to give a needed 'shock' to the meditator. The person who does this job is chosen on a rotation basis. While this posture is taken, often for long periods, thoughts, feelings, ideas and bodily sensations arise and there is awareness of them. If dissatisfaction arises, or excitement, the practitioner just continues sitting. The breath is watched, as a 'swinging door'. The teacher Dōgen also recommended particular care in maintaining collectedness as one leaves the posture. After sitting, Zen can continue in any activity. Awakening is always in the present.

The Japanese Zen attitude to posture provides an enactment of its teachings. Buddhahood, one's original nature to be brought into being, is expressed through the body's wholehearted engagement in the correct form. By 'just sitting' one lets oneself be a Buddha. The word Zen is derived from the word for meditation, *dhyāna* (Sk)/*jhāna* (P). By the time it has evolved in Japanese Zen, its associations have become rather different. Eastern forms of Chan, Seon, Thien and Zen share close affinities with one another, which differentiate them from other forms of Buddhist practice. While the element of concentration is still sometimes present, these schools include a great emphasis on processes of knowing, movement and awakening. In the various practices of Zen meditation, a quality of deep alertness, tranquillity in process and an understanding of change itself, within the mind and outside, are embodied. Eastern forms of Chan, Seon, Thien and Zen teach a kind of meditation resembling that taught in India, but they have created quite a different sort of spiritual path.

BUDDHISM, KŌAN, HAIKU AND THE ARTS

Soon after its arrival in Japan, Buddhism started to inspire and influence the form and content of an already sophisticated literature. One kind of *waka*, an early verse form, was supposedly shaped by Shingon theory in its thirty-one-syllable structure (5–7, 5–7, 7), said to emulate the thirty-two marks of the Buddha: the last, the thirty-second, is too sacred to be included. The haiku, a seventeen-syllable poem (5–7–5), has a particular association with Zen, and is characterized by sometimes startling physical observation, appreciation of the natural world and a zest for the moment. A famous haiku by an early master, Bashō (1644–94), describes 'an old dark sleepy pool', disturbed by the unexpected jump of a green frog: 'Plop! Watersplash!' It seems almost leaden to try and explicate the depth of associations, such as the traditional Japanese linkage of frogs with spring and the contrast between old and new in such haikus: the externally described image explodes into the mind's 'ancient' reverie with the fresh immediacy of a still-surprising moment of awakening (*satori*). Other Zen poems, in various genres, are characterized by a comparable delight in the haphazard, the momentary and the seasonal. In a poem 'composed while lighting incense', Gidō Shūshin (1325–88) describes the moving snows on the mountains and the nightly return of the stars. Buddhahood, he says, cannot be pinned down, 'like carving nicks on the side of the boat to mark its place in the river!' (Pollack 1985: 51). The Rinzai monk, Jakushitsu Genkō (1290–1367), describes phenomena as like dew, lightning or a deceptive dazzle of light: daily life and his routine continue. 'I eat my white rice, watch the green mountains' (Pollack 1985: 52). An earthy, rueful humour characterizes the poems of many Zen monks, describing their sack-like bodies and angular bones. Thanking friends for some tea, Shūshin, for instance, describes the steps by which an 'old and greedy' man prepares for meditation rather than an afternoon nap: 'With a ladle-full of its clear flow I boil some icy stream – How the lingering taste concentrates my divided mind! (Pollack 1985: 134). Indeed some Japanese poetry seems honed as a tool for Buddhist understanding. The mind that knows the natural world with full awareness brings into being, through accuracy of description, original Buddhahood:

All beings by nature are Buddha,
as ice by nature is water;
apart from water there is no ice,
apart from beings no Buddha.

Hakuin Ekaku (from 'A Song of Zazen, trans. Aitken 1991)

There is certainly something that 'thaws' the mind in the humour and precision of some of the best Zen poems.

CHIYONO (MUGAI NYODAI, 1223–98)

Many Japanese women, from all social classes, became nuns and some were highly esteemed teachers of meditation. Early Japanese women's writing had also always been characterized by inventiveness, confidence and grace: it was customary to compose *waka* verses on all kinds of occasions, as love-letters or records. Many nuns brought such finely tuned skills to bear upon the fruits of living the holy life, or, if from a low social class, learnt to compose verse as part of the training of a meditative life. A famous story is told of one of the first Zen women teachers, the nun Chiyono, who studied Zen under Bukko of Engaku. For a long time she could not obtain results from her meditation. At last, one moonlit night, she had to carry water in an old pail, which was bound with brittle bamboo. The bamboo finally broke, the bottom fell out of the pail, and the reflected light of the moon disappeared into the soil along with the water which had shown it. At that moment Chiyono was awakened, and wrote the following poem:

This way, that way
I tried to hold the pail of water together,
The bamboo strip was weakening and just about to ...
Break.
Suddenly the bottom fell out:
no more water!
no more moon in the water!
Emptiness in my hand.

SHAKYŌ

While Indian traditions, retained for so many centuries by *bhāṇakas* through techniques which ensured the correct transmission of the texts, were largely governed by orality and the exploration of sound, Eastern Asian countries from the earliest days also linked Buddhist meditation to the art of writing and calligraphy. These practical activities, seen as enactments of *dharma* in the physical world, continued to flourish even at times when Buddhism itself was less overtly influential. The practice of writing texts, Shakyō, has always been considered deeply meritorious, with its golden age seen as the period from 1050 to 1250. It is said that one cannot write properly if one is upset or disturbed or angry: the activity itself is also said, over a period of time, to free the mind from some defilements. In Japan in particular the copying of *sūtras* and the art of calligraphy were developed as discrete spiritual disciplines, requiring awareness of the chanted syllable or text, bodily posture, hand, breath, brush, ink and paper, all working together as one. This applies not only to the copying of *sūtra* collections but also to skills involved in executing one simple brush stroke as a test of meditative mastery, spontaneity and skill. The perfect painting of a single line or the *siddhaṃ* of the circle is seen as the consummate expression of purified mental state and its consequent imprint upon a physical form. The origin of all syllables,

Figure 11.3 **Calligraphy on a temple wall in Shikoku, Japan**

expressed either through voice or paint, lies in and will lead the practitioner to the *dharmadhātu*. So, for instance, the Japanese tantric syllable *hri* is taken to represent Amitābha, an embodiment of the power of that principle. When the syllable is drawn or recited, that power is established in the world. In order to express it the practitioner needs to make gradual preparations on the heart, mind and body. Training for the execution of a single *siddhaṃ* may take three years, over which time the practitioner, through repetition and reverence, fine-tunes his or her painting skills and actions. For the fulfilment of the practice, in Japan the calligrapher dons robes, pays homage and sits at a special table laid out with implements for painting, which are treated as ritual objects. With the execution of the *siddhaṃ*, it is said, the practitioner finds the *dharmadhātu*, the source of the syllable, as it is made manifest.

The five virtues of Shakyō, in which each word or syllable is seen as the expression of a new encapsulation of the Buddha nature, are expressed in the following way:

1   Venerating the letters with your eyes
2   Keeping the letters in your heart
3   Chanting the letters with your mouth
4   Writing the letters with your hands
5   Becoming one with the Buddha.

In Japan, particularly popular texts are the *Heart-Sūtra*, the twenty-fifth chapter of the *Lotus-Sūtra*, on Avalokiteśvara/Guan Yin and his/her compassion, the *Diamond-sūtra*, and the *Amida-sūtra*. The benefit accrued from such activity is not considered to be confined to oneself: after World War II many lay people dedicated themselves to shakyō to offer merit for those lost in the war.

Calligraphy is also considered an adjunct of Zen practice, with 'no method' and so no standard procedure. The practitioner makes a deep bow and sits on the heels to maintain close contact with the ground, keeping the centre of gravity below the navel. The practitioner fills the brush with ink, holds it above his or her head, 'in the world of *mu*', (emptiness), and takes a deep breath. Grasping the brush with a firm hand, he or she starts at the lower left-hand corner of the paper and makes a diagonal stroke, or writes *ichi*, 'one', in any one of a number of established styles. The stroke is written as slowly as possible, on the expiration of the breath, as if wielding a very heavy sword.

BUDDHIST ARTS

A number of other activities, still very popular in Japan, were shaped by Buddhist meditative practice and its particular relationship with Shintō, Dao and Confucianism. Such arts (dō), derived from Chinese counterparts known as *gongfu*, are not exclusively martial, though many are so. They include gardening, flower arranging (*kadō/ikebana*), and the way of the bow (*kyudō*).

Kyudō

The latter is typical of the martially based arts in that it has evolved over centuries, in this case through what seems to be the absorption of Zen and Shintō influence on an ancient, possibly Chinese, ceremonial tradition. Tracing ancestry of such disciplines is tricky: it is certainly true that some can be overeager to find historical meditative associations, but in considering Asian cultures, based so much in orthopraxy, there are risks also in excessive 'deconstruction', an approach that can overlook the traditionally salvific associations of ritual practice. In this case, at any rate, the use of the bow in a manner linking ritual and spiritual training seems at least early modern. Ritual activity concerned with the care and use of the vast bow (*yumi*) of bamboo, wood and leather, dates back to the tenth century, influenced by a Shintō appreciation of weapons as magical objects: depictions of warriors with bows in art from the sixth century suggest it had acquired some emblematic role even earlier. During the thirteenth century, in a high point of Samurai activity, Zen principles started to inform the training. Aphorisms such as 'one shot, one life' and 'shooting should be like flowing water', started to be employed, a measure of the way the bow was esteemed as a means of awakening awareness and readiness to act. By the seventeenth century, when the bow had ceased to be used as a martial weapon, *kyudō* emerged as a discrete discipline, a process fully codified by the nineteenth century. Months of preparation involving breath control, care in establishing action from the 'tanden' below the navel and repeated action are needed to discover the 'way' of the correctly shot arrow from the very large bow. After sitting meditation and careful preparatory work, the target can be hit cleanly, subject and object unified in a clear enactment of Zen and Samurai principle. The popular book by Eugen Herrigel, *Zen in the Art of Archery* (1953), is regarded by some as unrepresentative of real practice and too 'Germanic'. It is, however, a simple and eloquent work, understandably interpreting Zen through Herrigel's cultural heritage: its account of learning through a teacher has done a great deal to further interest in both Zen and Kyudō around the world.

The seven tea rules (*Shūun'an-hekisho*)

Another such ritual activity is the tea ceremony. Tea was introduced to Japan from China, along with some ancient communal customs such as that of a group of monks all drinking tea together from one large bowl, a measure of the longstanding importance attributed to social cohesion for spiritual work – and the health-giving properties of tea. The Rinzai monk, Eisai Zenji, brought tea plants over from China and recommended the beverage as a cure for sleepiness in meditation. In the early modern period the ceremonies associated with tea drinking assumed a different kind of formality under the auspices of Japanese Zen teachers.

In the tea ceremony, *chadō*, Zen principles are enacted through a fusion with Daoist understanding of action in accordance with the 'Way', Confucian care for manners and a Japanese love of a ritual in an appropriate setting. The ceremony is peculiarly expressive for its scrupulous formality and gracious restraint: a single ritual event is supposedly refined to become a tool for arousing awareness and inner peace so that eventually, through care and repetition, wisdom may arise. It is supposed to bring into being four basic principles: Harmony (*wa*), Respect (*Kei*), Purity (*Sei*) and Tranquillity (*jyaku*).

Various fifteenth- and sixteenth-century manuals on the subject give guidelines for the ceremony, which indicate its association with Buddhist doctrine, and that at one time, at any rate, it was considered a full spiritual training. The tea-house – the 'hut of emptiness' – is approached through a beautifully maintained garden, of rocks, stones and sand. Before a ceremony water is sprinkled on the stepping stones so that, slippery, they are trodden slowly and with grace. Hierarchy is acknowledged by the straightness of bamboo; flow by moss and the meander of the path. Patterns of light and shade, in stones and architecture, smooth the way from exterior to interior space. The garden demonstrates the gardener's attunement to the seasons and the natural environment. The gardens of one tea master, the architect and calligrapher Koburi Enshū (1579–1647) were considered particularly noteworthy. The garden path (*roji*), it is said, should make manifest (*ro*) the heart (*ji*): by following the natural curve of the surroundings and demonstrating an attunement with the design of the garden, it should reveal the practitioner's inner nature.

Figure 11.4 **A Japanese garden. This sort of garden is not walked upon but viewed from the side. Stones are placed on carefully raked sand.**

On his or her arrival, the host welcomes the guest into the hut with a humility and friendliness that should be echoed in the recipient: to enter the low door of the hut all must crouch. Status is of no importance. Each guest is greeted in the manner in which, it is enjoined by the manuals, all events in daily life should be welcomed by the practitioner. All instruments associated with the ceremony should be brought out and put away in the guest's presence. Some manuals warn against excessively rich or showy implements as detracting from the kindly austerity of the ceremony: old and well-worn are preferred. Bitter-green matcha tea is used. There is no climax to the ceremony; no one moment is more important than any other. Each movement and preparatory action should be performed with care, and there should be awareness of events occurring in the world around, particularly the seasonal: wind, sun and rain outside the hut may be commented upon by participants. Discussion should be limited to observations about the immediate surroundings, or, where appropriate, *dharma*.

Seven rules were formulated by a great Tea Master, Sen Rikyū (1522–91), well illustrated in the following story:

A disciple of Sen Rikyū once asked this question:

'What precisely are the most important things that must be understood
and kept in mind at a tea gathering?'

Sen Rikyū answered: 'Make a delicious bowl of tea; lay the charcoal
so that it heats the water; arrange the flowers as they are in the field; in
summer suggest coolness; in winter, warmth; do everything ahead of
time; prepare for rain; and give those with whom you find yourself every
consideration.'

The disciple, somewhat dissatisfied with this answer because he could
not find anything in it of such great importance that it should be deemed a
secret of the practice, said, 'That much I already know....'

Rikyū replied, 'Then if you can host a tea gathering without deviating
from any of the rules I have just stated, I will become your disciple.'

S'Oshitsu Sen (1979: 30)

The tea ceremony, like so much in Japan, is not always self-consciously
'Buddhist'. It is included here as it demonstrates one way that in Japan,
Buddhist principles of mindfulness, stillness in movement and respect for
other beings have become deeply interwoven with ritual. It is not clear
whether the ceremony offers guidance now in the full development of
mindfulness and concentration: at one time it appears it did.

Japanese history has seen some particularly violent periods, during which
Buddhist practice become less evident. Divisions between feudal lords from
1333 to 1573 and the military dictatorship, which lasted from 1603 to
1867, did not foster spiritual practice. Shintō also underwent a great revival
in the late nineteenth century, although Buddhism was never superseded. In
the twentieth century Buddhism to a certain extent flourished, particularly
after the Second World War. Sōtō Zen has been popular, as have the Pure
Land traditions. A number of chanting groups have been successful. It has
famously been said that the Japanese are born into Shintō ceremony, marry
with Christian and die with Buddhist.

CONCLUSION

Meditative practice in Japan shares many characteristics with that of its
neighbours. In the development of the idea of Buddhahood as achievable
by anyone, in this body, attitudes to sitting and conducting meditation
were gradually transformed. In Japan, a profoundly mimetic culture, theory
embedded itself in practice: ritual and behaviour 'in the moment' are seen
as expressions of doctrine. Ritual seems also to have influenced doctrine,

Figure 11.5 **Statues of the Buddha at a temple in Shikoku**

in the incorporation of Shinto deities, the emphasis on physical movement and posture in some schools as ways of bringing into being Buddhahood, and the further development of chant as a salvific practice. Many Japanese enjoy activities such as martial arts, calligraphy and gardening, all loosely aligned to Buddhist practice. Buddhism seems to have grown into a number of areas of life in the whole nation, and it is often difficult to attempt to separate that, or, in some cases, meditation, from them.

TIMELINES

552	Introduction of Buddhism from Paekche, Korea
594	Buddhism proclaimed state religion
741	*Golden-Light Sūtra* distributed to all provinces by order of emperor
788	Founding of Tendai in Japan and Enryaku-ji Temple on Mt Hiei by Saichō (767–822)
806	Kūkai (774–835) returns from China
818	Saichō codifies regulations for monks of Mt Hiei
847	Ennin returns from China to found Tendai
903–72	Kūya and Pure Land Buddhism
1133–1212	Hōnen and consolidation of Pure Land
1141–1215	Eisai Zenji and introduction of Rinzai Zen

1173–1262	Shinran
1185–1392	Kamakura period
1200–53	Dōgen and establishment of Sōtō Zen
1522–91	Tea master Sen Rikyū
c.1570	Persecution of Buddhism in Japan
1868–1912	Renewed suppression of Buddhism

FURTHER READING

Bielefeldt, C. (2004) 'Japan', Robert Buswell Jnr. (ed.), Encyclopedia of Buddhism, 2 vols., New York: Macmillan, 1, 384–91.

Bucknell, R. and Kang, C. (1997) The Meditative Way: Readings in the Theory and Practice of Buddhist Meditation, Richmond, Surrey: Curzon 64–5, 146–58.

Cousins, L.S. (1985) 'Buddhism', in Hinnells, J.R. (ed.) A Handbook of Living Religions, Harmondsworth, Middx: Penguin, 278–343.

Dobbins, J.C. (2004) 'Exoteric/Esoteric Kenmitsu Buddhism in Japan', Robert Buswell Jnr. (ed.), Encyclopedia of Buddhism, 2 vols., New York: Macmillan, 1, 271–5.

Gomes, L.O. (2004) 'Meditation', Robert Buswell Jnr. (ed.), Encyclopedia of Buddhism, 2 vols., New York: Macmillan, 2, 520–30.

Harvey, P. (1990) Introduction to Buddhism: Teachings, History and Practices, Cambridge: CUP, 161–9, 270–9.

Hammitzsch, H., Lemesurier P. trans., (1977) Zen in the Art of the Tea Ceremony, Tisbury, Wiltshire: Element.

Heine S. and Wright D.S. (eds) (2000) The Kōan: Texts and Contexts in Zen Buddhism, Oxford/New York: OUP.

Heinemann, R.K. (1991) 'The World and the Other Power: Contrasting Paths to Deliverance in Japan', in Bechert, H. and Gombrich, R. (eds) The World of Buddhism: Buddhist Monks and Nuns in Society and Culture, London: Thames and Hudson, 231–79.

Herrigel, E., Hull, R.F.C. trans., Suzuki, D.T. intro., (1953) Zen in the Art of Archery, London: Routledge and Kegan Paul.

Hurvitz, L. (1976) Scripture of the Lotus Blossom of the Fine Dharma (The Lotus Sūtra): translated from the Chinese of Kumarajīva, New York: Columbia University Press.

Onuma, H. with Deprospero, D. and J. (1993) Kyudo: The Essence and Practice of Japanese Archery, Tokyo: Kodansha International.

Pollack, D. (1985) Zen Poems of the Five Mountains, New York: Scholar's Press.

Sen, S'O. (1979) Tea Life, Tea Mind, London: Wetherhill.

Stevens, J. (1995) Sacred Calligraphy of the East, 3rd edn., Boston/London: Shambala.

Suzuki, S. (1991) Zen Mind, Beginner's Mind, New York: Weatherhill.

Teiko, Y., Peterson, R. and C. trans. (1988) Japanese Esoteric Buddhism, Boston/London: Shambala.

WEBSITES

'Chado, the way of Tea': http://japanhouse.art.uiuc.edu/oldsite/tea/1/4/1_4_1.html

Timelines: http://www.wsu.edu:8080/~dee/ANCJAPAN/TIMELINE.HTM

'The Japanese Garden' (July 13, 2007): http://learn.bowdoin.edu/japanesegardens/

Kōans and Sūtras:

Aitken, R. Roshi trans. (December 1991): 'Diamond Sangha Zen Sutras', http://www.ciolek.
com/WWWVLPages/ZenPages/Daily-Zen-Sutras.html#HAKUIN
http://www.buddhistinformation.com/on_the_life_of_dogen_zenji.htm
http://www.meditationproject.org/Many_One.htm
http://www.ashidakim.com/zenkoans/zenindex.html
http://www.angelfire.com/realm/bodhisattva/chiyono.html

Meditation Around the World
Twelve

Universally Good lives peacefully in all lands
Avatamsaka-Sutra (Thomas Cleary trans.)

THE BUDDHA

The image of the Buddha is the focus of devotional attention in most of the Buddhist schools covered in this book. Over the last two thousand years countless people, from varied cultures, in all kinds of states of mind, have sat down and looked at this simple form. There they have found reassurance, guidance, inspiration and, sometimes, teaching for meditation. Has the chin dropped? Is the mind settled? Are the knees supported well? How do these factors affect thought and action, as well as meditation? Awakening, in stillness and wisdom, is something that exists in present conditions. The image of the Buddha has been watched, explored and translated into physical form by many different peoples in highly various ways. Where people practise meditation, after some time new approaches, intellectual emphases and formulations emerge. Some might turn their minds to philosophy, debate or action. Some turn to discussion and some to silence. Just as the ways that people are drawn to Buddhist meditation now are diverse, so they seem to have been in the past. The Southeast Asians, it seems, were attracted to a meditative system and a soteriological framework. The Tibetans were inspired by the experiences suggested in the *Tantras* and the possibility of being a meditating scholar. Daoists, already interested in the development of the breath, investigated breathing mindfulness. Other Chinese schools found intellectual inspiration from Buddhist meditative practice and probed the limits and use of language itself. The Japanese focused on the efficacy of ritual and the suggestive bearing of the figure of the Buddha as a teacher. Many Eastern countries employed the meditative use of chant. All found the Buddha a guide and inspiration. This book has attempted to show some ways these attractions deepened, evolved and, in the end, transformed some meditative practice. It is a subject worthy of much more study.

FOUR DIRECTIONS

For the purposes of this book, the boundaries of East, South and North Asia have been used in a loose way to describe generic forms of Buddhism. The categories are not rigid, and there have often been contacts between groups over the last two thousand years which have taken influences in directions counter to the original transmission of the teaching. The ordination line was re-introduced into Sri Lanka from Thailand, for instance, and waves of Chinese immigration since the twelfth century have had some influence on Thailand and meditative practice there. Recently Chinese travellers have imported Tibetan Buddhism back into China, renewing a contact that has ebbed and flowed since the twelfth century. All these currents have created many different influences and cross-influences, often going on over centuries. But it is not a case of a constant flow making a kind of Buddhist 'soup' of undifferentiated contributory elements. Some countries have had little contact with other regions where Buddhisms and meditations of quite a different kind have evolved. Such isolation can be particularly interesting: after a period of separation for over a thousand years, Nepal, for instance, still uses a *siddham* script also employed in Japan, evidence of how ancient elements have been preserved and protected in different contexts.

DIFFERENT FORMS OF BUDDHISM

The separate identities of Buddhisms and the meditations involved in them, seem one of the main reasons why Buddhism is so attractive to the modern world. Its specificity, local colouring and highly differentiated methods appeal to very different kinds of people. In Britain, for instance, there are now, according to the 2001 census, 150,000 Buddhists; in America three to four million (see Appendix A). But these, like those in many European countries, are varied, some coming from new immigrant groups, some from different religious backgrounds and some from longstanding communities. The kind of person attracted to the austere simplicity of Japanese Zen may be of a very different type and temperament from the person attracted to the rich smells, colours and textures of Tibetan Buddhism. 'Protestant Buddhism', while used as a term of perjoration by some for those adhering to an understanding derived from early Western readings of Theravāda texts, has produced many lifelong Buddhists in Britain who have brought a new and often highly conscientious element to the practice of the Southern schools. How these will all evolve, perhaps only time will tell.

What does seem to be the case, however, as scholarship, travel and personal practice makes this subject more accessible, is that some of the categories that have been used in the West to describe schools of Buddhism are less rigid and distinct than was previously supposed. Early Pāli texts and the practices of Southern traditions contain features found in other schools, such as the use of visualization and ritual, and demonstrate in abundance qualities for which they are not always given credit, such as a strong emphasis on loving-kindness and compassion. Chan/Zen/Seon/Thien schools often exhibit a great reverence for textual work, devotional practice and humility, again against conventional stereotypes. Contrary to their popular image, Tibetan Buddhist texts and practitioners can be quite mundane and pragmatic in encouraging a straightforward level of basic mindfulness of one's own body and feelings as well as others. The schools, texts and teachers of Buddhism, if given loyalty, have some experience of eliciting qualities in time in people in areas that might not at first be expected.

Many schools share far more features in common than is often supposed. The eightfold path often features; the doctrine of dependent origination always does in some form. Many traditions have the interplay of *samatha* /*śamatha* and *vipassanā* /*vipaśyanā* as an important dynamic within their meditative texts and practice, which is seen sometimes in the discussion of a relationship between concentration (*samādhi*) and wisdom (*prajñā*). While they often differ in the priority they would assign to one of them, in most cases they state that in the end both are necessary for salvation. *Sīla*, or good conduct in the world and generosity are also key elements in almost all forms of Buddhism. The principle of non-harm characterizes all forms of Buddhism, though how this is interpreted in some schools may differ radically.

The figure of the Buddha provides a still point and focus for devotional practice in most Buddhist traditions. How this figure is interpreted, honoured and emulated varies greatly. From the experience of Buddhists 'on the ground', all probably feel an affinity with other forms of Buddhism. Many, however, if not most, naturally enough, prefer to practise in the way that is traditional for them, and which has contributed to their own cultural background. This may be quite different from other forms. Those brought up in one Buddhist country may well have had little or no contact with the rituals and methods of other Buddhist regions, which may have developed on lines which seem quite unusual or strange. Cultural cross-references and impressions are impossible to assess and quantify in a book of this kind. For instance Nepal is now receiving many Buddhist visitors as pilgrims from other countries, and it is difficult as yet to see what effect this will have on the form of Buddhism there. At the moment it has its own hybrid, as do some other Buddhist regions, and how this will develop through so much contact with other cultures is difficult to assess. For these, and many other reasons, Buddhism's heterogeneity is not something to be underestimated. It really is different in different places, and, from the point of view of the subject of this book, much of its strength in various cultures depends upon the way local practice has accommodated and supported the practice of meditation and vice versa.

WESTERN BUDDHISM

Yet another dynamic has been introduced by the idea of 'Western Buddhism'. This needs to go in inverted commas, as perhaps the other categories should too, because forms of Buddhism in what we call the West are even more highly differentiated. Most of the major traditions described in this book have now become well established in countries where Buddhism is new. It is early days to assess how this will work. What is American Buddhism? What is British Buddhism? It may be that the categories which are most suitable for defining traditions in the last century become unsuitable as Buddhist meditations and practices are imported into new countries and different cultures. This process has been going on for some time and involves, literally, millions of Buddhists. Pure-Land Buddhism, which came first to the States via Japanese and Chinese railroad workers in the nineteenth century, now has practitioners who have been American for generations. Those who follow Nichiren and Sōka Gakkai movements, who number millions globally, have also now been established, sometimes for several generations, in different countries. The latter part of the twentieth century saw devastating political upheaval in Cambodia, Myanmar, Laos and Vietnam, instigating waves of emigration from these countries. These groups, also numbering millions, may well also be developing different identities from those in their land of origin. The Tibetan diaspora, another product of migration prompted by the devastation within the homeland since 1950, often practise with greater attention to traditional practice than is always possible in the homeland, a feature also perhaps often a characteristic of migrating groups.

DIFFERENT KINDS OF BUDDHISM

At various times attempts have been made for Buddhist groups to work together, though a unified, homogeneous form is not seen by many Buddhists as necessary or desirable. The first of these was by Colonel Olcot in the nineteenth century, in what was then Ceylon. Recently there has been much more in the way of co-operation between various groups that acknowledges individual ways of working. The International Vesakha Conference in Bangkok has been one such venture, which has promoted some happy and even eccentric encounters between Buddhists of different nationalities and traditions, from countries as varied as Israel, Serbia, Ghana and New Zealand as well as from traditionally Buddhist ones. The Dalai Lama has also acted as a spokesman for Buddhism worldwide. The schools of Buddhism do, however, remain very different in meditation practice and doctrine. The *Avataṃsaka-Sūtra*, a text which became an inspiration for many Eastern Buddhists, speaks of a vast jewelled net, throughout the universe, which reflects in each crystal all the other crystals in the whole. This image seems to apply to the diversity of and within various traditions. There are all sorts of colours, depths and brilliances as comparable ideas and forms of meditation practice in different traditions seem reflected in one another. The difficulties and dis-eases of the human mind are delineated, often in great detail. There is also a sense of its inherent health, sometimes formulated as a radiance, sometimes as its potential for awakening, sometimes as an innate knowledge, a Buddhahood that is already there. Beings need to work for their own salvation, but can help others too. These needs, found in different conditions, are formulated by various traditions in various ways.

Certain ideas in the history of Buddhism have provided great inspiration and guidance for meditators, whether or not they follow the particular school with which that idea has been associated. The three lines of Bodhisatta/Bodhisattva, dedicated to the wellbeing of others; the *paccekabuddha*, who finds a way on his or her own; and the arahat, who finds awakening through hearing the teaching, are all expressions of vows that can transform the practice of meditation. Usually some sort of progression is seen; but some teach that these motivations may be suitable at different stages for different people. The area of motive, for Westerners, may be mysterious and not even recognized by themselves. I have met English Buddhists who say they started meditation for all sorts of reasons. Three examples spring to mind. One friend met someone at a pop festival who said that meditation was more 'cool' than drugs. Another desperately fancied someone handing out leaflets for a meditation class. Another claims to have had nothing else to do on Sunday afternoons, when classes were held. All of these people are still practising, thirty years later, tirelessly, in different traditions. Many of those who stated more 'noble' aspirations are not. What people think or say they are doing may be quite different from what is happening. I suspect these people of English articulations of what has become for them a form of the Bodhisattva vow!

There are, however, certain formal stages of commitment within many traditions. These often involve taking refuge as a starting point for meditation. Other expressions of commitment are often formulated and given privately, at the discretion of those teaching. All Buddhist teachings and teachers, in all traditions, stress the importance of wishing for the wellbeing of others and indeed all sentient beings. All regard it as essential for awakening. It is worth bearing in mind that some also teach that one should remember to wish well for oneself, and that loving kindness and compassion do not seek to impose their wishes on others.

The rich and manifold nature of these expressions are also a product of their separateness. Buddhism tends to form relationships with the traditions already existing in a country, such as Brahminism, Daoism and Confucianism, as well as with local 'deities' and popular forms of practice. This is evinced in the great variety of meditations or adaptations of traditional forms that have evolved in different settings. Particularities that are the product of adaptation seem to be an essential part of Buddhism's integration into the language and rituals of different regions. The image of the jewelled net is useful here: the radiance of a tradition seems to come from local separateness as well as affinity.

As Buddhism and its meditation practices travels, these adaptations are occurring in many ways. Waves of emigration of Buddhists, often now several generations down the line, the global trend for backpacking when young and visiting other countries, the accessibility of teachings on the internet and the movement of many teachers from Asia to centres in the West, are all having an impact. The movement of Westerners to Asia to ordain and practise meditation in a traditional context sometimes encourages locals to look at their own schools of Buddhism and the practice of meditation in a new light. Buddhism is becoming global, but many Buddhists and meditators hope that it retains and, in new contexts, develops some local identity and character.

RITUAL AND DEVOTION

There is a clear and important differentiation between meditation for *jhāna* or *vipassanā*, which involves sitting down and doing a meditation practice away from distractions, and practices for daily life and living in the world. Many walking practices require this seclusion too. Many rituals, chants, mindfulness techniques and other activities that support these are, however, also sometimes considered necessary complementary exercises. In most traditions, as we have seen, they form a large and significant part of daily practice.

An important distinction must be made between the kind of sustained sitting practice that needs regular sessions and the full attention of the practitioner, and things that can be done as part of a daily routine. Historically, and in a modern context, most traditions of Buddhism recommend, for meditation leading to *samatha*, and most forms of *vipassanā*, a period of time, however short, where it is the main object of attention. They also recommend making a clear mark between this sort of practice and activities of the day, so as to develop more fully mindfulness and concentration. Most traditions of Buddhism also have methods for setting aside daily preoccupations and worries and entering a meditation session. For some these are devotional, for others simply marking a space and time set aside from other activities.

There are also a number of features, however, called *bhāvanā* in Pāli and Sanskrit traditions and with counterparts in other traditions, which are not quite the same as meditation, but which complement, nourish and bring into the world the effects of meditative practice. Such ceremonies as the sharing of merit in Southern Buddhism, dedications for the welfare of other beings and the various localized rituals that link to different forms of practice, provide precise, formal ways of enacting the eightfold path in a particular setting. Such features do not necessarily involve deeper cultivation of *samatha* and *vipassanā*, but are considered essential for certain types of individuals as ways of developing an attitude helpful to meditation practice, and allowing motivation to be purified. Some ensure that the elements of *sīla*, described as right speech, right action and right livelihood, as well as generosity, are maintained. Others, that at the level of right view and right intention the mind is open to ideas such as 'non-self' and willing to try new directions in meditation.

Ritual elements in particular may contain a kind of seed understanding. The offering of flowers in Southern Buddhist countries, for instance, with chanting, is intended to still the mind to calm (*samatha*) and introduce a touch of insight (*vipassanā*): the flowers are described as going towards dissolution. The effect of offering flowers in such a ritual, and the 'letting go' (*cāga*) involved should not be underestimated for those of a certain temperament. On a purely anecdotal level I know many people, often non-Buddhists, who have been helped by rituals of this kind. One woman, not a Buddhist, told me that when apparently near death in a Tibetan hospital, she heard some monks at the next-door bed chanting and making offerings for someone else: she feels they helped her too. The space such rituals create do seem to help some to recovery – or, if the practitioner is clearly dying, for them to die in peace. It is considered very helpful for the next rebirth if the practitioner him or herself can 'let go', in the same way as offering flowers, lamps or incense, at the moment of death.

The idea of rebirth, and that birth and death are stages in a longer process, has often made Buddhist principle attractive through ritual as much as through the transmission of ideas. At some funeral ceremonies water is poured at the end to benefit all beings around, and to share merit with the dead. Everyone joins in the offerings of food, clothes, lights etc. and calls on other beings to take delight in these too. Such a ritual is an enactment of a perspective that allows the working of *kamma* to be seen as operating over lifetimes, as well as from moment to moment or within one lifespan. The mysterious singleness of any one birth or death is not denied. The perspective that the doctrine of *kamma* offers, however, is felt to allow a greater freedom and balance in relationships with others. Such rituals can share merit with parents, relatives and friends who may have died unhappily. They may wish any other 'ghosts' around in unhappy rebirths happiness. These are conducted in a context where there is a larger, subliminal sense of *kamma* operating on a vast as well as small scale. These ceremonies, performed with monks around who splash water on participants as they chant and offer blessings, can make such events memorable occasions, and sometimes even happy ones, for children too. Such patterns are replicated in other Buddhist rituals, in other regions, which cannot be discussed more fully here.

Meditation seems to need some sort of 'soil' to grow in, which *bhāvanā* of many kinds helps to provide and strengthen. The way this happens appears, in most cultures, to make creative and exploratory use of local customs, stories, myths and practices. Alan Sponberg (1986) has noted that we need to look at the way Buddhism was absorbed in new regions historically if we are to understand something of the way to do this in new contexts now. There is a real difference between the practices, even of neighbouring

Figure12.1 **Little girl chanting in Japanese temple**

regions, associated with ritual, ceremony and ideas connected with daily meditation, that demonstrate how this process has occurred. The chanting traditions are a good example of this. Their evolution has involved centuries of care, exploration and adjustment to language, metre, custom and local verse forms. Some are considered salvific in themselves, others as part of a path of meditation and insight.

THEORY AND INTELLECTUAL INVESTIGATION

Investigation and the awakening of the intellect also seems to have accompanied the spread of meditation. *Abhidhamma*, analysis of dependent origination and its implications and the inspirational philosophical methods of India, China and Tibet, are rightly the objects of challenging scholarly discussion. They have also, however, been closely associated with meditative work, and continue to be so in those countries where they are still examined, debated and argued over as applicable systems for understanding the mind, its processes and its relationship to the world around. Even the system that apparently rejects doctrinal exploration, the Chan/Zen tradition, has proved creative in its intellectual formulation: the *kōan*, the haiku and many forms of poetry evolved from Buddhist meditative practice. It is as if meditation awakens interest in using the intellect too, or perhaps needs it: Tibetan monks 'work out' the intellect through a vigorous system of challenge and debate on doctrinal points. Disciplines connected with the intellect in turn inspire further meditative exploration.

The eightfold path seems, historically, to have inspired a creative and ongoing process of adjustment and evolution in its application. Complete as an embodiment of principle, it seems however, to thrive in the incomplete, the open-ended and the changing. It inspires, at times, reformulation and exploratory work. Perhaps it always needs to be true to its name and to be 'awake' in order to be 'Buddhist'. It will be interesting to see how the many Buddhist meditative traditions develop in new contexts. Historically, Buddha figures start to look like the nationality of the country in which they are made. Qualities of stillness, alertness and sometimes humour are present, but take various different manifestations. In the same way, Buddhist theory, meditative practice and chant forms seem to develop in time new forms and particularities. Meditators and their groups have to deal with a number of issues, which include awareness of local customs, the need to apply for planning consent for meditation centres, kindliness to neighbours and creative adaptation to sometimes very complex theory systems. This needs time, patience and the willingness to look for the middle way in apparent contradictions.

LAY PRACTICE

As the practice of meditation and Buddhism moves into the twenty-first century, a number of interesting associated questions are being asked which are worth briefly considering. There has been an unprecedented increase in lay meditative practice in the late twentieth and twenty-first centuries, which some say is not typical of Buddhism as the monastic orders have usually been the main practitioners. This may be the case, but a few things should be said about this.

First, the majority of Buddhists must have been lay in the past: they did not always practise what we call meditation. But meditation must have been practised by some of the laity. In Southeast Asian countries, ordination may be undertaken for shorter times and most men become monks for what is usually a three-month period as they enter manhood. This practice is ancient. Historically many males, at least, must have practised some meditation and some, presumably would have continued at home, or at a time of crisis. Monasteries throughout Southeast Asian countries are full of women visitors, practising bhāvanā, in the form of offering food, chanting, performing ritual offerings and helping out, but also sitting in practice. The Indian example of the sannyāsin, the one who devotes him or herself to meditation in the last stage of life, still continues in spirit in such countries. Early Buddhist texts speak of members of the laity of both sexes having special meditative attainments and describe the laity wearing white for the day and doing meditation practice. There have also, historically, been Buddhist movements, particularly those associated with the Northern schools, where lay meditators have been prominent. The *Vimalakīrtinideśa-Sūtra*, popular in China, describes in eulogistic terms the life of an enlightened householder. As was noted in Chapter 9, lay practitioners in ancient China spoke of reconciling spirituality with a Confucian, householder life. Another dyanamic is introduced by the consideration that in some Japanese and Tibetan orders, marriage may be allowed as an aspect of the priestly role. This could include meditative practice too.

Historically, lay practice itself has sometimes been described. The Korean, Jinul, spoke of the potentially salvific effects of chanting, for the laity as well as the monastic orders, when pursued with an appropriate level of commitment that also included *samatha* and *vipassanā* elements. The various forms of Japanese Buddhism involving chanting may not always make such claims for their practices, but they seemed to have adapted in their own countries of origin and in other ones to lay practice. The dissemination of Chan and the Pure-Land across large proportions of China was associated with lay practice. Indeed the laity may be in a good position to practise some forms of *bhāvanā* that act as a support to meditation. Many traditions, such as *gongfu* in the East and the forms of dance and chant in other Buddhist countries, suggest that various forms of *bhāvanā*, while not leading directly to *jhāna* or *vipassanā*, are richly diverse supports for it, expressing its effects through action. These features seem to be needed for the meditation tradition to continue in a healthy way and are encouraged by the monastic orders. They do not exclude the practice of sitting meditation.

Many teachers recommend lay practice for Westerners, as the familiarity of one's own country and routines can, oddly enough, be more supportive when starting meditation. We do not have centuries of acculturation and the emotional support offered in Asia, though some choose to go there and ordain. Many distinguished meditation teachers from Asia now visit the West for extended periods and teach here. An understandable objection to practising meditation in the householder life that is sometimes expressed is that it encourages people to renounce sex. I have never heard this idea promulgated for the laity by monks. The happiness of the monastic life is inspirational, and always stated to be higher by the Buddha, but it is not for everyone.

This is a far-ranging and too-brief discussion of a number of issues in an under-researched area. The examples mentioned here suggest some possibilities and historical precedents. There are probably now far more meditators amongst the laity than there were in many places, at many times, in Buddhist history, but it is not a new phenomenon. Modern lay practitioners who practise meditation may not need such validation from the past, but it is gratifying. Another point could be made: there have been meditative disciplines, such as some theory systems, which require education, and some populist movements, such as the chanting methods of Eastern Buddhism, aimed primarily at large populations. Certainly the holy life is considered more suited to meditation. I am aware, however, of no period in Buddhist history, in which status, class or education has been considered a factor affecting the ability to practise meditation, for either the purposes of concentration or insight.

BUDDHISM THROUGH WESTERN EYES

The 'West' has a long history of contact with Buddhism: an early Indo-Greek king, Menander, became a Buddhist and Gandhāran Buddhist art was to some degree influenced by Greek classical style. St John of Damascus even brought the name Josaphat (Bodhisattva) to the West in his account of the lifestory of a hero who, in the early modern period, is canonized as a Christian saint. St John, however, would probably have never heard the word 'Buddha'. The interesting problem of interpreting key Buddhist notions has always been a constant feature of the transmission of Buddhism as it had contact with very different cultures. William of Rubruck (c.1210–70), a Flemish Franciscan monk, visited Mongolia in the thirteenth century. Here are his comments on the 'Friars' he encountered in Karkoram:

> ... they keep their heads uncovered as long as they are in the temple, reading in silence and keeping silence. And when I went into one of their temples at Caracarum, and found them thus seated, I tried every means of inducing them to talk, but was unable to do so. Wherever they go they have in their hands a string of one or two hundred beads, like our rosaries, and they always repeat these words, on mani baccam, which is, 'God, thou knowest,' as one of them interpreted it to me, and they expect as many rewards from God as they remember God in saying this.
>
> Waugh (2002: XIII)

This is suggestive writing, as clearly the monks and Rubruck did succeed in finding some sort of way of discussing their spiritual practice, despite a cultural gulf. Presumably both sides made quite an effort: the Buddhists to explain in terms they felt the newcomer would understand and the newcomer to interpret.

It took, however, many centuries before the key ideas of Buddhism started to be understood a little by those in non-Buddhist countries. Charles Allen, in The Buddha and the Sahibs (2002), has pointed out that while the Orientalists from the West may have imposed something of their vision on the countries with which they were in contact, we owe them a debt of gratitude for their philological and comparative work in opening up these cultures to Westerners. T.W. Rhys Davids, a great humanist and scholar of Pāli, was in part instrumental in effecting a change of perception:

> The distinguishing characteristic of Buddhism was that it started on a new line, that it looked at the deepest questions men have to solve from an entirely different standpoint ... For the first time in the history of the world, it proclaimed a salvation which each man could gain for himself, and by himself, in this world, during this life.
>
> Rhys Davids (1881: 28–9)

Edwin Arnold's Light of Asia (1879) on the life of the Buddha, was one of the best-selling poems of the Victorian period: Arnold lived in Japan and wrote about the forms of Buddhism there. Indeed the arts have been one means whereby Buddhist thought has been disseminated. There is animated discussion about the Bodhisattva as early as in George Eliot's Daniel Deronda (1876). Kipling's Kim (1901), by showing a Buddhist lama in a sympathetic light, did something to disseminate a sense of Buddhist practice. In America the popularity of Jack Karouac and the beat poets in the mid-twentieth century has also made 'Zen' a household word. America now has a number of the world's largest temples for many Buddhist traditions.

As Buddhism is becoming a little more familiar in non-Buddhist countries, the practice of its meditation, once thought very odd, has received some favourable publicity. This raises some questions as to how it will eventually be integrated into contexts where it has been unfamiliar. Two important areas are its relationship with Christianity and the scientific world.

Figure 12.2 **Japanese tea garden at Golden Gate Park, San Francisco, California**

CHRISTIANITY AND BUDDHISM

Do Buddhists feel the need to convert others? One feature of Buddhism as it has travelled has been in the effects on other traditions, and vice versa, which have not always involved conversion. No claims could be made for Buddhists on the whole being less aggressive than other humans, in other traditions, but there is no concept of a holy war. In practice, Buddhism has often adapted to a different environment with an interactive adjustment to native traditions and practices. How is this process of acculturation working in a Christian setting?

The Christian tradition has its own heritage of spiritual practice and meditation. Indeed it also has a long history of adaptation in different cultures, as seen in, for instance, the South American lodges for worship of the Virgin Mary, Afro-American gospel singing and the slow osmosis whereby Christian ritual has become mixed with Pagan festivals in Europe. Some of the interpenetrating temporal symbologies in Buddhist countries, such as those used for the days of the week in Thailand, seem analogous to those found in systems meshing Christian, Classical, 'Pagan' and neo-Platonic elements in early modern Europe. Western weekday symbology (Sunday/ sol/solitude/one associations, for example), seems directly comparable (see Fowler 1964: 63ff). From the meditative point of view, there seems to be a distinction in both traditions between a quiet which employs discursive thought and one that does not. St Richard's dictum was that 'Meditation investigates, contemplation wonders'. This perhaps corresponds to the difference between some forms of bhāvanā, such as the rcollections in Buddhaghosa's system, along with the first jhāna, where there is thinking about the object and sustained thought, and the other three jhānas. These latter are said to be characterized by an internal silence, and a successive purification of feeling through joy, happiness and one-pointedness. Cousins (1989) has demonstrated that the stages of prayer described by St Theresa seem to have close affinities with the stages of jhāna as described by Buddhaghosa. At any rate, on a purely practical level, contemplative nuns and monks find Buddhist meditative advice helpful and challenging. 'Conversion' is not an issue: they explore as Christian practitioners some Buddhist meditation techniques and sometimes derive a new way of approaching their own practice from Buddhist ideas. Conversely, Buddhist traditions in the West seem to be being influenced by their own native traditions. Monastic orders in Britain, such at Cittaviveka, the British Theravādin Saṅgha home at Chithurst in Sussex, and Throssel Hole Zen priory in Northumberland, inevitably draw upon some memory of the life of monks and friars in Britain. Many meditators in Buddhist traditions enjoy reading St Theresa, St John of the Cross and Julian of Norwich because they feel some sense of affinity, as they discover something about their own cultural background that might not have been evident before. It seems that after a time people who have found a home in one meditative tradition also feel they can learn from those in others.

PHYSIOLOGY AND THE PRACTICE OF MEDITATION

Buddhist understanding is percolating through to the scientific world view in ways that affect not only the interpretation of Buddhist meditative techniques but also the perception of those disciplines that examine them. There are a number of fronts in which Buddhism and its meditative systems have been investigated. These fall mainly into two categories: the reappraisal of modern scientific, physiological and psychological terminology and investigation of the physiological effects of meditation practice on the brain, blood pressure and nervous system. This is still in very early days and the work needs as much attention to paradigms of analysis as clinical observation. Perhaps just as the Chinese found when trying to import Buddhist terminology that seemed strange to older Daoist and Confucian models, or the Tibetans to their own cultural models, it seems our basic systems of thought rest on quite different assumptions and nuances.

Buddhism challenges the unconscious preconceptions of much modern scientific analysis. According to the doctrine of dependent origination, any sense of self as a fixed, permanent entity that survives after death is eternalism, one of the extremes avoided by the Buddha. The other extreme, however, is annihilationism, the view that nothing continues after death. The Buddhist middle way lies in the freedom from the view-making which needs and requires any variety or combination of these standpoints to sustain an 'I' or fixed identity. Many Buddhist thinkers argue that much modern scientific analysis – indeed much that even asserts its affinity with Buddhist doctrine – has its roots in what would be termed, within the Buddhist understanding, a profound annihilationism. Many Buddhists – including scientists – argue that psychological investigation that assumes that 'self' is in some way a property of the physical brain, for instance, rests on a materialist view of consciousness and the body. An onus of 'proof' is then required for any other stance, that does not share these assumptions. Do these assumptions themselves need scrutiny?

In some scientific fields Buddhist terms and understanding have been explored to suggest new paradigms and ways of interpreting unfamiliar events. Murray Gell-Man named his nascent system of sub-atomic particle theory 'the eightfold way' in 1964, an early formulation of 'quark' theory. The movement in modern physics to assess the importance of the 'subject', the mind, in measuring and hence creating events perceived as 'object', such as the atom or its contributory elements, has also been interpreted through Buddhist understanding. Certainly modern debate amongst physicists seems remarkably like that conducted by Nāgārjuna and his contemporaries, for whom the nature of flux and the substantiality of emptiness were seen as phenomonological as well as ontological problems, requiring both meditative and philosophical precision.

Recently investigative methods that display affinities with Buddhist ideas have also been evident in clinically investigative disciplines such as physiology, with an increased emphasis on process rather than substances. In *The Music of Life* (2006), Professor Denis Noble argues that the only sequences of events that can be interpreted as programmatic do not inhere in the body or even the genetic programme, but in the biological processes themselves: a sense of 'self' arises from process rather than from 'thingness'.

His work seems an interesting and challenging application of the doctrine of dependent origination.

In the area of research work on meditation is ongoing, but in early stages. Some cognitive behavioural therapy works on arousing mindfulness through challenging the area of the mind associated with identification or perception (saññā). Such schools attempt to change the way in which difficulties are identified and hence considered problematic. The inherent health of the mind, an idea suggested in many schools of Buddhism, is not articulated but is implied in psychological systems which have an emphasis on arousing awareness at the sense-doors as a means of combating depression. The word 'mindfulness', with explicitly Buddhist connotations, is now frequently employed. The Oxford Mindfulness Centre, for instance, has had an unusually high success rate of 50 per cent non-recurrence within a year when using awareness techniques with those suffering from depressive illnesses.

Scientific research work on longstanding practitioners of meditation has produced favourable results. A decrease in blood pressure has been recorded, an increased production of seratonin and increased strength in the immune system. Regular meditators exhibit a detectable increase in the ability to enter hibernatory, relaxed states like sleep with full awareness. Dr Herbert Benson of Harvard University (Benson *et al.* 1990)has identified a consciously applicable 'relaxation response' associated with those practising various forms of meditation. Professor Owen Flanagan at the University of Wisconsin/Madison has discovered indications such as better health and an increase in the psychological and physiological effects associated with happiness and wellbeing amongst meditating subjects. These factors are also evident in those who have been practising for short periods of time.

How such study will affect whether people actually want to practise meditation remains to be seen. It could arouse confidence where traditional rationales for this might not. The Dalai Lama has pointed out the great disparity between the indisputable, but subjective reality of consciousness and the third-person voice required for scientific observation. The dynamic between these two is ongoing, and seems to be influencing ways of interpreting scientific events. He points out that both require constant testing, by different means:

A comprehensive scientific study of consciousness must therefore embrace both third-person and first-person methods: it cannot ignore the phenomenological reality of subjective experience but must observe all the rules with scientific rigour.

Dalai Lama (2005: 134)

Does this have bearing on individual practice? Perhaps meditation helps to see the mysterious in the familiar (*samatha*), and to find that what seemed mysterious is natural and down-to-earth (*vipassanā*). As the Dalai Lama points out, the rules of science and meditation are not so different: both require experimental evaluation, of different kinds. What seems important is whether their rules are well maintained, and observation is always refined.

CONCLUSION

In this chapter some of the factors that have accompanied the spread of Buddhist meditative practices and Buddhism and its meditative traditions have been considered. The various identities of different groups, and the way they have evolved and adapted, have been discussed. The emergence of international interest in the subject has been explored, with some discussion of its impact both on Christian practice and scientific thought.

MEDITATION

A final word should concern the actual practice of meditation. Here it needs to be stressed that in most schools of Buddhism, consistency in one method is considered essential. Textual evidence and the writings and talks of experienced teachers stress the importance of finding a school of practice in which one feels at home and sticking to it: dig one hole and dig it deep! Meditation objects, as we have seen in the varied countries discussed, are multifarious, carefully developed and specific to temperament. It is usually advised that they are given personally by a teacher after some consultation. Often specific practices are geared to go with other ones in a particular school. Many take a long time to reach fruition, and consistency and some regularity are essential. Teachers assign meditation objects on the basis of their own lineages and schools, which provide a refuge in times of difficulty. They help people over tricky patches and it is considered important by most schools to be steadfast in this regard. These elements, which include reasonably regular discussion about the practice with a teacher and, if possible, practice in a group, have ensured the continuity of the meditative tradition over centuries.

The Buddha started with the physical body as the ground for the eightfold path and for the practice of meditation. On one level, the discovery of the middle way lies, in practice, in the balance of the physical body and in whether the knees are reasonably supported in meditation. At various times, both from the evidence of history, from records of personal practice and from the guidance of the eightfold path, it also needs other things. In Myanmar it might be some *abhidhamma* to test the intellect; in Eastern Buddhist contexts a kōan, that lets the inherent contradiction of a single statement rest in the mind. Others may find a ceremony involving chanting and generosity, which develops an equilibrium that can give and receive, helps meditation. All of these, it is said, may help develop the meditation object: perhaps increasing enjoyment of the breath, at a happy balance between self and other, knower and known.

For any single meditator, the refuge of the Triple Gem is advised. This involves three things. The first is trust that there is a teacher in the possibility of awakening; the second a willingness to explore a given system of procedures and the third an underlying respect and confidence in others who have tried and are trying this way. How we formulate these refuges will no doubt be constantly reassessed as Buddhist meditation continues to be practised.

THE EIGHTFOLD PATH

... the direction, as it were, of that path lies not in the plane of our own life at all – it is as though at right angles to it: a new direction

Ven. Ananda Metteyya Thera
(Alan Bennett, one of the first Westerners
to practise meditation as a Buddhist monk)
in 'Buddhist Self Culture', *The Buddhist Review*, 1914

TIMELINE

c.300 BCE	Greek presence in Bactria
c.150 BCE	Indo-Greek king Menander/Milinda converted to Buddhism
c.600	St John of Damascus writes story of *Barlaam and Josophat* (Bodhisattva), a hero eventually incorporated amongst Christian saints
c.1210–70	William of Rubruck, who met Buddhist monks in Mongolia
c.1850	Start of wave of immigration of Japanese and Chinese Pure-Land Buddhists into America
1881	Growing interest in the USA and UK in Buddhism: the Pāli Text Society founded in London
1950	Tibetan diaspora after invasion by Chinese
1959	Dalai Lama flees Tibet

FURTHER READING

Allen, C. (2002) *The Buddha and the Sahibs: the Men who Discovered India's Lost Religion*, London: John Murray.

Benson, H., M.S. Malhotra, R.F. Goldman, G.D. Jacobs, and P.J. Hopkins (1990) 'Three case reports of the metabolic and electroencephalographic changes during advanced Buddhist meditation techniques', *Behavioural Medicine*, 16: 90–5.

Bluck R. (2002) 'The Path of the Householder', *Buddhist Studies Review*, 19: 1, 1–18.

Bluck R. (2006) *British Buddhism: Teachings, Practice and Development*, London: Routledge.

Cousins, L.S. (1989) 'The Stages of Christian Mysticism and the Path of Purification: Interior Castle of St Teresa of Avila and the Path of Purification of Buddhaghosa', Werner, K. ed., *The Yogi and the Mystic: Studies in Indian and Comparative Mysticism*, London: Routledge, 103–20.

Flanagan O. (2003) 'The Colour of Happiness', *New Scientist*, Issue 2393: 24 May.

Fowler, A. (1964) *Spenser and the Numbers of Time*, London: Routledge and Kegan Paul.

Gell-Mann, M. (2008) in *Encyclopedia Britannica*: http://www.britannica.com/eb/article-9036327

Heine, S. and Prebish, C. (eds) (2003) *Buddhism in the Modern World: Adaptations of an Ancient Tradition*, Oxford: OUP.

Houshmand, Z., Livingston R.B., and Wallace B.A. (eds.) (1999) *Consciousness at the Crossroads. Conversations with the Dalai Lama on Brain Science and Buddhism*, New York: Snow Lion Publications.

Lama, Dalai (2005) *The Universe in a Single Atom: the Convergence of Science and Spirituality*, New York: Morgan Road Books.

Lancaster, B.L. (1997) 'On the stages of perception: towards a synthesis of cognitive neuroscience and the Buddhist Abhidhamma tradition', *Journal of Consciousness Studies*, 4 (2), 122–42.

Noble, D. (2006) *The Music of Life*, Oxford: OUP.

Prebish, C.S. (1979) *American Buddhism*, North Scituate, MA: Duxbury Press.

Rhys Davids, T.W. (1881) *The Hibbert Lectures: Lectures on the origin and growth of Religion, as illustrated by some points in the history of Indian Buddhism*, London and Edinburgh: Williams and Norgate.

Rockhill, W.W. trans. (1900) *The journey of William of Rubruck to the eastern parts of the world, 1253–55*, London: Hakluyt Society.

Sponberg, A. (1986) 'Meditation in Fa-hsiang Buddhism', Gregory, P.N. ed., *Traditions of Meditation in Chinese Buddhism*, Kuroda Institute: Studies in East Asian Buddhism, 4, Honolulu: University of Hawaii Press, 15–43.

Waugh, D.C. (2002) 'William of Rubruck's Account of the Mongols' http://depts.washington.edu/silkroad/texts/rubruck.html#buddhism

WEBSITES

Research on meditation and mindfulness techniques:

Research conducted by the University of Wisconsin/Madison, Prof Flanagan received widespread publicity 22–24 May 2003. See:

http://www.londonbuddhistvihara.org/happiness.htm

http://focus.hms.harvard.edu/1996/Mar1_1996/Off_the_Quad.html

http://www.waisman.wisc.edu/brainimagingfund/research-happiness.html

Williams, M. (2008) University of Oxford Centre for Suicide Research, 'Mindfulness Based Cognitive Therapy and the prevention of relapse in depression':

http://cebmh.warne.ox.ac.uk/csr/mbct.html

(2008) University of Wales, Bangor, Centre for Mindfulness Research:

http://www.bangor.ac.uk/mindfulness/

(2008) University of Massachusetts Center for Mindfulness in Medicine, Healthcare and Society:

http://www.umassmed.edu/cfm/index.aspx

Mind and Life Institute website:

http://www.mindandlife.org/

Brief Glossary

E = English, C = Chinese, J = Japanese, K = Korean, P = Pāli, Sk = Sanskrit, T = Tibetan, V = Vietnamese

BUDDHAS, BODHISATTVAS, GODS, AND PEOPLE

Akṣobya 'Imperturbable': one of five 'self-born Buddhas' said always to have existed.

Amida: Japanese combination of Amitābha (infinite light) and Amitayus (infinite life) into Buddha Amida, worshipped in Japanese Pure Land.

Amitābha 'Infinite light' Buddha: one of five Buddhas of Northern Buddhism said always to have existed. Invoked by Pure Land chant.

Amoghasiddhi 'Infallible success': one of five 'self-born Buddhas' said always to have existed.

Ānanda Buddha: Gotama's attendant.

An Shigao (fl. 148): Iranian monk who introduced breathing practices and textual translation into Chinese.

Avalokiteśvara (Sk) / Chenrezig (T): embodiment of the compassion of all Buddhas.

Ayya Khema (1923–97): twentieth-century German Buddhist nun.

Ba khin, U (1889–1970): Burmese lay meditation teacher who emphasized insight, speed and a lack of ritual in daily practice.

Bodhidharma (470–543): meditation teacher, of legendary fame, considered by Chan school to be its first patriarch.

Buddhabhadra (359–429): Kashmiri Sarvāstivādin monk who translated *Avataṃsaka-Sūtra* for the Chinese.

Buddhadāsa (1906–93): teacher of breathing mindfulness, who placed some emphasis on *samatha* practice.

Buddhaghosa (c.5th century CE): Buddhist scholar, author of *Visuddhimagga*, and supposed composer of many other commentarial works.

Buton (1290–1364): Tibetan librarian, scholar.

Chah, Ajahn (1919–92): Thai forest meditation teacher.

Dalai Lama: 14th current incarnation of Tibetan religious leader.

Daoan (312–85): meditative monk who introduced techniques into China.

Daochuo: Pure Land teacher.

Dōgen (1200–53): founder of Japanese Sōtō Zen school.

Düsum Khyenpa (1110–93): the first Karmapa of Tibetan Kagyu school.

Eisai Zenji (1141–1215): founder of Japanese Rinzai Zen school.

Faxian (337/8–422): first Chinese pilgrim to travel to India and return.

Fazang (Fa-tsang 643–712): Huayan teacher and author.

Goenka (1924–): Indian follower of U Ba Khin, who has established *vipassanā* meditation centres throughout the world.

Gotama Buddha (d. 404 BCE): name of historical Buddha, sometimes called Śakyamuni.

Guan Yin: Chinese goddess of compassion.

Hōnen (1133–1212): Japanese Pure Land teacher.

Huineng (638–713): Chinese Chan teacher.

Huiyuan (334–416): monk who introduced meditative techniques into China.

Jinul (Chinul 1158–1210): Korean Seon teacher.

Jizang (549–623): exponent of Madhyamaka form of Buddhism in China.

Kūkai (774–835): Tendai monk, introduced the Mantrayāna to Japan.

Kumarajīva (344–413): Central Asian monk who imported Buddhist teachings to China.

Kūya (903–72): Japanese monk who taught Pure-Land chant.

Laozi (Lao Tsu): Chinese philosopher, associated with Dao, who lived sometime after the 6th century BCE.

Liangjie (807–69): founder of Chan Caodong school.

Lokakṣema (b. 147 CE): Indian teacher who brought Buddhist texts, developed around the meditation of the recollection of the Buddha, to China.

Mahasi Sayadaw (1904–82): Burmese *vipassanā* teacher.

Manjuśri: Northern Bodhisattva associated with wisdom.

Mantrayāna: esoteric form of Buddhist practice based on mantra.

Milarepa (1052–1135): celebrated Tibetan *mahāsiddha*, literally 'one of great powers'.

Nāgārjuna (c.150–250): one of the greatest Buddhist thinkers, who challenged the basis of philosophical discourse and, hence, meditative investigation, by challenging concepts of substantiality and conventional duality.

Nichiren (1222–82): Japanese founder of chanting movement.

Padmasamhava from Uddiyāna: founder of Nyingma School in Tibet.

Ratnasambhava 'Jewel-born One' or 'Origin of Jewels': one of five 'self-born Buddhas' of Northern Buddhism.

Saddhatissa: twentieth-century Sri Lankan teacher and monk.

Śākyamuni: term used by Northern schools of Buddhism to describe Buddha Gotama, the historical Buddha, a Sakyan.

Śāntideva (c.685–763): Indian Buddhist teacher and writer.

Sāriputta (P) / Śāriputra: Buddha Gotama's chief disciple.

Shandao (Shan-tao 613–81): Pure Land teacher.

Shenxiu (606–706): Chinese Chan teacher.

Shinran (1173–1262): pupil of Honen and founder of Jōdo-shin-shū.

Shōtuku (573–622): Japanese king who brought kingdom to Buddhism.

Tanluan (T'an-Luan 476–542): author of first Chinese work on Pure-Land.

Tārā: Indian and Tibetan goddess of compassion.

Upatissa (4th century?): author of the *Vimuttimagga*, the *Path to Freedom*, which lists meditation objects and describes methods.

Vairocana 'Resplendent': one of five 'self-born Buddhas' of Northern Buddhism, who 'have always existed'.

Wonhyo (617–86): Korean Buddhist teacher and synthesizer.

Xuanzang (596–664): Chinese pilgrim to India.

Yeshe Tsogyal: yoginī and Tibetan queen.

Zhantan (711–82): Tiantai teacher.

Zhiyi (Chih-I 538–97): synthesizer and founder of the Tiantai school of Buddhism; developed a meditative method based on the Mahāyāna notion of emptiness and Madhyamaka logic.

SOME SCHOOLS

Caodong (Ts'ao-tung): Buddhist school founded in 9th century.

Chan (Ch) / Seon (K) / Zen (J) / Thien (V): Buddhist meditation school, founded in China, which has had immense popularity. The word is derived from the Chinese transliteration of jhāna/dhyāna meditation.

Confucianism: traditional way of Confucius, the 6th-century BCE philosopher, who stressed social harmony through attention to behaviour in a hierarchical societal organism.

Dao (Tao) the 'Way': ancient philosophy of China, based on teachings of Laozi (Lao Tsu).

Faxiang: early Chinese Buddhist school based on the Indian Yogācāra school.

Gelug: one of three new Tantric schools of Tibetan Buddhism.

Hīnayāna: literally the 'lesser vehicle', a term used by those following the Mahāyāna schools, which placed more emphasis on the Bodhisattva vow, for Southern schools.

Hossō: early Japanese Buddhist school.

Huayan (Huayen): major school of Chinese Buddhism which based teaching on *Avatamsaka-Sūtra*.

Jingtu (C): Pure-Land Buddhist School.

Jōdo (J): Japanese Pure-Land School.

Jōdo-shin-shū (J): 'True Pure-Land School'.

Kadampa: Tibetan school of Buddhism.

Kagyu: one of three new Tantric schools of Tibetan Buddhism.

Kegon: school of Japanese Buddhism.

Madhyamaka: Indian school of Buddhist philosophy.

Mahāyāna 'Great Vehicle': term used by Northern Buddhists, particularly Tibetan, to describe their commitment to the Bodhisattva ideal.

Moguk: Burmese school of meditation.

Mūlasarvāstivādin: early Indian Buddhist school.

Nichiren: Japanese Buddhist school.

Nyingma: oldest validated Tibetan school.

Pure Land: name of a heaven realm, of Buddha Amitābha/Amida/Amitabha; also associated with schools of Buddhism: Jingtu (C), Jōdo (J), and Jōdo-shin-shū (J).

Rinzai: Japanese Zen school.

Sakya: one of three new Tantric schools of Tibetan Buddhism.

San-lun: three-treatise school of early Chinese Buddhism, based on the Indian Madhyamaka school.

Shingan: Japanese School

Sōka Gakkai: Japanese school founded in 1930.

Sōtō: Japanese Zen school.

Theravāda: school of Southern Buddhism.

Tiantai (T'ien-t'ai, Tendai (J)): Chinese school which moved to other Eastern countries.

Vajrayāna: Diamond or Thunderbolt school of Northern and Eastern Buddhism.

Yogācāra: early Indian meditative and theoretical school.

SOME TEXTS

Abhidhammapiṭika: literally 'higher teaching', one of three 'baskets' of early Buddhist texts.

Ānāpānasati-Sutta: text on breathing mindfulness.

Avataṃsaka-Sūtra: Indian text that inspired Chinese Huayan school.

Diamond-sūtra: sūtra of Indian Prajñāpāramitā genre, favoured in Eastern Buddhism.

Heart-Sūtra: very short sūtra of Prajñāpāramitā literature, favoured in Eastern Buddhism.

Lotus-Sūtra: Sūtra of the Lotus Blossom of the Fine Dharma /Saddharmapuṇḍarīka-Sūtra (Sk), Miao-fa Lien-hua Ching (Ch), Myōhō Renge Kyō (J): highly influential text on the 'one vehicle' to Buddhahood.

Pārinibbāna-Sutta: text on the approach to death of Buddha Gotama.

Prajñāpāramitā-Sūtra: Indian Buddhist text on wisdom.

Pratyutpanna-Sūtra: Indian text on meeting manifold Buddhas 'face-to-face'.

Sāmaññaphala-Sutta: one of principal Southern texts on meditation.

Satipaṭṭhāna-Sutta: text on foundations of mindfulness.

Sukhāvativyūha-Sūtra: the principal texts of the Pure Land school.

Sutta-piṭika: one of three 'baskets' of early Buddhist texts of particular occasions of teaching.

Vinayapiṭika: one of three 'baskets' of early Buddhist texts pertaining to monastic discipline.

SOME TERMS

Abhidhamma (P) / *abhidharma* (Sk): literally 'higher' teaching; delineation and analysis of relationship between mind, mental states, matter and the unconditioned.

Ālayavijñāna storehouse: the seed bed of consciousness described by Yogācāra school.

Bardo (T): in Tibetan Buddhism, intermediate state between death and conception.

Bhakti devotion: movement that became popular in all Indian religious traditions in the first centuries CE.

Bhāvanā 'bringing into being': the culture of the mind of which meditation is a major part.

Bhavaṅga: underlying consciousness to which mind of any being returns at rest; governed by moment of death in previous life.

Bodhisatta (P) / *Bodhisattva* (Sk): being bound for, or to enlightenment/ awakening.

Buddhānussati (P) / *Buddhanusmṛti* (Sk): the recollection of the Buddha, the 21st meditation object described by Buddhaghosa, developed and extended in various Buddhist traditions to include mantra, visualization, mantra linked to breath meditation, a walking practice on his thirty-two marks and, subsequently in China, insight practice.

Cetanā (P): volition.

Citta (P): consciousness, mind.

Dāna: generosity, the first perfection, used to describe ceremony of food offering in Southern Buddhism.

Dhamma (P) / *dharma* (Sk): law, what is right. More specifically, the teaching of the Buddha and the second refuge of the Triple Gem of Buddha, *dhamma/ dharma* and *saṅgha*. When in plural it usually refers to events – things that occur.

Dharmadhātu: the state of the mind in non-duality.

Dharmakāya: the 'truth-body' of Northern Buddhism, the ultimate nature of the enlightened mind and the ultimate expanse of existence.

Dukkha: variously translated as suffering, dis-ease or unsatisfactoriness, it is the basic condition of all beings and all existence. It is the first of the four noble truths, and is to be 'understood'.

Dzogchen: central teaching of Tibetan Nyingma school.

Ekayāna (one vehicle): a way transcending three paths, of salvation for the human race from the wheel of suffering and rebirth (*Lotus-Sūtra*).

Gongan (C) / *kōan* (J): statement or question for meditator that encapsulates teaching, to arouse awakening.

Gongfu/Kung fu: art, often martial, that can embody teaching.

Hwadu (K): the 'head' of a *gongan*; the pith.

Jhāna (P) / *dhyāna* (Sk): meditative state of confidence, mindfulness, effort, concentration and wisdom which deepens and is aroused by *samādhi* concentration. Particularly emphasized by Samatha meditation schools, it is described in early texts as essential for awakening/enlightenment.

Karmapa: name for highest teacher of Tibetan Kagyu schools.

Kasiṇa: device for calm meditation (described by Buddhaghosa).

Kusala: healthy, skilful, good opposed to *akusala*.

Linji (Lin Chi): School of Chinese Buddhism.

Mahāmudrā: Tibetan Kagyu system of theory and meditation.

Mappō: age of spiritual decline.

Magga (P) / *marga* (Sk) path: the eightfold path that leads to the end of suffering, the fourth noble truth, to be 'brought into being'.

Nembutsu: Pure-Land chant.

Nianfo (Nien-fo): remembrance of the Buddha.

Nimitta: mental image in meditation.

Nirvana (E) / *nibbāna* (P) / *nīrvāṇa* (Sk): derived from the word to 'extinguish' or 'put out' a flame, it is that condition, described as 'peaceful', where there is freedom from suffering. Sometimes known as the 'unconditioned' compared with the 'conditioned' world of existence. The third of the four noble truths.

Panjiao (P-an chiao): classification of texts according to hierarchical importance, using five stages of the Buddha's teaching career.

Paññā (P) / *prajñā* (Sk) wisdom: associated with the first two path factors of right view and right intention, it is the intuitive wisdom that is particularly cultivated by *vipassanā* schools, though it is also considered essential for *samatha/śamatha*.

Pārami perfection: quality developed by a Bodhisattva.

Paritta (P): chants for blessing and protection.

Pūja: homage, chant.

Samādhi: concentration.

Samatha (P) / *śamatha* (Sk): calm.

Sanzen: teaching that occurs between teacher and pupil (Rinzai).

Sati: mindfulness.

Shakyō: meditative calligraphy.

Shikantaza: 'just sitting' (Zen).

Shintō: way of the gods; indigenous ancestor and spirit worship of Japan.

Siddhi: literally 'power' (*iddhi* (P)).

Stūpa: shrine built to house relics and as object of veneration.

Sukhavati: heavenly realm, the Buddha field in Indian and Eastern Buddhism.

Śūnyatā: emptiness; teaching of Indian Buddhist philosophy that accompanied spread to Tibet and the East.

Sutta/Sūtra: text.

Tanhā (P): desire, the second noble truth, that is to be 'abandoned'.

Tantra: kind of practice usually involving invocation, visualization and worship of a deity, Buddha or Bodhisattva with the intention of finding union with those qualities.

Tathāgatagarbha: the seed of Buddhahood, emphasized by Chinese schools as a representation of the potential for Buddhahood in all beings.

(ti)piṭika: the three 'baskets' of texts in Sanskrit and Pāli Buddhism.

Tulku: incarnate lama in Tibetan Buddhism.

Vinaya: one of the three baskets of texts, pertaining to the monastic code of discipline. When lower case, *vinaya*, generic term for a monastic code.

Vipāka: result of volition (*cetanā*) and action (*kamma*).

Vipassanā/vipaśyanā: insight.

Yan: diagram embodying meditation teaching.

Yogi/yoginī: meditator m. and f.

Zazen (J): 'sitting opening the hand of thought'.

Appendix A

How many Buddhists are there in the world? Most of the population of Southern Buddhist countries and Japan say they are Buddhist. Several million people claim to be Buddhist in Korea and China. Numbers in Tibet are difficult to assess. The Tibetan diaspora now numbers millions, as does that from many other Buddhist countries, living as refugees or willing migrants in a worldwide movement of populations and ethnic groups. In Australia, there are now about 200,000 Buddhists – oddly enough the same percentage of the population, about 1 per cent, as in the late nineteenth century, when Chinese workers arrived, attracted by the Gold Rush. In America, an estimate in 2006 assessed three to four million, of whom 75 per cent are of Asian origin; the study of Buddhism in America has now become a separate academic subject. The 2006 census in New Zealand revealed 52,392 Buddhists, one of the two largest non-Christian groups there. In Mongolia, a programme of rebuilding and initiating Buddhist monasteries has been ongoing since 1990, though no numbers are available. Overall, the Buddha Dharma Education Association estimates that there are 350,000,000 Buddhists in the world – about 6 per cent of the population.

But statistical surveys make no assessment of practice. Of these, how many practise meditation? How many people practise Buddhist meditation who are not Buddhist? It is not clear how this sort of thing could be quantified. Helpful statistics are certainly provided by the great recent interest in practical books on meditation and a considerable increase in the number of meditation centres around the world. Large audience figures for films such as 'Seven Years in Tibet' and 'Kundun', along with the high profile of monks such as the Dalai Lama and Thich Nhat Hanh, have ensured that Buddhist meditation is at least discussed and considered. At an international level, Buddhist meditation is now recognized as helpful: doctor's surgeries in the UK, as in many other countries, exhibit leaflets encouraging meditation as a way of reducing blood pressure and stress.

This does not, of course, mean that many people do it. Although it has proved remarkably resistant to social upheaval, it is, as the Buddha indicated, an adventurous activity. It is, perhaps, just for the few, and they select themselves.

NUMERICAL ASSESSMENT OF BUDDHISTS:

America (2006): http://buddhistfaith.tripod.com/pureland_sangha/id65.html
Australia: http://www.buddhanet.net/whybudoz.htm
Mongolia: http://www.multifaithcentre.org/images/content/features/mongolia/essay.htm
New Zealand: http://www.methodist.org.nz/index.cfm/Touchstone/February_2007/Census___religion
Worldwide (2007): http://www.buddhanet.net/e-learning/history/bud_statwrld.htm

The Postures of the Buddha
Appendix B

In Thailand a posture of the Buddha is linked to each day of the week. Those born on a particular day of the week are thought to have a special affinity with the posture of that day.

Some Thai day symbolism is based on the Chinese system, which takes Monday as the first day of the week, while some takes the Indic system of Sunday as the first day. This particular list employs the Indic sequence, with the addition of an extra posture for Wednesday, making the number up to eight.

Sunday
Open-eyed
posture

Monday
Preventing
calamities

Tuesday
Reclining Buddha

Wednesday (morning)
Holding an alms bowl

Wednesday (evening)
Resting with monkey
and elephant

Thursday
Meditation

Friday
Contemplation

Saturday
Seated under
the nāga hood

Index

Where terms have counterparts in several languages the sequence of the book is used: for instance Pāli followed by Sanskrit, as in *abhidhamma/abhidharma*. For some Tibetan and Chinese names and terms common alternative spellings are given in brackets after entries: Wylie and Wale-Giles respectively. For reasons of space abbreviations are very short: C = Chinese, E =English, K = Korean, J = Japanese, P= Pāli, S=Sanskrit, T= Tibetan.

Theravada Buddhism

A Social History from Ancient Benares to Modern Colombo

Richard Gombrich

Theravada is the branch of Buddhism found in Sri Lanka and parts of south-east Asia. The Buddha preached in north-east India in about the fifth century BC. He claimed that human beings are responsible for their own salvation, and put forward a new ideal of the holy life, establishing a monastic Order to enable men and women to pursue that ideal. For most of its history the fortunes of Theravada, the most conservative form of Buddhism, have been identified with those of that Order. Under the great Indian emperor, Asoka, himself a Buddhist, Theravada reached Sri Lanka in about 250 BC. There it became the religion of the Sinhala state, and from there it spread, much later, to Burma and Thailand.

Richard Gombrich's book, widely recognised as the classic introduction to the field of Theravada Buddhism, shows how Theravada Buddhism has influenced and been influenced by its social surroundings. He explores the influences of the Buddha's predecessors and the social and religious contexts against which Buddhism has developed and changed throughout history.

ISBN13: 978-0-415-36508-6 (hbk)
ISBN13: 978-0-415-36509-3 (pbk)

Introducing Buddhism

Charles S. Prebish and Damien Keown

'An up-to-date textbook for beginners as well as advanced students of Buddhism. Its clear structure helps beginners getting oriented in the complex field of Buddhism, and its respective chapters are rich in detailed information for students who already have some basic knowledge. Instructors and students alike will appreciate its didactic tools. I have used this book in my classes, with great success.'

Oliver Freiberger, University of Texas

Introducing Buddhism is the ideal resource for all students beginning the study of this fascinating religion. Damien Keown and Charles S. Prebish, two of today's leading Buddhist scholars, explain the key teachings of Buddhism, and trace the historical development and spread of the religion from its beginnings down to the present day. A chapter is devoted to each of the major regions where Buddhism has flourished: India, south-east Asia, east Asia and Tibet. In addition to this regional focus, the introduction takes contemporary concerns into account, covering important and relevant topics such as Engaged Buddhism, Buddhist ethics, and Buddhism and the Western world, as well as a chapter devoted to meditation.

Introducing Buddhism also includes illustrations, lively quotations from original sources, learning goals, summary boxes, questions for discussion and suggestions for further reading to aid study and revision.

World Religions Series
Edited by Damien Keown and Charles S. Prebish

ISBN13: 978-0-415-39234-1 (hbk)
ISBN13: 978-0-415-39235-8 (pbk)

Available at all good bookshops
For ordering and further information please visit:
www.routledge.com

Buddhist Meditation

An Anthology of Texts from the Pali Canon

Edited by Sarah Shaw

Meditative practice lies at the heart of the Buddhist tradition. This introductory anthology gives a representative sample of the various kinds of meditations described in the earliest body of Buddhist scripture, the Pali canon.

It provides a broad introduction to their traditional context and practice and supplies explanation, context and doctrinal background to the subject of meditation. The main themes of the book are the diversity and flexibility of the way that the Buddha teaches meditation from the evidence of the canon. Covering fundamental features of Buddhist practice such as posture, lay meditation and meditative technique, it provides comments both from the principal early commentators on Buddhist practice, Upatissa and Buddhaghosa, and from reputable modern meditation teachers in a number of Theravadin traditions.

This is the first book on Pali Buddhism which introduces the reader to the wide range of the canon. It demonstrates that the Buddha's meditative tradition still offers a path of practice as mysterious and awe-inspiring yet as freshly accessible as it was centuries ago. It will be of interest to students and scholars of Buddhism as well as Buddhist practitioners.

Sarah Shaw is on the steering committee of the Oxford Centre for Buddhist Studies and practises with the Samatha Association of Britain.

ISBN13: 978-0-415-20700-3 (hbk)
ISBN13: 978-0-415-20701-0 (pbk)

Buddhist Thought

A Complete Introduction to the Indian Tradition

Paul Williams and Anthony Tribe

'Though there is no shortage of introductions to Buddhism on the market, I found this one compelling reading, for the ideas are presented with logical cogency and stylistic clarity. The summary of the Buddha's own views would be hard to better.'

Richard Gombrich, Balliol College, Oxford

Buddhist Thought guides the reader towards a richer understanding of the central concepts of classical Indian Buddhist thought, from the time of Buddha, to the latest scholarly perspectives and controversies. Abstract and complex ideas are made understandable by the authors' lucid style. Of particular interest is the up-to-date survey of Buddhist Tantra in India, a branch of Buddhism where strictly controlled sexual activity can play a part in the religious path. Williams' discussion of this controversial practice, as well as of many other subjects, makes *Buddhist Thought* crucial reading for all interested in Buddhism.

ISBN13: 978-0-415-20700-3 (hbk)
ISBN13: 978-0-415-20701-0 (pbk)

Related titles from Routledge

Mahayānā Buddhism

The Doctrinal Foundations
Revised Second Edition

Paul Williams

Originating in India, Mahāyāna Buddhism spread across Asia, becoming the prevalent form of Buddhism in Tibet and east Asia. Over the last twenty-five years Western interest in Mahāyāna has increased considerably, reflected both in the quantity of scholarly material produced and in the attraction of Westerners towards Tibetan Buddhism and Zen.

Paul Williams' *Mahāyāna Buddhism* is widely regarded as the standard introduction to the field, used internationally for teaching and research and has been translated into several European and Asian languages. This new edition has been fully revised throughout in the light of the wealth of new studies and focuses on the religion's diversity and richness. It includes much more material on China and Japan, with appropriate reference to Nepal, and for students who wish to carry their study further there is a much-expanded bibliography and extensive footnotes and cross-referencing. Everyone studying this important tradition will find Williams' book the ideal companion to their studies.

Paul Williams is Professor of Indian and Tibetan Philosophy and Co-director of the Centre for Buddhist Studies at the University of Bristol. The author of six books and an editor of a further eight, he is a former President of the UK Association for Buddhist Studies. Among his other books for Routledge is *Buddhist Thought: A Complete Introduction to the Indian Tradition* (2000).

ISBN13: 978-0-415-35652-7 (hbk)
ISBN13: 978-0-415-35653-4 (pbk)

Available at all good bookshops
For ordering and further information please visit:
www.routledge.com